MADE IN LYNN

The history of Scott & Son
and events in the town
1874 to 1971

by
Martin Scott

SUNBEAM PUBLICATIONS

Published in 2009 by Sunbeam Publications
scottandsonkingslynn@hotmail.co.uk

Origination and printing by:
The Complete Product Company
Unit 20a, Diss Business Park,
Hopper Way,
Sandy Lane,
Diss
Norfolk IP22 4GT

British Library Cataloguing in Publication Data
A catalogue record for this book is available from the British Library.

ISBN
978-0-9564571-0-3

ACKNOWLEDGEMENTS

It is unlikely that I would have started researching the history of Scott & Son if my brother Robin had not passed on to me an extensive archive of material relating to the firm and its business, including the very first ledger book, dating from 1892. My principal thanks, therefore, go to him for stimulating this initial interest, providing me with information and contacts to augment my lines of inquiry and spurring me on as the project has progressed.

One of the richest seams of illustrated material to have survived is the collection of annual catalogues issued by Scott & Son and I am indebted to my cousin Alan Scott for giving me several of these, together with some old photographs, and for his support and recollections.

My research has been greatly helped by my nephew, Edward Shepperd, who salvaged some irreplaceable relics from the clearance of the former family home in Dersingham, including the partial remains of the earliest surviving catalogue, dating from 1912. He enthusiastically sought out several significant historic pictures, articles and advertisements, copying some of these for me.

My initial research involved countless hours trawling through the newspaper archives held in microfilm form at the Lynn Library, and my thanks go to the staff there for their help. The records of planning applications and council meetings are held at the Lynn town archives and I am very grateful to Susan Maddock for assisting my research into these.

Another King's Lynn researcher, Stan Langley, has forwarded via Michael Allbrook much information of interest concerning Scott & Son and, particularly, about the occupancy of No. 97, High Street, and their help is much appreciated.

Having found the key dates, including the formation of the partnership between Alfred Jermyn and Thomas William Scott, my next task was to obtain images of the newspaper advertisement, notices and articles. For this I am greatly indebted to Ray Bathe of the Lynn News. His support was over and beyond the call of duty, involving lifting down the huge and weighty volumes of newspapers from the archive shelves, and then replacing them afterwards!

One of the most rewarding parts of the project has been through the contact that I have established with past members of staff of Scott & Son, their descendants or relatives. The first of those is John Mitchell, whose memories have helped me to contact others and to establish an extensive list of former staff. Others whom I have met, or been in contact with, are:- Ellen Bambridge; Daphne Baylis; Viola Betts; Muriel Browne; Doreen Chapman; Sandra Clark; Colin Delph; David Dixon; Richard Eke; Noreen Foulsham; Margaret Green; Paul Griffiths; Michael Hart; Mary Kettlewell; Irene Laws; Mary Loasby; Mary Mathers; Jenny Mitchell; Jean Nunn; Lynda Parker; Ann Pease; June Ranger; and Brenda Skoyles.

Former customers, or their descendants, have kindly provided me with some recollections and with copies of receipted bills from almost every decade since the 1890s. They include:- Raymond Askew; Jean Barber; Mary Billing; Martin Browne; Mrs Dawson; Tom Fayers; Daphne Harvey; Mr. C. Hodson; Jane Hurry; and Diana Smith.

Encouragement, information, anecdotes and photographs have come from my sisters Rosemary Harper and Heather Shepperd, and my cousins John Cox, Olwen Curtis, and Marian Conway.

I am most grateful to the following for their kind permission to reproduce photographs and illustrations:- Ellen Bambridge; Viola Betts; Muriel Browne; Doreen Chapman; the East Anglian Film Archive (UEA); the Eastern Daily Press; Michael Hart; John Mitchell; King's Lynn Forums; Irene Laws; the Lynn News; June Ranger; Rosemary Robson; Mr. James Tuck and the Francis Frith Collection.

Finally, many thanks are due to my wife Ann, and to my children Alice and Will, for their support and encouragement to complete this book.

CONTENTS

PREFACE

In the 1950s, as a young lad, I would sometimes accompany my father to the Tuesday market. My father, with a wry smile on his face, would stand and watch one stall-holder whose sales patter for his 'unbreakable' oven-to-table ware would often include, "… and if it does break, just take it along the street to Scotts who will replace it for you!" Scott & Son was that kind of shop. 'Along the street to Scotts' meant leaving the Tuesday Market Place at Jones and Dunn's corner and walking up the High Street to the junction with Purfleet Street. Jones and Dunn's gentlemen's outfitters was one of the long-established shops in King's Lynn, having been started even earlier than Scott & Son. Amongst the other older shops in the town were two of the largest, Jermyns and Catleughs, and two others that have left me with some particularly distinctive

memories. These were Plowright Pratt and Harbage in Norfolk Street, the ironmongery and hardware shop, with its smell of paraffin, and Ladymans in the High Street. Passing Ladymans, or more properly J. H. Ladyman & Co Ltd., an extraordinarily exotic smell of freshly roasted coffee beans would waft through the doors, spiralling upwards past the sign proclaiming '**The Gallery Tea Room**' and the big red teapot suspended out from the mock half-timbered gable high above the pavement. All of this was but of minor interest compared to the fascinating overhead wire cash dispensing system inside! The whiz, whir and click of the little containers shooting back and forth on the cables high above the heads of the customers was mesmerising, as were the actions of the counter staff and the cashier as they reached up to unscrew and screw-up the cash cartridges before pulling the lever to send them on their way again. I was waiting, doubtless, to see a collision or studying the cable network and trying to work out why they never did bump into each other.

Next to Jones and Dunn was Walton Bros, another long-established tailoring business, run by a family friend, Mr J. B. D. Walton. Now Mr Walton possessed an item of almost unique one-upmanship in those long-ago days when such things were a great rarity – a personalised number plate, JBD 1. This was much to be admired and was a great talking point. Doubtless he became fed up with people asking how he came to acquire it.

A little further along was Targett's stationery shop where you could buy all your correspondence needs from a most obliging Miss Madge Targett, a lady who was never without a lit cigarette. Two doors away was a shop that my father did not enter when I was with him, although I suspect that the odd crate or two of ale came from there on occasions – Peatling and Cawdron wines and spirits merchants. Across the road from Woolworths, on the corner of Norfolk Street, was the chemists Allen and Neale. Also on the left side of the street was the marvellously-named ladies' fashion shop of Modelia. This was in an age when the drapery shop assistants would clothe the tailor's dummies in modesty cloths when they were changing the window displays. Finlay & Co, the tobacconists, had a display of pocket knifes that was an irresistible magnet to a schoolboy out window shopping, as indeed was the barred window of Gallyon & Son, the gunsmiths. On the opposite side of High Street we would by now have passed the Easifit Shoe Shop, where comfortable shoes were guaranteed, Rivett's wool shop, Dolcis shoes, and Purdy the bakers, where delicious cakes could be bought and often were! Next was Burlingham's, a most classy jewellers, Head's dress shop, Brown Bros & Taylor (furniture), the leather goods shop of Rose's, Weston's dress shop, the Belfast Linen Warehouse Co., Ltd., Speed & Son's jewellers and the Scotch Wool Shop.

We had now reached Scott & Son, where I felt very much at home. Like some of the other, long-gone shops I have mentioned, it was stuck in a time warp and was rather old fashioned even by 1950s standards. My father, William Crawshay Scott jnr. and my uncle, Maurice Septimus Crawshay Scott (Mr Will and Mr Maurice to the shop staff), ran the store and shared a most dingy, stuffy and claustrophobic office, hidden away behind the cashier, telephonist and central office staff. Sometimes when I called to see my father, the staff would think that he was in the office, only to discover that he was not there. They had not seen him leave by the 'secret' escape door that was hidden behind the rolls of lino lined up vertically in a display rack!

However, I would much rather see him when he was walking the floor, usually in the china department. More welcoming, too, was the hardware department, where another uncle, Percy Cox, held sway and who was ever ready with a cheery greeting and a joke or two. Drapery, carpets and floor coverings were of no great interest to a small boy but there was a toy counter at the front of the shop and I would crawl under this to see if there were any discarded broken clockwork 'Triang Minic' cars. If I was allowed to take one of these away, I could usually manage to take it apart and mend it.

Upstairs was the furniture, which again was of little interest to me, but beyond this there was a secret attic where my father had a little hideaway. Underneath layers of dust were bent and battered display signs and stands, items from a long-forgotten age, bearing quaint and wonderful names, such as: 'The New ACME 55 Portable Cleanser-Wringer'; 'SAMSON Rollers'; 'The LITTLE PRIDE Mangle'; 'RIPPINGILLE'S Patent Oven'; 'The FLORENCE Stove'; 'The ARCTIC Footwarmer'; 'The EVERSTON Cold Safe milk cooler'; 'CONGOLEUM'; 'LINOETTE'; 'HAREFIELD Rubber Flooring'; 'RUBOLEUM'; 'DAMASCLENE'; 'REXINE'; and many others. Another exciting world lay out at the back of the shop where there was a rear access yard off Purfleet Street. Halfway down the yard stood a sticky pot of hot glue, gently bubbling away on a small gas ring and giving off a distinctive, and not entirely unpleasant, smell. This merged with the rather heady scent of French polish, emanating from the polish shop which was up a rather rickety set of wooden stairs that rose upwards from the floor adjacent to the glue pot.

Often, I would have to search further afield for my father, in the vast warehouse across the road in Purfleet Street where there was even more to discover, such as abandoned furniture, some of which had been brought in for repair but never reclaimed. This was the domain of Billy Green, the warehouseman, who was quite a small man. So small, in fact, that he could easily disappear behind the piles of furniture and crockery. On occasions a call would go out for him from Mr. Will or Mr.

Maurice, who would be taken by surprise when a figure would rise, Ali Baba–like, from within one of the large barrels in which the new china was packed! There was always a small item, such as an eggcup, hidden in the sawdust at the bottom of a barrel and Percy Green would have to climb

right inside to check the bottoms of the barrels.

Garaged at one end of the warehouse were the carpet fitters' vans. These were little Bradford vans that were powered, if that is not overstating the case, by two-cylinder horizontally-opposed engines that had not been changed in design since first being conceived by the Jowett company in 1906. They ran on 'the whiff of an oil rag', according to my father. It was said, and I am inclined to believe it, that when a van needed petrol the fitters would have a discussion to consider how long it was since it last had a refill.

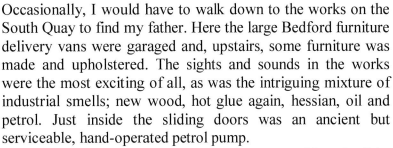

Occasionally, I would have to walk down to the works on the South Quay to find my father. Here the large Bedford furniture delivery vans were garaged and, upstairs, some furniture was made and upholstered. The sights and sounds in the works were the most exciting of all, as was the intriguing mixture of industrial smells; new wood, hot glue again, hessian, oil and petrol. Just inside the sliding doors was an ancient but serviceable, hand-operated petrol pump.

A part of the ground floor of the works was partitioned off by a heavy and really filthy canvas screen. When my father was busy upstairs, I would try to sneak behind this screen where, under thirty or so years of dust and dirt, stood a little boy's dream; a vintage, 1919 Sunbeam tourer. My parents always knew when I had made a clandestine visit to see the Sunbeam

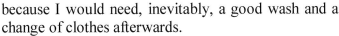

because I would need, inevitably, a good wash and a change of clothes afterwards.

Such was the world of Scott & Son, as seen through the eyes of a lad in the 1950s.

This is the story of a shop which, for some eighty years, was one of the most prominent independent retailing establishments in King's Lynn. Scott & Son was a traditional family firm, offering good value for money, combined with friendly, helpful service provided by attentive, hardworking and

knowledgeable staff. Advertising as 'Complete House Furnishers', this is exactly what they were, having the stock and complementary services to enable anyone about to set up home, or moving house, to order everything that they would need from the one supplier.

However, this is not simply a story about a shop. The business started out as an upholstery and cabinet making workshop and swiftly grew into a small factory. In their first thirty years of trading, most of Scott & Son's bedding and furniture was 'Made in Lynn'.

INTRODUCTION

Scott & Son's High Street furniture store was founded by my great grandfather, Thomas William Scott, and my grandfather, William Crawshay Scott snr., in 1892. Thomas had served an apprenticeship as an upholsterer and ran a small upholstery and cabinet-making business in Church Street for thirteen years. Then, in 1887, he accepted a partnership with Alfred Jermyn, Lynn's premier retailer, trading as Jermyn and Scott from premises in High Street and Union Lane.

When this partnership was dissolved in 1892, Thomas set up business at 89, High Street in partnership with his son. The business expanded into Nos. 93 and 94, High Street. Eventually it occupied the large block of property, Nos. 91 to 97, High Street, together with shops and a huge warehouse round the corner in Purfleet Street.

Throughout the first forty or so years, much of the furniture that Scott & Son sold was manufactured in their own works, firstly in St. James Street and later, from 1902 onwards, on the South Quay. Over time, the nature of the business changed, with fewer and fewer items being manufactured by the company. Nevertheless, Scott & Son maintained a small works and workshop facility throughout the 1950s and 60s, where they undertook some upholstery work, made up mattresses and chair frames and carried out furniture repairs for customers, including re-polishing.

Both World Wars were economic watersheds in the life of the nation. Years of scarcity in the availability of raw materials, goods and services, eventually gave way to rapid growth. The two wars also each marked a step-change in technology which stimulated the development of new methods of manufacture of furniture and goods for the home. For Scott & Son, these changes presented both opportunities, to increase the range of products made by other manufacturers, and challenges, to compete with big national furniture-makers and with the larger chain stores and cut-price retailers.

Between the two wars, Scott & Son embraced the new technologies, being amongst the first to run motor vans and, for example, offering the latest in mechanical organs and phonographs for the expanding music market.

After the Second World War, the firm prospered again in spite of the growing competition. Presciently, Oliver Jermyn, director of Jermyns the High Street department store (later Debenhams), in his capacity as President of Lynn Chamber of Trade had forecast in May 1933 that the national chain stores would drive the private traders from the High Street. By the 1960s the expansion of national chains that were able to offer all of the basic household necessities at rock-bottom prices had begun to have this predicted impact. In competition with Scott & Son there were, by 1970, some furniture and carpet warehouse outlets in the region. Furthermore, carpets made from man-made fibres were taking the demand away from the pure wool Axminsters and Wiltons. In due course, furniture was to become available off-the-shelf in flat packs to be transported home in the family car. China and glass and every-day kitchen utensils eventually became available at a wide range of stores, including out-of-town supermarkets and, of course, from catalogue companies.

In hindsight, it is clear that Scott & Son made the decision to close at the right time. Situated in the centre of the town, where the commercial rates were the highest and car access the least convenient, Scott & Son would eventually have found that their location, once their most prized asset, would have made them uncompetitive. They still retained vast warehousing facilities in Purfleet Street and the semi-redundant works on the South Quay, whereas the new breed of furniture retailers would operate from smaller and more efficient premises or edge-of-town trading estates.

The decision to close was necessitated by the fact that the partners had all of their financial assets locked-up in the company. It was inevitable, therefore, that they would have to rationalise their operations and release some of these assets. It was the partners' intention to continue trading by converting the warehouse into a retail outlet but eventually they were forced to close the shop and works, albeit reluctantly. In 1971 the site was sold for redevelopment and the shop closed.

The High Street / Purfleet Street corner is now occupied by Boots the Chemist and others. The warehouse in Purfleet Street has been radically refaced and adapted and is currently occupied by the Lynn News offices, a café bar, an estate agents, a hair salon and a tanning studio. The new-look buildings provide a much better setting for the views of Henry Bell's Custom House. The works on the South Quay have been replaced by riverfront apartments.

Like many people who eventually embark on researching their family history, I left it until it was too late to gather information from my parents. However, I have been able to consult my brother, Robin, and my cousin, Alan Scott, both of whom worked for many years at Scott & Son. Some papers from the time of my great grandfather, Thomas William, and my grandfather, William Crawshay Scott snr., have been passed down to me and I have used these to provide a framework for the early history of the firm.

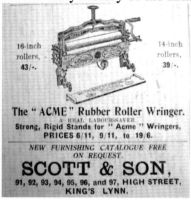

16-inch rollers, 43/-.

14-inch rollers, 39/-.

The "ACME" Rubber Roller Wringer.
A REAL LABOURSAVER.
Strong, Rigid Stands for " Acme " Wringers,
PRICES 6/11, 9/11, to 19/6.

NEW FURNISHING CATALOGUE FREE
ON REQUEST.

SCOTT & SON,
91, 92, 93, 94, 95, 96, and 97, HIGH STREET,
KING'S LYNN.

The local newspapers, available on microfilm at the King's Lynn Library, are invaluable sources of information and it is staggering how much information can be gleaned from these. Jermyn & Scott advertised in both the 'Lynn News and County Press' and the 'Lynn Advertiser'. The dissolution of the partnership in July 1892 was formally notified in both newspapers and, when Scott & Son set up shop in the High Street later that year, the new company started to advertise on a regular basis in the weekly press.

Besides providing an insight into the range of goods and prices offered by Scott & Son, these early advertisements often include details of the services they provided and clues as to the premises that they were occupying at the time. The newspapers also carry articles, and sometimes photographs, concerning newsworthy events, such as a fire at the St. James Street factory in 1898 and the remodelling of the High Street display windows in 1927.

Perhaps the most interesting memorabilia that have survived are the illustrated sales catalogues from about 1912 through to 1934. These give a fascinating glimpse of life in those times, in particular showing how household appliances and kitchen gadgets developed to ease the drudgery of housework. They also chart the progress in demand for some of the less utilitarian items, although Scott & Son never sought to cater for the luxury end of the market.

I have drawn on these catalogues extensively and have included copies of some of their illustrations to show the goods and services offered by the shop in the inter-war years.

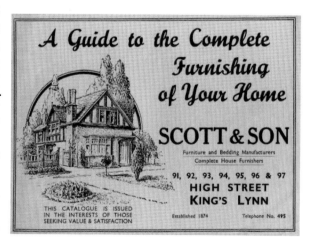

A Guide to the Complete Furnishing of Your Home

SCOTT & SON
Furniture and Bedding Manufacturers
Complete House Furnishers

91, 92, 93, 94, 95, 96 & 97
HIGH STREET
KING'S LYNN

THIS CATALOGUE IS ISSUED
IN THE INTERESTS OF THOSE
SEEKING VALUE & SATISFACTION

Established 1874   Telephone No. 495

Scott & Son did not produce any catalogues of their own after the Second World War. Like other large independent retailers, however, they were afforded the opportunity of having their company stamp on the catalogues of the furniture manufacturers whose goods they stocked or with whom they had an agency arrangement, such as Lebus of Tottenham. Interestingly, both Scott & Son and the Lebus company were to close within a few years of each other.

CHAPTER ONE
Thomas William Scott
and the Early Years
1874 – 1892

DISSOLUTION OF PARTNERSHIP.

JERMYN AND SCOTT.

NOTICE is hereby given that the partnership heretofore existing between us, the undersigned ALFRED JERMYN and THOMAS WILLIAM SCOTT, of King's Lynn, in the county of Norfolk, as cabinet makers, upholsterers and furniture dealers, under the style of "Jermyn and Scott," has this day been DISSOLVED by mutual consent. And notice is hereby also given that all debts, claims and demands against the said partnership will be paid and satisfied by Alfred Jermyn, by whom all debts due to the firm will be received.

Dated this 20th day of July 1892.

ALFRED JERMYN.

Witness to the signature of
   Alfred Jermyn,
EDWD. M. BELOE, Solicitor, Lynn.

THOMAS WILLIAM SCOTT.

Witness to the signature of
Thomas William Scott,
ROBT. A. WILKIN, Solicitor, Lynn.   [52340]

1. THOMAS WILLIAM SCOTT and the Early Years: 1874 – 1892

The two largest of the High Street shops during the first half of the 20th Century were Jermyns drapery and furniture store, founded by Alfred Jermyn, and Scott & Son, the house furnishers. The latter business was founded by Thomas William Scott as a small upholstery and cabinet-making workshop in 1874. For a period of five years, Thomas Scott was in partnership with Alfred Jermyn. Then, in 1892, he formed a partnership with his son William Crawshay Scott and they opened Scott & Son at 89, High Street.

Thomas William Scott was born in London in 1834. After schooling in Chatham, he moved with his mother and sister to Norwich where he was apprenticed to Clarke & Hunter, upholsterers of Dove Street.

On 10th December 1857, at St Margaret's Church, King's Lynn, Thomas married Elizabeth Davison, from Wickmere in north Norfolk. At the time of his marriage, he was living in New Conduit Street. By this date, he was already working as an upholsterer, possibly as an employee at an established King's Lynn workshop. In 1861, the family was living at Bedford Street. Thomas and Elizabeth had six children; five girls, one of whom died in infancy, and one boy, William Crawshay Scott, born on 5th August 1869.

Nothing is known of the work that Thomas was doing at this time but it seems certain that he was developing his cabinet-making skills and learning about the modern furniture manufacturing processes. In 1874, Thomas Scott

THOMAS W. SCOTT,
UPHOLSTERER, CABINET MAKER, &c.,

BEGS to thank the clergy, gentry and the public generally of Lynn and the surrounding district, for the favours bestowed upon him for the past seven years, and to inform them that he has opened the new and commodious premises, 15, CHURCH STREET with an entire New Stock of Upholstery, Cabinet and Bedding Furniture; also Iron Bedsteads, Fenders, Fire Irons, Coal Vases, &c. All goods not in stock made to order, or obtained upon the shortest notice.
All orders entrusted to T. W. S. will be executed with neatness, despatch and economy.

OBSERVE THE ADDRESS :—

15, CHURCH STREET (Opposite the Crown Hotel), KING'S LYNN.

branched out on his own, possibly renting a workshop in the St. James Street area of the town. In later years, Scott & Son were to use this year as the date that the firm was founded. Seven years later he was ready to start selling furniture from his own premises and on 7th January 1882 placed a notice in the Lynn Advertiser announcing that he was moving his business to 15, Church Street (illus. above).

KING'S LYNN.
—
Valuable Freehold Property.

To be Sold by Auction, by

MESSRS. MILES & SON,

ON FRIDAY, MARCH 24th, 1882, at the Globe Hotel, King's Lynn, at Six for Seven o'clock in the evening, the following

VALUABLE PROPERTY.

Lot 1.—All that well-built Freehold Shop and Dwelling-house with Cottage adjoining, situate on the south side of St. James' street, King's Lynn, in the occupations of Wood, Turner and Warnes.

This property will be offered in one lot, if not sold will be offered in two.

Thomas rented the Church Street house and upholstery shop for three years, until buying the freehold in October 1885 from Mr. Thomas Edward Bagge for £450.

Ambitious to expand his business, he set about purchasing property on the south side of St. James Street with a view to developing a modern furniture factory. The first property that he acquired comprised of a shop, house and cottage. The sale notice is illustrated, left.

Thomas William Scott bought this property on 24th March 1882, for £400. Two years later, in April 1884, he purchased further property, described as the **'Estate in St James Street'** from Mrs S.E. Haskins. In order to finance this latter purchase, Thomas took out a loan on mortgage from the King's Lynn and West Norfolk Permanent Benefit Building Society in the sum of £250. He paid this off at the rate of about £25 per annum through monthly instalments of £1 19s 10d until November 1891, when he paid the outstanding amount of £15 0s 8d in cash.

Although Thomas was now manufacturing furniture on a reasonably large scale, he did not have a sufficiently large retail outlet to match his output. Thomas decided to accept the offer of a partnership with the most prominent businessman in King's Lynn, Alfred Jermyn.

Alfred, who was the son of a farmer and miller from Wymondham in Norfolk, trained as a draper in Cambridge and moved to Lynn to take over John Thorley's drapery shop at Nos. 12 & 13, High Street in August 1872. By 1881, he had acquired No. 14 and was employing fifteen men, three boys and three women. On 17th December 1884 there was a disastrous fire at Jermyns' shop, which was totally destroyed. In 1885, Alfred Jermyn commissioned Lynn architect William Adams to design a new drapery store, which was opened later that year. It would appear that Alfred Jermyn bought the two fire-

MR. ALFRED JERMYN, J.P.

THE NEW

PALATIAL

FURNISHING

EMPORIUM,

KING'S LYNN.

damaged shops, Nos. 15 & 16, repaired them and opened a furniture department there. The furniture business did well enough for Alfred to decide to demolish the old buildings in 1887 and to build an extension to his '**New Bon Marché**', as he liked to call his shop. He again called upon William Adams to act as his architect. The building was to be a large new wing attached to the drapery store, with frontage to both High Street and Union Lane, the result being Lynn's largest comprehensive furniture shop and its first fully-fledged department store. Alfred would doubtless have been well acquainted with Thomas Scott because they both traded from the St Margaret's area of the town and he clearly considered him an able manager for this new enterprise. Indeed, it may well have been that Alfred was already buying furniture manufactured by Thomas Scott.

On 24th September 1887, he placed a notice in the Lynn News and County Press announcing that he was taking on a managing partner for his new furniture department (illus. right).

Although he was ten years younger than Thomas Scott, Alfred Jermyn was very much the senior partner, already running a thriving business from the largest retail premises in the town. He had other property in the town too, and was clearly able to raise capital for new ventures, such as the furniture department, without any difficulty at all. However, he seems to have let Thomas run the new department without too much interference. Indeed, the partnership announcement made it clear that Thomas Scott was in full control of the furniture side of the business. This included his St. James Street furniture factory, which at this date was probably mostly manual with, presumably, treadle-powered lathes and stitching machines. Thomas Scott can be credited, therefore, with the innovations and promotions that emanated from the furniture department over the next five years. Meanwhile,

ALFRED JERMYN

Respectfully announces that the

NEW FURNISHING STORE is rapidly approaching completion. He fully expects it will be so far advanced to enable the opening to take place early in October.

Mr. T. W. Scott (who for several years has carried on business in Church Street, Lynn) has come to an arrangement with Mr. Jermyn for the transfer of his entire business to the New Stores, and will become the Managing Partner.

Alfred Jermyn spent most of his time on that side of the business that appears to have interested him the most, clothing. Several of his drapery department advertisements proclaim that '**Mr Jermyn is just back from London**'. He travelled up to town regularly to survey the London fashion houses and returned with new stock for his clothes department. The new furniture department was opened on Michaelmas Day, Tuesday 11th October 1887.

It was housed in an imposing two-storey building designed in a similar, but not identical, style to that of the drapery store, to which it was an extension. The High Street frontage of the new department was 37ft long, about half that of the drapery shop alongside, with a fully-glazed ground floor comprising of two huge floor-to-ceiling plate-glass display windows, one each side of a central glazed entrance. Above these were five windows fitted with blinds and curtains to protect the goods on display on the first floor from fading in the sunlight. The vertical brick columns and horizontal timber floor beams of the High Street façade were clad externally in glazed tiles and the whole was surmounted by a decorative pediment in the form of an oriole dormer window giving light into the attic storage level. Over the heads of the first and ground floor windows, the tiled fascias bore the legend: **'JERMYN & SCOTT FURNITURE UPHOLSTERY AND BEDDING STORES'**. Along the 84 ft Union Lane frontage, the store had six bays, each glazed with full-height plate-glass display windows at street level. The upper windows matched those overlooking High Street, as did the tile-clad columns and fascias. The steeply-pitched and slated roof ran parallel to Union Lane, and along its ridge, silhouetted against the sky, were tall letters reading: **'JERMYN & SCOTT'**.

Together with the drapery shop, this new department formed a most magnificent-looking store (illus. above – Lynn Advertiser 5th July 1890) which was quite the largest and most imposing commercial establishment in the town. Doubtless many of the townspeople, who would be unfamiliar with city shopping in Cambridge, Norwich or London, would have gravitated to this end of High Street just to gaze in awe at this grand shop – the **'VICTORIA BON MARCHE'** as Alfred Jermyn now called it – and to wander around inside admiring the huge range of goods on display. In size, it was not to be rivalled until Thomas Scott had fully-developed his own store at 91 to 97, High Street. The other great independent retailing establishment in the town at this time was **'THE GREAT EASTERN STORES'**, a clothier's shop at the corner of Norfolk Street and Broad Street, founded by a young Scottish draper, Richard Catleugh.

Both Alfred Jermyn and Thomas Scott demonstrated care and concern for the welfare of their staff and for the interests of their customers. Jermyns' staff were provided with rest and refreshment facilities and some living accommodation was made available to them in High Street and in St. James Street. Some of Alfred Jermyn's drapery apprentices lodged with him and his family at his home, Burleigh House, in Goodwin's Road.

Jermyn & Scott's furniture department was an immediate success and the output from the St. James Street factory increased rapidly. On 29th October 1887, Jermyn & Scott placed an advertisement in the Lynn Advertiser (illus. right), extolling the merits of the new store.

Thomas Scott introduced hire purchase facilities for customers, together with a '**Furniture Club**', aimed at 'the working classes'. Through these initiatives, together with their policy of offering furniture at the cheapest possible prices, Jermyn & Scott aimed at enabling even the poorer families to comfortably furnish their homes.

They strived to live up to their self-proclaimed position as '**The People's Store**'. Their pre-Christmas advertisement in the Lynn News and County Press on 3rd December 1887, (illus. below) offered Christmas presents and decorations at '**Remarkably Low Prices**'.

Thomas Scott commissioned the building of a special furniture removal van and this was delivered to the firm by the end of December, 1887, when they announced their: '**NEW "SAFETY" REMOVING VAN, (Specially Built by CHILVERS), is now Finished and Ready for Use. Estimates given for Removal of Furniture to any distance, also for Warehousing.**'

THE PEOPLE'S FURNISHING STORES.

MESSRS. JERMYN & SCOTT

Respectfully invite all Visitors to Lynn to look over their Spacious

NEW SHOW ROOMS.

THESE ARE THE LARGEST IN THE EASTERN COUNTIES.

Well Lighted, Comfortably Accessible, and now contain a very Great Variety of the

MOST USEFUL, MOST MODERN & MOST PLEASING ASSORTMENT OF

HOUSEHOLD FURNITURE

MOST SUITABLE FOR EVERY HOME,

Whether it be Mansion, Hall, Farm Residence, Villa or Cottage,

At such Remarkably LOW PRICES that must command the purchase of this class of goods in Lynn, for which so many residents of the district have previously visited London.

JERMYN & SCOTT'S

NEW BEDSTEADS, NEW BEDDING, SPRING MATTRESSES,

OF THEIR OWN MANUFACTURE.

MAY BE RELIED ON FOR STRONG AND DURABLE WEAR AND TEAR.

ESTIMATES GIVEN FOR THE REMOVAL AND STORAGE

OF ALL CLASSES OF HOUSEHOLD FURNITURE.

JERMYN & SCOTT

Will exhibit in their

HANDSOME WINDOWS

A Large Display of Very Cheap

Fancy Furnishing Articles

Suitable for

CHRISTMAS PRESENTS & DECORATIONS.

The Remarkably Low Prices for their

GENERAL HOUSE FURNITURE

Has given great satisfaction to the

NUMEROUS VISITORS TO THEIR NEW STORES.

Messrs. JERMYN & SCOTT in order to give the same facilities as the London Furniture Houses, have now established "A Hire Purchase System," so that by easy Payments the Purchases become the entire Property of the Purchaser within One, Two, or Three Years.

Special Terms will be made by private arrangement to all who avail themselves of this system.

JERMYN & SCOTT'S Goods are all marked Cheap and cannot be excelled in Price.

JERMYN & SCOTT have also commenced a Furniture Club for the Working Classes, every information given to enquirers.

On 9th June 1888 Thomas Scott placed an advertisement in the Lynn Advertiser (illus. below left) announcing the issue of his first illustrated furniture catalogue. It is not known whether this was based on catalogues issued by other retailers, locally or from further afield, perhaps London, or whether it was an original idea. Either way, it was a bold advertising initiative and must have required a considerable input in terms both of time to compile the details, price list and illustrations, and also in financial outlay. The fact that the catalogues were to be continued on an annual basis thereafter indicates that this must have been judged to be a successful marketing strategy.

Alfred Jermyn doubtless invited Thomas Scott to accompany him on some of his trips to London so that they could assess the nature and strengths of the capital's furniture retailers. Jermyn and Scott aimed to match the London shops, not only in style and price but also in the terms of their hire purchase facility. Their greatest selling point, however, was the fact that the furniture and bedding was

SEND FOR

JERMYN & SCOTT'S

HANDSOME NEW FURNITURE CATALOGUE,

Several Hundreds of them are being posted this week over the district.

made at their own factory and that this allowed them to guarantee its quality. Increasingly, they emphasised this in their advertisements. In August 1888 they advertised '**BEDDING MADE UP IN OUR OWN FACTORY**'. In June of the following year, they offered '**DRAWING-ROOM SUITES – FIVE GUINEAS upwards, JERMYN & SCOTT'S Own Manufacture. DINING-ROOM SUITES – SEVEN GUINEAS upwards, JERMYN & SCOTT'S Superior Strong Make**'. Later that same year, they advertised their range of locally-made bedding:- '**IMMENSE STOCK OF BRASS-MOUNTED BEDSTEADS, MATTRESSES, FEATHER BEDS, PALLIASES, MADE AT OUR OWN NEW LARGE FACTORY. ALL CAN BE RELIED ON AS PURE, CLEAN AND STRONG MADE**'.

Thomas Scott's son William started working for his father in 1888 and learnt about every aspect of the manufacturing and retailing sides of the business at Jermyn & Scotts.

JERMYN & SCOTT
"MANUFACTURING FURNISHERS."

A trades exhibition was held in St James's Hall, County Court Road, Lynn from 29th October to 6th November 1888 and this provided an opportunity for the business to display their wares. The show was advertised as promoting innovation and on show were items such as 'Self-pouring Teapots' and the 'latest productions in Hot Water heating apparatus'. Thomas William Scott was a member of the organising committee, which was chaired by Henry Plowright, the town's foremost ironmonger.

TRADES INVENTIONS EXHIBITION.
ST. JAMES'S HALL, LYNN.
JERMYN & SCOTT
WILL HAVE ON SHOW A LARGE ASSORTMENT OF
HIGH-CLASS FURNITURE,
FOR BED, DRAWING AND DINING ROOMS,
OF THE LATEST STYLES AND IMPROVEMENTS. ALSO A GREAT QUANTITY OF
GLASS BRACKETS AND OVERMANTELS,
AND FANCY GOODS OF VARIOUS DESCRIPTIONS.
THE LATEST IMPROVEMENTS IN
BRASS AND OTHER BEDSTEADS.
JERMYN & SCOTT,
HIGH STREET, KING'S LYNN.

There was a grand opening ceremony to the exhibition at 4.00pm, performed by the mayor, G. S. Woodwark, supported by Weston Jarvis, Esq., M.P., Lord Henry Bentinck, M.P. and members of the Corporation. The large hall was decorated out as an 'Old Irish Town', with scenes of the Lakes of Killarney, the castles of Clonmines and Blarney complete, of course, with a replica kissing stone. 'By kind permission of Supt. Ware', the King's Lynn Police Band performed a selection of popular music on the first Monday afternoon and the first Tuesday evening. There were other bands, concerts, recitals and entertainments too, including 'Illusions' and 'Illuminations on the lawn'. The exhibition was open each day from 2.30pm until 10.00pm, extended to 11.00pm on each Tuesday. Day tickets were priced at 6d and a season ticket cost 1/6. Special train fares were available from all Norfolk stations and from Newmarket, Cambridge, Peterborough, Boston and Spalding and intermediate stations.

MESSRS. JERMYN & SCOTT
ARE CONSIDERABLY EXTENDING
THEIR FACTORY ACCOMMODATION.
THE NEW BUILDING
IS NOW NEARLY COMPLETE, WHICH WILL GIVE CONSIDERABLY
INCREASED ACCOMMODATION TO THEIR
FURNITURE MANUFACTURING DEPARTMENT.

In the Spacious Show Rooms in High street will shortly be displayed a number of exceedingly cheap Suites of Household Furniture, upon which the workmen have been employed during the winter months. Purchasers may have great satisfaction in knowing they can obtain as good value in their own neighbourhood, in securing reliable goods, and thus encourage the trade and labour of the district, instead of going to the trouble and expense of making their purchases in London, and not knowing how the goods will turn out after they arrive at home, very often broken and damaged in transit.

The St. James Street factory was improved by the erection of a new workshop, the plans being approved on 7th March 1889. A requirement of the Borough Council, in approving the plans, was:- 'Walls not of uncombustible (sic) materials. Passed subject to the wood panel work on front being replaced by brickwork'. Later that year, an application was submitted for a new furniture store to be built in a yard off Union Lane at the back of the High Street shop. The yard had lockable gates, giving access to an open-fronted furniture storage shelter, with timber posts supporting the roof. At the back of this was a lock-up furniture warehouse and to one side a long carpenters' shop. A coach house and stables completed the development.

The new factory building in St. James Street was soon completed and Jermyn & Scott advertised on 30th March 1889 (illus. above) that they had increased the stock that was on display at their shop.

Their first catalogue was clearly a success because on 4th May 1889 they advertised in the Lynn Advertiser that they were issuing 5,000 new ones.

Alfred Jermyn was keenly aware of what London shops had to offer and it is apparent that he was determined to match them for design, quality and, of course, price. The aim was to persuade customers within the wider district to shop in Lynn. Their slogan was 'London Style at London Prices' (illus. below right), which indicates that at this date the Capital was seen as providing the cheapest goods and that provincial businesses were trying hard to match the prices available there. For Christmas 1889 Jermyn & Scott advertised ideas for presents as well as decorations for the home. Decorative grasses and palms were traditional decorations at Christmastime and these were available in many of the Lynn shops. Amongst the items considered suitable as presents at Christmas were:- 'BAMBOO and LACQUERED TRAY WHATNOTS; MUSIC WHATNOTS; LADIES' WORK BASKETS lined and unlined in great variety; EGG POTS and CHAINS in various colours; ENAMELLED MIRRORS with Plush Brackets; RUSH and WICKER TABLES and CHAIRS; BLACK and WALNUT BENT-WOOD CHAIRS stuffed in Satin; OCCASIONAL CHAIRS IN VELVET of various colours; CANDLE and LAMP SHADES and VEILS; and a quantity of other useful Household Articles'.

DON'T GO TO LONDON FOR YOUR
FURNITURE,
WHEN YOU CAN SEE SUCH A SPLENDID AND VALUABLE STOCK AT
JERMYN & SCOTT'S,
WHO SUPPLY
LONDON STYLE AT LONDON PRICES,
Made in their St. James's Factory by their own Cabinet and Upholstery Employes.

Jermyn & Scott appreciated the benefit to their business of attracting as customers young married couples who were about to set up home for the first time. Consequently, they aimed some of their advertising towards this potential market. They appealed to these young couples to consider the availability of Jermyn & Scott's hire purchase system as a means of furnishing the whole of their first house. The illustration (above left) is part of an advertisement that appeared in the Lynn Advertiser on 27th April 1889.

ALL ABOUT TO BE MARRIED,
ALL REPLENISHING THEIR HOMES,
ALL WANTING CHEAP FURNITURE,
ARE INVITED TO PAY A VISIT TO
JERMYN & SCOTT'S
GREAT FURNITURE AND FURNISHING STOCK,
(IMMEDIATELY ADJOINING JERMYN'S DRAPERY STORE,)
SEE THEIR DURABLE HOME-MANUFACTURED
DRAWING & DINING ROOM SUITES,
At Six Guineas, Eight Guineas, Ten Guineas.

In September 1890 their third illustrated catalogue was issued. This time 20,000 copies were sent out, giving some measure both of the success of their previous catalogues and of the number of potential customers in their catchment area. White's trade directory of 1890 lists: 'Jermyn & Scott, cabinet makers, upholsterers, general house furnishers & manufacturers, 15 & 16 High Street & Union Parade factory, St James Street'. They were now capable of producing a full range of furniture and bedding at their St. James Street factory. Their capacity had increased, too, and the output from the factory was now sufficiently high for Thomas Scott to satisfy orders from London and from elsewhere in the country. It is likely that Alfred Jermyn had helped to secure these orders from outside their local area through his extensive business contacts in London, the Midlands and the north of England. These orders were certainly a coup for this young manufacturing company and Jermyn & Scott did not miss out on the promotional opportunities that this afforded them.

Throughout the month of January 1890, their advertisements mentioned the completion of a large London order, together with the fact that it had been safely delivered and that the customer was very satisfied (illus. above right).

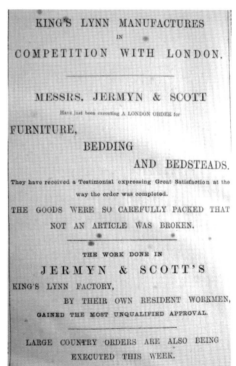

KING'S LYNN MANUFACTURES
IN
COMPETITION WITH LONDON.

MESSRS. JERMYN & SCOTT
Have just been executing A LONDON ORDER for
FURNITURE,
BEDDING
AND BEDSTEADS.
They have received a Testimonial expressing Great Satisfaction at the way the order was completed.
THE GOODS WERE SO CAREFULLY PACKED THAT NOT AN ARTICLE WAS BROKEN.

THE WORK DONE IN
JERMYN & SCOTT'S
KING'S LYNN FACTORY,
BY THEIR OWN RESIDENT WORKMEN,
GAINED THE MOST UNQUALIFIED APPROVAL.

LARGE COUNTRY ORDERS ARE ALSO BEING EXECUTED THIS WEEK.

Alfred Jermyn was content with the way that his partnership with Thomas Scott was working out, particularly because of his ability to delegate all of the management responsibilities of the furniture department. This gave him some time to devote to his London visits, to his role within the Wesleyan Methodist church and, increasingly, to his involvement in local politics. However, he was still in day-to-day control of the huge drapery half of the business and he decided to devolve management of this department, too. On 8th March 1890, he announced a second partnership, making it clear his intention to travel to London even more frequently. In the notice, Alfred Jermyn explained the need for the new partnership, saying that the drapery and carpet business '**has become such a Vast concern that he believes it necessary for the best Interests of the Public generally that more frequent Visits should be paid to the GREAT MARKETS OF MANUFACTURERS and FASHION, for securing the Latest Products at Prices that NONE CAN EVER BEAT**'.

The man chosen by Alfred Jermyn as his new partner was Mr. Charles William Perry, a 33 year-old draper who had been employed with Messrs. Footman, Pretty and Nicholson, of Ipswich. In choosing Charles Perry, it is clear that Alfred Jermyn found himself a dynamic and loyal partner, one who stayed with the firm for 37 years and whose sons became partners, too. Within a very short time, Charles Perry had made his mark on the advertising style of his department and he took more and more space in the weekly newspapers. Jermyn and Perry's advertisements were nearly always the largest in the local press.

A COTTAGE furnished for	·	·	£10.
A SMALL HOUSE furnished for	·	·	£25.
A VILLA furnished for	·	·	£50.
A SUBURBAN RESIDENCE for		·	£100.
A SMALL MANSION· for	·	·	£250.

An indication of the cost of furnishing the home in 1890 is provided by their advertisements giving the minimum costs to furnish various sized houses (illus. left). Jermyn & Scott's principal selling points for their own furniture were listed as:- **1. Every article may be relied on for wear. 2. All goods delivered free any distance. 3. Bedding, cabinet work and upholstery, are manufactured in our own factory. 4. All goods are warranted and exchanged if not approved. 5. Prices will bear comparison with any London and provincial houses. 6. Arrangements can be made for extending the payments over one or two years, if satisfactory reference be given. 7. Our testimonials express unqualified satisfaction with execution of orders.**

Advertisements at this date rarely included any illustrations of the wares being offered for sale. It was quite a bold departure, therefore, for Jermyn & Scott to include sketches of their furniture in the Lynn Advertiser on 22nd November 1890 (illus. right). It was not repeated and it must be presumed that this was a costly exercise and that they decided to rely on the distribution of their annual illustrated catalogues. The expression 'Art Furniture' was used in some of Jermyn & Scott's advertisements and apparently referred to the more ornately designed ranges with decorative inlay.

The traders at this date very often bought up the whole stock of others who were retiring or whose business had gone bankrupt. The bigger stores, such as Jermyns, would sometimes advertise a huge purchase from as far afield as London or the Midlands. In August 1891 Jermyn & Scott held another big summer sale and they included in it the entire stock of Mr. Whincop, a Lynn cabinet maker who was retiring from business. Born in about 1831 in Great Yarmouth, Robert Garwood Whincop was the son of a mariner who had brought his family to Lynn before 1841. Robert

had been in business as a cabinet maker and upholsterer on his own account for at least 37 years, first at Checker Street, then at Railway Road and finally at No. 32, Norfolk Street. It appears that Thomas Scott and his son William had a close relationship with the Whincops and that either Robert or his son helped at Scott & Son in the 1890s.

The furniture and bedding factory in St. James Street was often referred to as a 'Steam Factory', in recognition of the fact that the machinery was powered by a steam engine. The factory was housed in a two-storey building. The mattresses and bedding were manufactured on the ground floor, which also contained the stabling for the horses that drew the pantechnicon vans. Also on the ground floor was the machinery and engine house, which contained a steam engine, a gas engine and a steam chaff cutter. On the first floor were the cabinet making, polishing and upholstery workshops. In the yard were stacked piles of different types of timber used in the manufacture of the furniture.

Scott's steam factory was one of several manufacturing workshops in King's Lynn, there being other traders in the town who both made and sold their own products. Another factory in St. James Street was W.H. Johnson's steam cycle and machine works, manufacturing and selling cycles, perambulators and mail carts. Similarly, James Plowright was in the same line of business, operating out of his works at No. 27, Railway Road and Market Street. These two were amongst several familiar names that remained at the heart of Lynn's shopping centre well into the latter half of the 20th Century.

SALE! SALE! SALE!

In addition to the Great Sale now going on at Jermyn & Scott's,

THE ENTIRE STOCK
OF
MR. WHINCOP, CABINET MAKER,
Will be offered at ENORMOUS REDUCTIONS.

PAPER HANGINGS from 1d. per piece to clear lots.
ALSO OTHER BARGAINS IN CABINET GOODS.

THE GREAT FURNISHING EMPORIUM
OF
JERMYN & SCOTT
IS NOW OFFERING
SPECIAL ADVANTAGE TO ALL ABOUT TO FURNISH EITHER
COTTAGE, VILLA OR MANSION,
BY GIVING
2/- in the Pound discount for Cash for one month commencing
SATURDAY JULY 18th.
THE WHOLE OF THEIR MANUFACTURED STOCK
WILL BE OFFERED, CONSISTING OF

Drawing Room Suite	
Dining Room do.	Bedroom Suite
Breakfast Room do.	Dining Room do.
Library do.	Bathroom do.

ALSO
BEDSTEADS, PALLIASSES,
MATTRESSES, BEDS,
BOLSTERS, PILLOWS,
AND
EVERY REQUISITE FOR COMPLETE FURNISHING.

JERMYN & SCOTT,
LYNN.
[2290]

KING'S LYNN
TRADES AND INDUSTRIAL EXHIBITION,
WHICH WILL BE OPENED BY
H.R.H. THE PRINCE OF WALES,
ON SATURDAY, NOVEMBER 14.
JERMYN & SCOTT
WILL EXHIBIT FURNITURE OF THEIR OWN MAKE
At Stalls 3, 4 and 5.
A SPECIALITY
(One of our 'own ideas and made for this Exhibition.)
THE COMBINATION BOOK-CASE BEDSTEAD.
DRAWING AND DINING ROOM SUITES,
THE "FRAMES" OF THE LATEST DESIGN,
Which have been carefully selected for this occasion.
SEVERAL VERY HANDSOME
ROSEWOOD INLAID CABINETS & OVERMANTLES,
WALNUT CABINETS AND OVERMANTLES,
And a very great variety of Fancy Articles, consisting of
TERRA COTTA PLAQUES.
(These make a very handsome picture.)
Newspaper Racks, Plush Mirror Brackets, Hand Bags,
Some remarkably
CHEAP PICTURES, HANGING AND OTHER FLOWER POTS IN VARIETY.
A Quantity of Really Good Class Ware, consisting of
IMARI, KOLAN AND KAGA VASES, &c.,
ALSO
BISHUI CUPS AND SAUCERS,
RUSH AND WICKER CHAIRS AND OTHER GOODS,
AND SEVERAL VERY HANDSOME
DRAUGHT SCREENS & FURNISHING REQUISITES
JERMYN & SCOTT,
GENERAL HOUSE FURNISHERS,
HIGH STREET & UNION PARADE,
KING'S LYNN.

Another trades exhibition was organised in Lynn in 1891. At four o'clock on Saturday 14th November 1891 His Royal Highness the Prince of Wales performed the opening ceremony of the 'King's Lynn Trades and Industrial Exhibition' at St. James's Hall and Assembly Rooms. The exhibition ran for a week and included exhibits of the '… work of Her Royal Highness's Alexandra Technical Schools at Sandringham, and of Ladies and Gentlemen of the Town and District.'

This was a really big event in the life of the town and was promoted vigorously to attract visitors from throughout Norfolk and further afield. The Great Eastern Railway Company issued return tickets at the single fare rate on each day of the exhibition from every station in Norfolk, and from Lowestoft, Cambridge, Newmarket, Ely and all intermediate stations. Daily entrance tickets were 6d and 'Season Tickets' were 2/- and 5/- (which latter included the opening ceremony). The trades section included many of the leading trades people of the town, who had been encouraged to submit 'articles of their own manufacture and latest novelties in connection with their business.' Prizes, medals and certificates of merit were awarded in each of the various classes. Jermyn & Scott took three stands at the exhibition and certainly appear to have made every effort to impress with their specially-made items of furniture, as can be seen from their advertisement in the Lynn News and County Press, 14th November 1891 (left).

Thomas Scott's partnership with Alfred Jermyn continued until 1892. In the Lynn Advertiser on 2nd January of that year they advertised New Year gifts, including:- **'Oil paintings from 9d each; Scripture texts with enamelled frames at 6d each; Coloured Prints in frames of various colours. Imitation Painted Opals mounted on plush at 5d each; Photo Frames in gilt, oak and enamel; Hanging and other Flower-pots, Grasses, Bull-rushes; Brackets; and Lined Work Baskets'**. Their hire purchase scheme was proving very popular with their customers and there had been a significant take-up. The most popular items in the shop were their brass rail bedsteads, wire spring mattresses, wool overlays, feather bolsters and pillows. The bolster and a pair of pillows were offered together at 48/6. On 6th February of that year, they advertised their annual sale. The sale was to extend for one month and everything in the department was on offer, for cash only, at a discount of 10%. A similar advertisement appeared for the following four weeks but there were no more for Jermyn & Scott after 5th March 1892.

It is apparent that Thomas Scott had decided to set up shop on his own and that he and Alfred Jermyn were in negotiation over the termination of their partnership.

DISSOLUTION OF PARTNERSHIP.

JERMYN AND SCOTT.

NOTICE is hereby given that the partnership heretofore existing between us, the under-signed ALFRED JERMYN and THOMAS WILLIAM SCOTT, of King's Lynn, in the county of Norfolk, as cabinet makers, uphol-sterers and furniture dealers, under the style of "Jermyn and Scott," has this day been DIS-SOLVED by mutual consent. And notice is hereby also given that all debts, claims and demands against the said partnership will be paid and satisfied by Alfred Jermyn, by whom all debts due to the firm will be received.

Dated this 20th day of July 1892.

ALFRED JERMYN.

Witness to the signature of
Alfred Jermyn,
EDWD. M. BELOE, Solicitor, Lynn.

THOMAS WILLIAM SCOTT.

Witness to the signature of
Thomas William Scott,
ROBT. A. WILKIN, Solicitor, Lynn.   [52340

On 30th July 1892, in the Lynn Advertiser (illus. left), and on 6th August in the Lynn News and County Press, a formal notice announcing the dissolution of the partnership appeared. The signatures of Alfred Jermyn and Thomas Scott had been witnessed by their King's Lynn solicitors, Edward M. Beloe and Robt. A. Wilkin, respectively.

Although we have no details about the terms of the dissolution, the notices that Alfred Jermyn and Thomas Scott subsequently issued indicate how the main assets were divided. Alfred Jermyn bought out Thomas's interest in the retail business, including the remainder of the stock, while Thomas bought Alfred's share of the factory. This arrangement allowed Alfred to continue selling furniture without interruption from Nos.15 and 16, High Street. Thomas was now free to set up his own retail establishment but had to find suitable premises and then stock it with new furniture from his factory.

Thomas was now 58 years old and his son William was 23. The main motivation for Thomas to break away from Alfred Jermyn at this time may have been the desire to establish a business for his son to inherit. If he had wanted to do this, he could not have left it too much longer, and the appearance of Charles Perry as a much younger partner in the drapery department may well have prompted him to take action without further delay. Although he had nothing like the property portfolio that Alfred Jermyn held, Thomas William Scott owned property in the town and was able to raise capital to invest in the development of the new partnership with his son. The five years that he had been in partnership with Alfred Jermyn would have generated for him a not inconsiderable income and Thomas was now in a good position, financially, to lay the foundations of what was to become one of Lynn's largest stores.

The photograph above, courtesy of Irene Laws, shows Thomas William Scott sitting next to his wife Elizabeth, with their children standing behind. From left to right are:- Maria Thirza (b.1864); Emily Sarah (b. 1861); William Crawshay (b. 1869); Edith Jane (b. 1874); and Elizabeth Maria (b. 1858).

PLAN of HIGH STREET. c1890
SHOWING THE LOCATION OF
JERMYN & SCOTT'S FURNITURE STORE

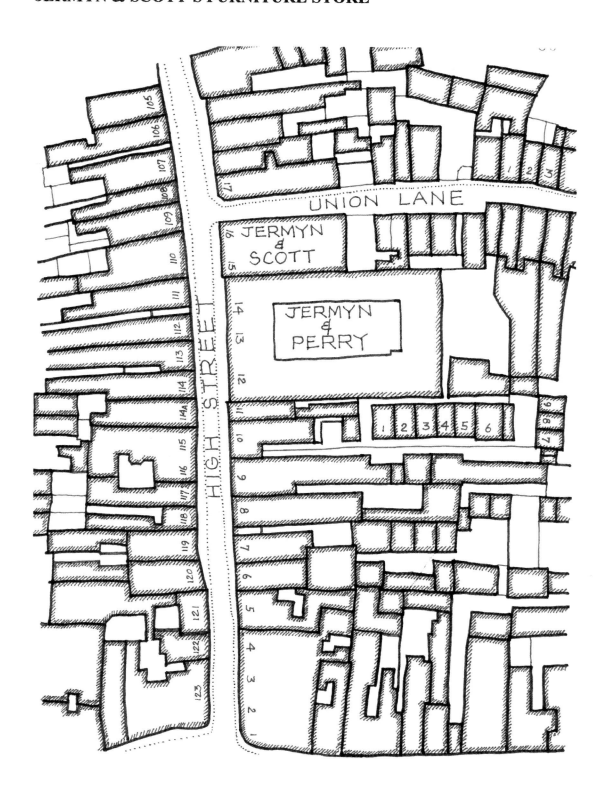

CHAPTER TWO
A shop on the High Street
Scott & Son: 1892 - 1900

2. A Shop on the High Street: Scott & Son 1892 - 1900

The photograph below shows Thomas William Scott, standing far right, and his son William Crawshay, centre, in front of Scott & Son's first shop at No. 89, High Street and dates from about 1892.

The search for suitable High Street premises in which to set up the new shop was made easier by the number of empty properties and the frequency with which existing traders were moving. The advertisements in the Lynn News and the Lynn Advertiser in

MR. THOMAS W. SCOTT,

WHO for many years carried on a good business as Cabinet Maker and Upholsterer in Church Street, King's Lynn, until five years ago, when he introduced his business into High Street, under the name of JERMYN & SCOTT,

BEGS TO GIVE NOTICE

That he has Dissolved Partnership with Mr. Jermyn, and intends to carry on business, with his son as Partner, in Church Street, under the name of

SCOTT AND SON.

the summer of 1892 contained a few to choose from and one, in particular, which remained vacant for several weeks. This was No. 89, High Street, on the western side, eight shops along from the Purfleet Street junction. The shop had been occupied by J. H. Reddie & Sons, music sellers and pianoforte and harmonium dealers. Josiah Henry Reddie and his sons Ferdinand and Percy were moving from No. 89 into No. 42, High Street, just across the road. The owners of the property put it in the hands of Lynn estate agents Miles & Son, who advertised it to let in June, offering occupation on the 24th of the month. It is not known when Thomas and William Scott first showed an interest in renting the premises, but further advertisements appeared throughout June and July, the last one being in the Lynn Advertiser on the 30th of the latter month. However, they had the choice between this shop and the one next door, No. 88, which was also advertised to let in July 1892.

It is apparent that they had not secured the tenancy of suitable premises prior to the dissolution of the partnership with Alfred Jermyn, because the first notice placed in the newspapers by Thomas Scott announcing the new partnership contained only the Church Street address (illus. above). They moved quickly, however, and on 16th August they announced in the Lynn News that they were opening their new shop at No. 89. Incidentally, Reddie and Sons, whose move to No. 42 created the

opportunity to set up shop here, were to be taken over by Scott & Son in January, 1903.

In addition to their Church Street Shop, they have opened the Extensive Premises,

No. 89, HIGH STREET,

(LATELY OCCUPIED BY REDDIE & SONS, MUSIC SELLERS.)

STEAM FACTORY: ST. JAMES'S STREET.

SEE OUR FUTURE ADVERTISEMENTS. 62329

Evidently, on learning that Thomas was setting-up shop at No. 89, Alfred Jermyn offered the opinion that this was unwise because it was at 'the wrong end of High Street'.

By September 1892, Scott & Son's business was well under way and they began to advertise their furniture, emphasising the quality and value for money. The fact that they made the furniture themselves was their greatest selling-point and, as manufacturers, they were also able to make items to their customers' requirements and they advertised 'SCOTT & SON are Manufacturers, therefore can produce a better article, for less money, than people who Buy and Sell. Special sizes in MATRESSES and PALLIASES made on the shortest notice and NOT CHARGED EXTRA'. Although their Lynn competitors could offer some of these benefits, Scott & Son's factory had a wider range, especially for bedding, and a greater output. Amongst the other furniture retailers in the town were Cole & Co., of 13, London Road, who had their main shop in Station Road, Newmarket; Trenowath Bros., at 73 & 74, High Street; and, of course, Alfred Jermyn, who announced the establishment of Jermyn & Sons, 'THE COMPLETE HOUSE FURNISHING STORES'. In his advertising at this date, Alfred Jermyn played on the strength of having the largest store of its kind in the Lynn area. The words he used were either 'The Largest Furniture Show Rooms in the Eastern Part of England' or 'The Largest Furniture Store This Side the County'. Although he announced that the new store was to be known as 'Jermyn's Furniture & Complete Furnishing Stores', it was never referred to in this way in advertisements after 6th August 1892.

IMPORTANT NOTICE.

THE STEAM FACTORY IN ST. JAMES'S STREET is now the Sole Property of SCOTT and SON (who were the Buyers, Managers and Manufacturers of JERMYN & SCOTT,)

Scott & Son included a notice concerning their factory in the Lynn Advertiser on 3rd September 1892 (illus. above), the wording of which gives a clue as to the nature of the relationship between Alfred Jermyn and Thomas Scott in the management of the furniture department during their partnership. From this it becomes clear that Alfred Jermyn had delegated the running of his furniture business to his managing partner, Thomas Scott. There is no doubt, therefore, that Thomas had demonstrated considerable business acumen in developing such a dynamic business. Although he had to leave this behind when he broke with Alfred Jermyn, he retained the steam factory in St. James Street and was soon able to build up his new business with fresh stock.

Scott & Son banked with Sir E. H. K. Lacon of Lacons, Youell & Co., at the King's Lynn Bank, in High Street, where they secured an overdraft by depositing the deeds of a property in St. James Street on 5th September 1892. Then, on 27th October 1892, they paid £500 for a 'Shop cottage and ground at St James Street' and it was for the purchase of this property that Scott & Son needed the overdraft from their bank. It is interesting to note that Thomas describes himself as a 'Cabinet Maker' when signing the agreement to purchase this property, whereas in every census from 1851 to 1891 inclusive, he gives his occupation as 'Upholsterer'. In addition to being a banker, Sir

Edmund Henry Knowles Lacon was the proprietor of the Norwich brewery that bore his name and a Member of Parliament. He lived at Ormesby Hall. His King's Lynn Bank was at No. 65, High Street, on the corner with the Tuesday Market Place. It moved into new premises diagonally opposite, at the corner of the Tuesday Market Place and Surrey Street, in 1897. The name of the bank became Lacon, Youells and Kemp, which amalgamated with the Capital and Counties Bank in 1901. The latter became part of Lloyds Bank in 1918.

Also in 1892, Thomas William Scott made an effort to acquire what appears to have been a substantial property in the High Street, but was unsuccessful. According to an account for services provided by his solicitor, David Ward, Thomas had instructed him to negotiate with a Miss Jackson for a house and shop 'lately occupied by Mr Taylor.' Miss Jackson said that she had been offered £1,500 and so Thomas offered £1,550 but this was declined. It is likely that his failure to secure this property led to him setting-up Scott & Son in No. 89, High Street when it became vacant. Intriguingly, the property concerned may well have been No. 114, High Street, directly opposite Jermyn & Perry, which was occupied at this time by Charles Henry Taylor, a grocer. Alfred Jermyn later bought this property, so it appears that he could have been the one who out-bid Thomas Scott!

It was inevitable that Scott & Son would find themselves going head-to-head with Jermyn & Sons for the furniture retail market in King's Lynn. This battle is reflected in the wording of the advertisements placed by the two companies in the

THE CHEAPEST AND BEST
BEDSTEADS, BEDDING AND GENERAL
HOUSE FURNISHING STORES
IN NORFOLK
IS
SCOTT AND SON'S.
All about to Furnish would do well to inspect their immense Stock.

two local newspapers over the next few years. By October 1892, it was becoming apparent that both Jermyns and Scotts were conscious of the claims that the other was making about their prices and services through their advertisements. The grounds for this advertising rivalry were quickly established. Each was anxious to be seen to:- be the largest store in the region; stock the most comprehensive range of goods; be able to undercut their rivals in terms of affordable furniture, with regular emphasis on the cheapness of their stock; be selling furniture of the best quality and durability. In due course, they would also each be promoting their own easy payments arrangements.

On 1st October, Jermyn & Sons advertised that they were the 'LARGEST AND CHEAPEST COMPLETE HOUSE FURNISHING STORES WITHIN A RADIUS OF NEARLY FIFTY MILES'. The following week Scott & Son responded to Jermyn & Sons' claims by advertising that they were 'THE CHEAPEST AND BEST BEDSTEADS, BEDDING AND GENERAL HOUSE FURNISHING STORES IN NORFOLK'. They advertised special lines that they had just manufactured at their factory in St. James Street. These were drawing-room and dining-room suites in 'Cretonne, Leather, Leather Cloth, Plush, Tapestry, Velvet, and Saddle-bags'. These were priced from £3/3/0 to £8/15/0. Their principal boast was always that they could guarantee the purity of the bedding that they manufactured:

WRINGING & MANGLING MACHINES CHEAPER than EVER.
SCOTT & SON have just made a large contract with the Makers for WRINGING AND MANGLING MACHINES, whereby they can offer them at exceptionally low prizes, namely, from 25 6.
CARPETS! CARPETS!! CARPETS!!!
TAPESTRY CARPET 1/3½, 1/6½, 1/9½ yd. TAPESTRY SQUARES, 3 yds. × 3½ yds., from 34 6.
KIDDER SQUARES, 3 yds. × 3 yds., from 22/6.
BRUSSELS SQUARES, 3 yds. × 3½ yds., from 48 6.
FLOOR CLOTHS, ALL WIDTHS AND PRICES.
RUGS! RUGS!! RUGS!!!
3/6, 3/11, 4/9, 5/11 to 23/6.
SPLENDID ASSORTMENT IN DOWN QUILTS, from 15/ to 40/.

'SCOTT & SON, being Bedding Manufacturers, can warrant everything being pure and clean'. Having introduced a savings scheme and hire purchase arrangements when in partnership with Alfred Jermyn, it is not surprising that Thomas Scott did the same at his new shop as soon as he was able to make the necessary financial arrangements. Back at the other end of the High Street, Jermyn & Sons were doing likewise and, consequently, another selling point for the two companies became their hire-purchase arrangements. On 29th October 1892 Scotts proclaimed that 'All should join Scott & Son's Furniture Club. Their Hire Purchase System gives great Satisfaction. Terms on Application'. Jermyn & Sons responded on December 3rd by claiming to have 'The Most Popular Hire Purchase System by which Anyone can Furnish a House for a few Pounds down'.

In addition to the furniture and bedding lines that Scott & Son manufactured at their St. James Street factory, their shop stocked an expanding range of products made by other manufacturers. In order to be competitive, they sought to secure contracts with some of these manufacturing companies for the supply of their products in quantity. On 3rd October 1892, they advertised that they had secured a large order for wringing and mangling machines at competitive prices (illustrated on the previous page). They also stocked a wide range of carpets, floor cloths and rugs.

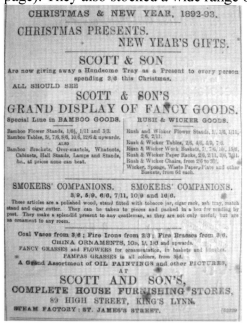

Christmas and New Year presents in 1892/3 were rather utilitarian by today's standards, although Scott & Son tried hard to cater for people's leisure interests. In their advertisement placed in the Lynn Advertiser on 7th January, illustrated on the following page, they offered a tray as a present to everyone spending 2/6. Items of a decorative nature, rather than those serving an entirely functional purpose, were advertised, including china ornaments, oil paintings, fancy grasses and flowers for decoration and a range of '**Fancy Goods**'. The smoker was well catered for by the offer of a range of '**Smokers Companions**' from 3/9 all the way up to 16/6: '**These articles are a polished wood stand, fitted with tobacco jar, cigar rack, ash tray, match stand and cigar cutter. They can be taken to pieces and packed in a box for sending by post. They make a splendid present to any gentleman, as they are not only useful, but are an ornament to any room**'.

The following year, the advertising war between Scott & Son and Jermyn & Sons continued unabated, with each vying to be seen as having the biggest furniture store offering the widest range of products at the cheapest prices. In an age when there was no Advertising Standards Authority to regulate the use of superlatives, they each sought to outdo the other. Scott & Son invited potential customers to '**GO TO SCOTT & SON'S (WHO ARE MANUFACTURERS) WHERE YOU CAN SEE THE LARGEST STOCK OF HOME-MADE FURNITURE IN THE DISTRICT AT PRICES NOT TO BE EQUALLED**'.

Other traders in the town seem to have felt compelled to join in this competitive advertising battle, even if they were not selling the same type of goods. Ladymans, whose advertisements were usually quite restrained, proclaimed that '**LADYMAN'S TEAS ARE THE BEST**'.

However hard Scott & Son and the other Lynn traders tried to outdo each other with the inventiveness of their advertisements, none of them could match the idiosyncratic and amusing approach adopted by Richard Catleugh, whose '**Great Eastern Stores**' were situated at the corner of Norfolk Street and Broad Street. On his arrival back from his trips to Scotland, he would place the cheery greeting '**RICHARD IS BACK!**' at the top of his advertisement.

His trademark invitation to customers to come and inspect his stock was '**U KUM ANN C 4 U R Selves**', which seems remarkably like a nineteenth century precursor for today's text-speak. Having stocked his store with some new purchases from London, Richard Catleugh came up with a most bizarre, but attention-catching, start to his advertisement in the Lynn Advertiser on 11th March 1893 (illus right).

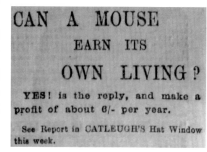

Jermyn & Sons, meanwhile, were busy re-inventing themselves under various new names, including: '**JERMYN & SONS, GIGANTIC FURNITURE STORES**' and '**JERMYN & SONS, EASTERN COUNTIES' FURNISHING STORES KING'S LYNN**'.

Perhaps Scott & Son found this name-changing rather unsettling because they then started to advertise under the name of T. W. Scott & Son (illus. above left). This lasted for a period of eight weeks until May 20th 1893, when they reverted to Scott & Son. It is perfectly possible that there was a serious discussion between father and son over the way that the company was styled. All the evidence suggests that William, even though he was only 23 at the time, was sufficiently strong-minded to assert his rights as a partner. He may well have been sensitive about the use of his father's initials in the company title for this series of advertisements. Alternatively, this may simply have been a copy-writer's mistake. There are very many examples of typographical errors in advertisements from this period, including traders' names and addresses.

As the year wore on, Scott & Son started to be a little more relaxed in their approach to advertising, reducing it to a single column, which made it half the size of those placed by Jermyn & Sons. They even missed a couple of weeks in August, perhaps when either father or son were on holiday. They were now advertising their household removal service in lock-up 'PANTECHNICON VANS by Road or Rail. Estimates Free' (illus. above right from Lynn Advertiser 24th June 1893).

Scott & Son's advertisement in the Lynn Advertiser on 13th January, 1894, invited readers to write for a copy of their illustrated catalogue and price list. Although this was the first occasion that Scott & Son had advertised the availability of their illustrated catalogues, it seems likely that they would have started producing them almost immediately that the new partnership started trading in 1892. It was, after all, Thomas Scott who had first introduced these annual catalogues when in partnership with Alfred Jermyn, in 1889. Scott & Son probably made their catalogues available at their shop for customers to pick up and take away but did not promote them more widely until 1894. Jermyn & Sons, however, were advertising their version of the furniture catalogue from 1892 'BY POST THIS WEEK. We present to our clients throughout the entire district TWENTY-SIX THOUSAND (26,000) PROFUSELY ILLUSTRATED CATALOGUES - COMPLETE HOUSE FURNISHING - COMPLETE BEDDING LISTS - COMPLETE BEDSTEAD CATALOGUE - ONE OF THE MOST USEFUL GUIDES TO HOUSE-FURNISHING EVER PUBLISHED - AT PRICES NONE CAN BEAT'.

It is not known whether any of these 19th Century catalogues have survived. However, it became quite a tradition for both Scott & Son and Jermyn & Sons and, presumably, some other local companies, to issue comprehensive, illustrated catalogues annually. In the case of Scott & Son, this practice continued right up until the commencement of the Second World War.

Next door to Scott & Son, at No. 88, High Street, were the offices, warehouse and works of the Lynn News & County Press Co., Ltd. In July 1892 they had announced that the Company had 'purchased the premises occupied by Mr. R. Nurse, in Purfleet-street (with adjoining property) and intend to erect there a new and commodious Printing Office etc, etc'. They were selling-off their stock of books and stationery in anticipation of the move. In due course, they vacated their warehouse at the rear of No. 88, and this gave Scott & Son an opportunity to expand.

On 14th April 1894 Scott & Son included a statement in their advertisement in the Lynn Advertiser announcing that they had opened further showrooms in the warehouse at the rear of No. 88 (illus. right). Their expansion into the former Lynn News warehouse allowed them to create twelve showrooms.

Whilst Jermyn & Sons and Jermyn & Perry together regularly occupied two complete advertising columns, by 1894 Scott & Son were content with a quarter of that amount and would not advertise every week. However, the war of superlatives continued on and off, with both claiming to be the biggest and best in their particular field. Scott & Son were 'The UP TO DATE COMPLETE HOUSE FURNISHERS - ACKNOWLEDGED BY ALL TO BE THE CHEAPEST IN THE TRADE'.

In 1894 the company advertised that they held over £3,000 worth of stock. As an incentive to customers, they offered two shillings in the pound discount (10%) for cash. Drawing and dining room suites cost from £3 to £25 and all were made by the company at their St. James Street works. Evidently, they were doing a brisk trade that year and in their advertisement in the Lynn Advertiser on 7th April 1894 they claimed that they had been unable to satisfy the demand for their suites (illus. left).

The range of services offered by the Company included the recovering, re-polishing and repair of furniture and the remaking of mattresses 'equal to new', and they also offered 'FUNERALS completely furnished.'

On 8th August 1894 William Crawshay Scott married Florence Emily Hampton, the daughter of William Hampton, a tailor of Priory Lane, King's Lynn. They went on to have seven children, five girls and two boys; William Crawshay jnr., born 10th September 1901, and Maurice Septimus Crawshay, born 5th July 1913, both of whom were to enter the business.

The only ledger book to have survived dates from these early years of the Scott & Son partnership, between 1892 and 1896. Being located in the heart of Lynn's High Street, it is not surprising that many of the other traders there were clients of Scott & Son. Indeed, over 50 of the 104 individual businesses in the street traded with them during these first four years.

Amongst their very first clients was Messrs. Jermyn & Sons, the family company formed by Alfred Jermyn to run his furniture department after Thomas Scott's departure. It may be that Jermyn & Sons needed a few

months to recruit all the skills they required to continue the cabinet-making and upholstery sides of the business. In July, 1892, Scott & Son fitted some chair cushions for them. They also supplied them with 850 tiles for a shed - possibly in the yard off Union Lane. These tiles were most probably surplus to their requirements at the St. James Street factory premises. Also that month, they supplied Jermyn & Perry with 4yds. of blue check linen tick at 3/6 per yard.

Many of the earliest transactions related to repairs to furniture, re-polishing and re-upholstery. A significant amount of this work was undertaken for the brewers and for individual publicans and they completed jobs at over 25 public houses during this period. Most of these were in Lynn, including work for Mrs. Wenn at No. 123, High Street, Mrs. Holdcroft at the Queen's Head, 45, High Street, and Mr. Oliver Rowell at the Volunteer Stores in Union Street (above left). They travelled further afield for some of this work, including to the Plough Inn and the County Arms at Terrington, the Ship Inn, Narborough, the Plough Inn, Snettisham, the Norfolk Hero, Stanhoe and the Le Strange Arms at Hunstanton.

Thomas Scott was already acquainted with Thomas Edward Bagge, head of Messrs. W & T Bagge & Son, the King Street brewers, having purchased No. 15, Church Street from him in 1885. Mr. Bagge and his family placed a considerable number of jobs with Scott & Son, both for the brewery's chain of pubs and personally for their residences. He bought and hired furniture from the company and used them to move furniture for him. In March 1893 Mr. Bagge arranged for them to supply 4yds. matting for the 'Royal Standard', situated in County Court Road, on the site of the former St. James Church which had been demolished in 1854 (illus. above). In June that year they re-stuffed and covered one of the bar seats at the 'Greyhound', 25, High Street, using best leathercloth, at a cost of 15/9. They did a similar job in April, 1894 at the 'Duke of Fife', 5, Saturday Market Place, again using best leathercloth, at a cost of £1/9/3.

When Mr. Bagge was living at Islington Hall, near Tilney, he hired four large easy chairs from Scott & Son for a fee of £1. Later he moved to Gaywood Hall, the family home where he had been born in 1838, and they transported his furniture from Islington for him, also hiring out to him six chairs for a shop that he had in the vicinity. In total, the value of Mr. Bagge's business with Scott & Son amounted to over £60 during their first three years of trading. The sketch of Mr. Bagge (right) appeared in the Lynn News & County Press on 21st January 1893.

MR. THOMAS EDWARD BAGGE.

One of their earliest removal contracts was for the Rev. Pryor B. Whalley, who was living in King Street in 1893. The Rev. Whalley had been curate of East and West Wretton for several years, during the time that his father had been the rector there. Scott & Son moved his furniture by rail in one of their pantechnicon vans and stored it for him for a time, at a total cost of £1/15/7. Some of the Rev. Whalley's furniture needed repair, although not as a consequence of any damage caused during transportation. Scott & Son effected these repairs at a cost of 9/6. One year later, the Rev. Whalley was on the move again, taking up the living of St. Paul's Lakenham, Norwich, and Scott & Son again moved his furniture for him, this time at a cost of £4/15/0.

In addition to deliveries and removals that started or ended at Lynn, Scott & Son undertook more complicated journeys. On 30th July 1894 they moved two pantechnicon vans full of furniture from Little Dunham, near Swaffham, to Totham, near Bishop's Lydeard, Taunton, Somerset, for a Mr. Womack. Their fee was £15 and the rail bill £17/2/0. The total weight that was transported was 3tons 12cwt 3qr 12lb, which was charged at 4/9 per cwt on the railway.

The removal of furniture by horse-drawn pantechnicon van and rail was not a straight-forward operation by any means and each journey required a considerable amount of planning. Despite this careful planning, however, there was still plenty that could go wrong. Horses had to be hired to pull the pantechnicon at the end of the rail journey and they could not be kept waiting indefinitely if the

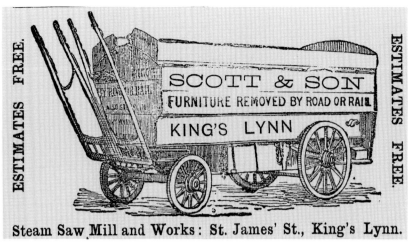

Steam Saw Mill and Works: St. James' St., King's Lynn.

train was late. The pantechnicons had to endure some rough handling and sometimes suffered damage that required repair before the horses could be hitched up to complete the journey. The furniture suffered frequent breakages while being transported by rail, although Scott & Son prided themselves in the careful packing and safe handling of customers' goods. If delays and problems arose, the only form of communication between Scott & Son's men and the client or the shop in Lynn was by telegram.

In December 1895 they moved Mr. George Grimson's furniture from 38, Marine Parade, Yarmouth, where he had a boarding house, to the 'Gun Inn', Tower Street, Lynn, where he became the licensee for a short time. Their fee was £6/10/0 and the rail charge was £5/15/0 for 2tons 3cwt of furniture. Some china was broken in transit and the bill was reduced by 10/- in compensation. Mr. Grimson appears to have enhanced the atmosphere in the 'Gun Inn' by the introduction of some musical clocks and he bought three of these from Scott & Son during the year or so that he was in Lynn. However, the pub trade was not to his liking, apparently, and he returned to the boarding house business in Yarmouth in 1897, with Scott & Son again transporting his furniture for him. On this occasion, they charged him 1/- for the cost of a telegram sent during the move.

In the three years 1894 to 1897, Scott & Son made 36 claims to Mr. Knights, the Great Eastern Railway Company's local manager, for breakages incurred transporting goods, mostly on journeys from London to Lynn or vice versa. One claim was settled on behalf of the Great Northern Railway Company, following damage to four chairs in transit from Glasgow to Lynn. The number of claims made reflects the frequency with which Scott & Son were moving furniture on the Lynn to London route - at least once per month.

Damage to the van was the cause of the most serious problems that they encountered. On 9th August 1895 they claimed for the delay of one of their vans at Cambridge. The van could not proceed any further without repair, which included having two bolts made up to replace those that had been lost. Four of Scott & Son's men had been sent with the consignment and they were held up at Cambridge overnight. The claim to the Great Eastern Railway Company, including the cost of the repairs, the new bolts and the overnight accommodation for the four men, amounted to £2/16/6, which was settled in full. There was negotiation over some of the claims, of course, and the Railway Company would occasionally refuse to cover the total amount requested. In one instance, they would not agree to pay for damage to two marble washstand tops, for some reason, and paid only half of another claim.

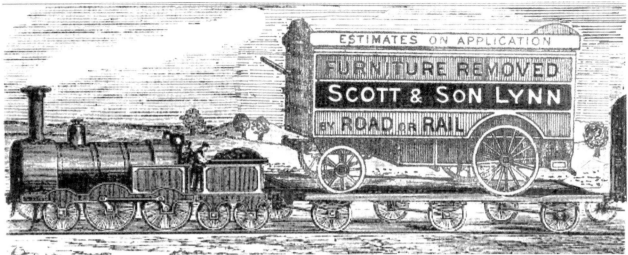

Almost any item was prone to damage in transit on the railway, including fragile items such as mirrors, picture frames, glass-topped dressing tables and chimney glasses for oil lamps. More sturdy items suffered too, and the ledger entries detail the extent of the damage, e.g., 'Sideboard back, bottom plinth and pillars broken' (16th May 1896), 'Wardrobe Panel broken and cornice smashed to pieces' (28th October 1896), 'Birch Washstand completely smashed' (29th October 1896), and '12 bags flocks damage by water' (26th October 1894).

One journey, in December 1895, was particularly fraught. The client's house was at Harrow-on-the-Hill, Middlesex, and Scott & Son's men were there with horses awaiting the arrival of the van. However, it was so badly damaged that the railway personnel could not unload it at Harrow and it had to go on to the terminus at Stanmore, where it was taken off in the goods yard. The horses had to be driven to Stanmore to fetch the van but, before they could do so, it had to be repaired. Unfortunately, the men could only fix the damage temporarily but it was sufficient to get the van back to Lynn for permanent repairs to be done. The Railway Company paid for the delay, the extra cost of transporting the van from Stanmore to Harrow and for the two sets of repairs.

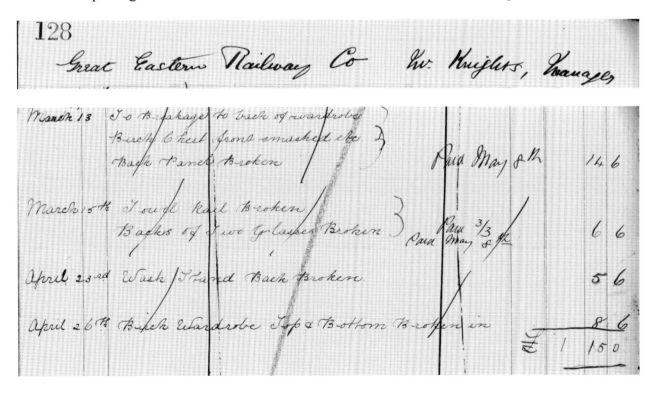

Scott & Son were frequently called upon to move furniture locally, sometimes from one room of a house or commercial premises to another or from one Lynn address to another. In March 1894 they moved Thomas C. Green's furniture from No. 44 to No. 84, High Street, at a cost of 12/6. T. C. Green advertised as a 'Merchant Clothier, Tailor, Hatter, & Men's Clothier'. Later that year they moved Mr. T. Green snr's furniture from High Street to Checker Street. Longer distances within the county were common, with Norwich being a regular destination and, in November 1895, they moved furniture to Norwich from Lynn for the Singer Company, bringing another load back again (illus. above).

The job of getting large items of furniture into and out of the houses in High Street was almost as difficult as it was at small rural cottages. Mr. Charles Barrett was one of Lynn's best known grocers at this time (illus. right c1900). He had been born in Bluntisham, Huntingdonshire, and he called his shop at No.100, High Street 'Bluntisham House'. In April 1893 Scott & Son supplied him with a new birch wardrobe for £5/18/6 but they had to dismantle it at the foot of the stairs, carry it up to the bedroom in pieces and reassemble it. For this they charged 5/-. Moving Charles Barrett's piano was also problematic and they had to get it in through the window.

Mr. Herbert Le Grice's business was that of Le Grice Brothers 'Fancy Drapers' at Nos. 21 and 22, High Street, which he founded in 1888 with his elder brother, Charles. In June 1896 Herbert left the High Street house to live in Gaywood and Scott & Son moved his furniture. This was another case that involved lifting a piano out of a window. Herbert also bought some new furniture from Scott & Son for the Gaywood house, including a bedroom suite in satin walnut for £12/12/0, a bedstead and spring mattress and a kitchen dresser. The firm was often called upon to alter curtains and blinds when clients moved from one house to another and the Gaywood house had a bay window, which necessitated altering curtain poles that Herbert had brought with him from High Street. The total cost of the removal, new furniture and work at the house amounted to £22/2/0, which made it one of Scott & Son's larger contracts, in monetary terms, in the early years.

Another job that same month indicates the extent to which Scott & Son would carry out work to help their customers move into a new house. Their client was Mr. Murrell, who paid a total of £24/17/10 for the removal of his furniture and for new items and for work at the house. They supplied stair carpet and rods, fitted floor coverings, curtains and poles, picture hooks, and towel rails and they hung the pictures and fitted the blinds. They also made a linen cupboard under the cistern for Mr. Murrell. Once again, the removal of a piano necessitated lifting it out of a window.

Amongst the customers who placed large individual orders with Scott & Son during this period was Mrs. Ellen A. Cracknell, a widow, who bought £31/11/4½ worth of furniture and furnishings for a house in Carmelite Terrace, Lynn. She bought many of the items needed to furnish a house from scratch, endorsing Scott & Son's constant claim to be 'Complete House Furnishers'. Her order included linoleum, floor canvas, stair baize, stair rods, curtains with all the fittings, window blinds, a three piece suite in green velvet, a dining table, Pembroke table, bedstead, mattress, pillows, bolster, hearthrug, door mat, toilet set, towel rail, coal scuttle, slop pail, knife box, dust pan, waste basket, and kitchen fender. It would appear that Mrs. Cracknell subsequently ran into financial difficulties and was declared bankrupt. In December 1895, Scott & Son received the first of three payments from the court. The total that they received against their outstanding account was £10.

Mrs. Cracknell was not the only customer who found it difficult to complete the payments on their purchases from Scott & Son. Few paid the full amount straight away and it was usual for the payments to be spread over several months.

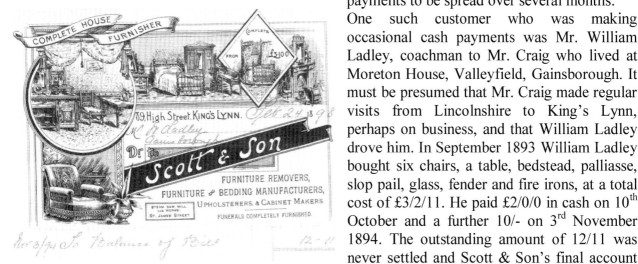

One such customer who was making occasional cash payments was Mr. William Ladley, coachman to Mr. Craig who lived at Moreton House, Valleyfield, Gainsborough. It must be presumed that Mr. Craig made regular visits from Lincolnshire to King's Lynn, perhaps on business, and that William Ladley drove him. In September 1893 William Ladley bought six chairs, a table, bedstead, palliasse, slop pail, glass, fender and fire irons, at a total cost of £3/2/11. He paid £2/0/0 in cash on 10th October and a further 10/- on 3rd November 1894. The outstanding amount of 12/11 was never settled and Scott & Son's final account (illus. above), drawn up on 24th February 1898, was never presented. It would seem that either Mr. Ladley ceased employment with Mr. Craig or that the latter stopped visiting Lynn and Scott & Son decided to write off the outstanding amount.

Another debt that was pursued through the County Court concerned furniture supplied to Mr. G. Rix Wells (aka George Rix) of Dersingham on 13th June 1893. He bought a suite in green velvet (£8/15/0), four chairs (3/3 each), chest of drawers (24/6), and a dining table (£1/4/6). The total bill was a not insignificant £13/13/9 (illus. above). George had been born at Gayton in about 1861, the son of Henry and Ann Rix. He went to St. James School, London Road, King's Lynn. Henry Rix was a farmer at Hall Farm, Gayton between 1861 and 1871 and was married to Ann Wells, who came from Dersingham. On the death

of his maternal grandmother, Mary Wells, George Rix inherited a considerable estate, left in the will of his grandfather, John Wells, a Dersingham publican. George, who apparently never worked for a living, set himself up in some style, with a butler, cook and domestic servants and proceeded to spend his inheritance. He changed his name to Wells and called his large house in Manor Road, Dersingham 'Wellswill' (illustrated left). Unfortunately for Scott & Son, the purchases from their shop were made when George's money was already spent and they had to apply to the court for payment of their account. On 1st July 1893 they received £8/0/0 cash from the County Court in King's Lynn but the remaining £5/13/9 had to be written off. (In a rather bizarre postscript, William Crawshay Scott jnr., grandson of Thomas William, bought 'Wellswill' in 1953. He lived there with his family for many years, having first changed the name of the house to 'Woodroyal').

The works of renovation and repair carried out by Scott & Son were many and varied. One of the smallest was the repair of a pair of bellows for Mr. Marshall of St. Ann's Street, Lynn, at a cost of 3d. Chair casters were often replaced, but usually as part of a larger job, such as a new leg. In May 1895, they provided and fitted a new flywheel to a wringer for Mr. William Linnett Smith, a butcher of 54, London Road, at a cost of 3/-. Having supplied him with a new wringer barely six months earlier, for £1/7/6, Scott & Son must have been attending to a machine that had suffered accidental damage rather than one with some manufacturing fault. They advertised that they sold the sturdiest of wringing and mangling machines and that they would repair faulty goods.

One of their earliest repair contracts was for Mr. Richard Charles Wales, licensee of the 'Rummer Inn', on the corner of Tower Street and St. James Street. In July 1892 they repaired a frame to a couch (1/6), a linen horse (6d), a towel horse (6d), a brush handle (3d), a small chair (1/3) and a work table (1/9). In the following year, they fitted out the pub with eight window blinds at a cost of £8/8/0.

Local social clubs (illus. right) were good clients and often called upon Scott & Son to move furniture from one club room to another and to hire extra chairs and tables when needed for special functions. On several occasions they did work for the YMCA, re-polishing and re-upholstering some chairs for them in August 1893, moving goods to the club rooms in December of the same year and hiring them some furniture 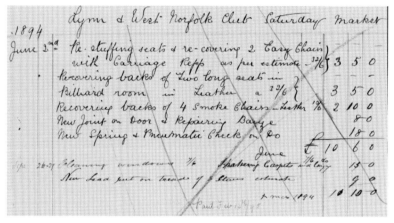 at the same time. In December 1894 they loaned some tables and chairs to the club for their Christmas dance, at a cost of 10/-

The King's Lynn Working Men's Conservative Club was situated in St. Ann's Street prior to moving to St. James Street in 1894. Scott & Son helped to maintain the club's billiard table and its other furniture and equipment. In 1893, they recovered the billiard table for £5/10/0 and also returned the ivory billiard balls which had become misshapen. They made shades for the billiard table lights, too, and renovated the long smoking-room seats and ten chairs in February 1894. When the club moved premises to St. James Street, they transported the billiard table across town for them and installed it at the new venue. They fixed the marker board and took down one of the internal doors, re-hanging it so that it opened the other way. Other work for the club included laying new lino and carpet and they even repaired one of the billiard cues.

An occasional job entrusted to Scott & Son was the re-polishing of sets of bowls. This was usually on behalf of a local pub, such as the 'Greyfriars Tavern' in London Road. The licensee there in August 1894, was Alfred Drake, who paid Scott & Son 2/- to have a set of bowls re-polished. Two years earlier, they had charged 1/- for a similar job to William Henry Brown, builder, of 30, London Road. Mr. Brown built Scott & Son's 'New Shop' at Nos. 93 & 94, High Street, in 1899.

In the years before the invention of the vacuum cleaner, carpets needed to be taken up for shaking and cleaning. Trenowath Brothers were the principal firm that did this work in Lynn but Scott & Son also offered the service to their customers. In March 1894, they were commissioned by Mr. Page of the Provincial Bank, Tuesday Market Place, Lynn to recover some chairs and to clean the carpets. The work entailed re-covering an easy chair in **'figured rep. with plush borders'** (£1/16/0), re-covering a couch in moquette (£1/12/0), and cleaning and shaking two carpets (2/6 each), totalling £3/13/0.

Arthur Robert King was the chief cashier, later (1894) manager, at Lacon & Youell, No. 65, High Street, where Scott & Son banked. He placed numerous orders with them between 1892 and 1896. Most were for his domestic, rather than business, requirements and a significant proportion was for the repair of a child's chair and mail cart. Arthur and his wife Elizabeth had a young family and they must have given the furniture at No. 65 some hard times. Between 1892 and 1895, their children's chair was repaired nine times, the crib was repaired once and the mail cart, bought new from Scotts on 22nd July 1893 for £1/1/6, was mended eight times. Tragically, Mr. and Mrs. King's daughter Ellen Victoria died in October 1893 aged six. Scott & Son made the coffin for her funeral. In addition to these domestic repairs, Scott & Son made and repaired furniture for the bank, including two office stools covered in pig skin with matching footstools. Two other office stools were re-upholstered, also in pig skin, and they supplied a letter rack, paper rack and a notice board covered in green baize.

One of the biggest jobs in 1894 was the moving of goods for a firm from Peterborough that was opening a branch in Lynn. The firm was Custance & Son, **'Practical, Clerical and Livery Tailors, Breeches Makers, Hatters, Hosiers, and Juvenile Outfitters'.** The branch manager was George Burton Custance, who had a First Class Certificate from the Tailor and Cutter Academy in Drury Lane, London and who promised men 'a perfect fit'.

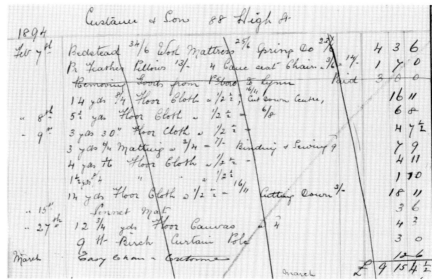

The shop that Custance & Son had chosen for their King's Lynn branch was No. 88, High Street, next door to Scott & Son. Doubtless Thomas and William Scott would have met George Custance when he came to inspect the premises. However it came about, the two firms did business with each other and Scotts moved George's furniture for him from Peterborough to Lynn in February 1894. They also supplied a bedstead (34/6), wool mattress (25/6), spring mattress (23/6), pair of feather pillows (13/-), and four cane seat chairs at 3/6 each. The total bill, which included some floor cloth, amounted to £9/15/4½. Some additional furniture was transported from Peterborough by train in May and Scott & Son collected the van from the station and took it to No. 88, High Street where it was unloaded, the bedsteads re-assembled and the curtain poles altered and fitted. George Custance had two pianos and these were re-polished by Scott & Son, bringing the total bill to £11/18/4½. The bill was settled in an interesting manner. Scott & Son rented out some space in the outbuildings at No. 88 and £3 of the bill was paid off against rent that was due. A further £3/5/0 was accounted for by the value of a new bespoke jacket and waistcoat that William Scott had ordered from George Custance. The remaining £5/13/4 was paid by cheque, the settlement being made very promptly after completion of the work. Very few payments by cheque are recorded in this ledger.

The re-polishing of pianos was a regular job for Scott & Son at this date. Some polishing was undertaken on pianos situated in private houses, as in the case of those belonging to George Custance. They were also called out to clubs and other venues to do this type of work. However, by far their greatest amount of work came from the piano dealers in Lynn, who regularly called upon their skills to renovate pianos that had been out on hire.

J. H. Reddie & Sons, who had previously occupied No. 89 but had moved to No. 42, High Street, called upon the services of Scott & Son to re-polish pianos on average once per month. Some of these jobs involved polishing only one part of the piano, usually the side or front panel. It is likely that these had become bleached by the sun as the instrument stood in the front room of the person to whom it was on hire. Reddies had supplied a grand piano to the 'Duke's Head' in the Tuesday Market Place and Scott & Son were called out to re-polish this instrument at the hotel.

Pamment & Smith were another of the principal music dealers in the town and were established around the same date as Scott & Son, in about 1892, when they took over the premises at No. 90, High Street, moving to No. 5 in 1901. Thomas Smith was a blind piano tuner and music teacher and lived at his parents' house at No. 50, High Street until he formed a partnership with Robert W. Pamment, an organist and music teacher. Thomas married Robert's sister Charlotte in 1896. Over the years, Scott & Son carried out a considerable amount of work for Pamment & Smith, including moving and, mostly, polishing pianos. The charges for their work were based upon the time taken to re-polish a piano, typically between 5½ hours (4/3) and 8½ hours (6/6). Most of the work for Pamment & Smith was carried out at their High Street shop but some was done at their clients' premises.

In August 1893 Hepzibah Pamment, Robert and Charlotte's mother, died and Scott & Son made the coffin at a cost of £3/10/-. The first coffin that they had made was for the funeral of Mrs. Fanny Nears Rye in October 1892, made from pitch pine with brass engraved plate and handles, at a cost of £3/15/0. Fanny was the wife of Stephen Rye, a plumber of 85, Norfolk Street, and she died at the age of 34, leaving two young sons.

Another tragic case was that of Mr. and Mrs. Brown who had just moved to Lynn. In June 1895 Scott & Son repaired an easy chair for them and then supplied them with a new cradle and pram blanket. However, by the beginning of the following month their baby daughter, Alice May, had died and Scott & Son made the coffin (16/6) and provided the coach for the funeral (7/6).

One of the larger and longer removal jobs undertaken by Scott & Son was a van full of furniture that had to be transported from Carlisle to Middleton Towers for Mr. and Mrs. Saunders in 1895 at a cost of £24/0/0. A further load of loose furniture, weighing 4tons 8½cwt, brought the bill up to £41/15/0. The bulk of this bill was settled by a cheque for £19/4/2 and two £10 notes. However, the remaining amount of £2/10/0 was not settled until two years later. In September 1895 they furnished three servants' bedrooms at Middleton Towers and the bill at that date amounted to £15/0/0, which included the outstanding sum, and this was paid in January 1897.

Clement Royd Bentley, of West Bilney Hall, settled his bill for £17/19/8 rather more promptly. Scott & Son were brought in to strip down and varnish the woodwork in the bedrooms, landings and stairs. The work was started on Friday 11th August 1893 with one man and an apprentice travelling by train from Lynn. They worked on the bedrooms for 10 hours that day and the same on Saturday 12th, using two gallons of stain and three of varnish. They returned on Tuesday 5th September and again on Thursday 7th to finish this part of the job and to lay carpets. Meanwhile, a team of three men were tackling the landings and the stairs, using chemical paint stripper before staining and varnishing the wood. They travelled each day in a horse and cart, for the use of which Scott & Son charged 3/- per day. The men worked a minimum of 7½ hours and a maximum of 11½ hours each day to complete the job, every day from Monday 11th September to Tuesday 20th, apart from Sunday 17th.

Scott & Son worked for several of Lynn's best-known businessmen, including George S. Woodwark, of Thompson, Patrick & Woodwark, timber and slate importers, who was a former town mayor (1885/6). In 1896/7 they undertook twelve jobs for him, most of which were carried out at his house in Goodwin's Road. These included repairing a skylight and a washstand, replacing sash cords and window catches, re-fitting Venetian blinds, replacing a bedstead rod and fitting a new leg to a dining room table.

Two other of Lynn's most prominent men were the engineers Alfred Dodman and Frederick Savage and both placed work with Scott & Son. For the former they made a deal table covered in best leathercloth for the steam tug 'Star' at a cost of 8/6 (illus. above) and they also supplied him with some furniture for his house.

The order placed by Frederick Savage was one of the largest, in monetary terms, recorded in the period 1892–1896. Frederick Savage bought land for development in Lynn, where workers' houses were built in North End near his St. Nicholas Ironworks and in Gaywood Road, where nine executive villas were built. In Lowestoft, he built shops with houses attached. His biggest project there was for three shops with houses above on a corner site fronting London Road and Waveney Road, known as 'Turret House'. The houses were for the benefit of his children and grandchildren and Scott & Son provided much of the furniture for one of these. The furniture supplied included many of the items required to furnish an empty house, including: a three piece suite (£8/8/0); Persian bedstead (£4/18/6); spring mattress (35/6); tin toilet set (10/6); wool mattress (30/-); overmantel (£6/8/6); sideboard (£6/10/0); four cane seat chairs (4/- each); birch Duchess pair (£5/17/6); three pairs of ornaments (7/6); night commode (35/6); set of toilets (17/6); bamboo table (15/6); paper rack (3/6); wicker table (8/6); towel horse (5/-); coal vase (8/6); skin mat (4/6); six fans (1d each); a tray glass (5/3); and a toilet table (4/6). They also renovated some other items of furniture, repairing and re-polishing four cane chairs and re-upholstering an iron-framed couch. Everything was transported to Lowestoft for £4/10/6 and the total bill of £52/4/10 was settled by cheque.

In May 1896 the firm undertook a contract at the Town Hall for the King's Lynn Corporation. They laid linoleum in the Council Chamber, two other rooms and the landing, at a cost of £32. They made a large kneehole writing desk for one of the offices for £9/15/0 and repaired, cleaned, re-polished and re-lined an office table for 18/0. Three chairs in the Borough Surveyor's office were re-polished and re-covered in Morocco leather at a cost of 17/6 each. Amongst other items was an office table in oak for £2/15/0, three chairs for the visitors' room at 10/6 each and a new chair for Mr. Barrett's office. They laid new lino in the Town Clerk's office and supplied him with two new office chairs, at 4/6 each, and three office stools.

Another large order recorded in the first ledger was placed by Emma Louisa, the wife of Thomas Baker, a confectioner of 10, West Street, Cromer, in July 1896. There were 77 items on the initial order (illus. above right), including lengths of fabric and floor coverings. It appears that Mr. and Mrs. Baker had recently moved from a shop in East Dereham and were changing their old furniture for new. They had also just started a family and needed to furnish the children's rooms. The total cost of their first order was £73/4/7 and Emma paid a first instalment of £20 cash on 10th July, and arranged for payments to be made over a two year period. She signed an agreement to this effect, specifying that further instalments were to be made in October 1896; September 1897, and September 1898. Following completion of the agreement, Mrs. Baker bought some further items and the total bill, before interest, amounted to £81/3/4. This bill was settled on 30th September 1898 in accordance with the agreement.

By now King's Lynn had developed a tradition for holding trades exhibitions in the town, although not on a regular basis. They had been held in 1885, 1886, 1888 and 1891. In February 1897 (illus. left), another such exhibition was promoted and managed in Lynn by Mr. G. M. Bridges at St. James's Hall. Kelly's Directory for 1896 lists Benjamin Bridges as the hall keeper, so this may have been a relation of his. The arrangements for the exhibition were co-ordinated by a committee of tradesmen, under the joint chairmanship of Mr. Henry Plowright and Mr. Thomas William Scott. Henry Plowright's business was that of Plowright, Pratt & Skevens, ironmongers and heating engineers, of 8, Norfolk Street and Broad Street. Amongst the members of the organising committee was William Crawshay Scott. A large number of the articles on display at the exhibition had been made in the Alexandra technical school at Sandringham, established some nine years earlier and in which the Prince and Princess of Wales took a great interest. As a consequence of this, their Royal Highnesses the Princess of Wales and Princess Victoria decided to look round the trades exhibition while they were in the town visiting the hospital. On the opening day, Wednesday 10th February, their Royal Highnesses drove from Sandringham House in an open carriage to Lynn. They visited the hospital first before going to St. James' Hall. While the Princesses were at the hospital the mayor, Mr. S. A. Gurney, performed the opening ceremony at 3.00pm in front of Town Councillors, the organising committee, the exhibitors and several prominent townspeople. Resplendent in his chain of office, attended by the mace and sword bearers and accompanied by Lord Walsingham, High Steward of the borough, the mayor had processed from the Town Hall, followed by the councillors and civic dignitaries. When they reached County Court Road, which was festooned with flags, they were met by a great crowd of people who were awaiting the arrival of the Royal visitors.

The opening address and welcome was delivered by Henry Plowright. The Mayor then performed the opening ceremony and Lord Walsingham proposed a vote of thanks. The speeches had been kept short and were timed to be over before the two Princesses arrived. As they approached the hall, Mr. A. H. Cross of Sandringham sang the first verse of the National Anthem and the audience joined in, accompanied by Mr. H. B. Collins on the piano. The Mayor and Lord Walsingham greeted the royal guests who were then escorted round the trades displays by Messrs Bridges and Winch, with Thomas Scott and Mr. H. Johnson bringing up the rear. After looking round the stalls, the two Princesses and their attendants were given tea in a room that had been especially furnished for the occasion by Scott & Son. Tea was served by Charles Winlove Smith, whose confectionery business was at No. 50, High Street. After the Royal visitors had left, the band of Messrs. Jones and Wright struck up to entertain the guests who then toured the stands.

The Lynn Advertiser for Friday 12th February 1897 gave a description of Scott & Son's exhibition stand: **'Messrs. Scott & Son, of High street, furniture and bedding manufacturers, upholsterers and cabinet makers, have a stand near the entrance to the hall, upon which they exhibit a handsome mahogany drawing suite of their own make in the Louis XV style, with cabinet, overmantel and table to match; mahogany inlaid Chippendale drawing-room suite, in Genoa velvet with cabinet and overmantel *en suite*, bed-room suite in satin walnut and rosewood, with bedstead of satin walnut and brass; odd chairs, handsomely in-laid; a splendid assortment of genuine antique furniture, consisting of bureau beautifully in-laid, very old and good half-circle in-laid sideboard; and a rare and good glass top tea table'.**

At the end of the exhibition, on Tuesday 16th February, Mr. Bridges laid on a tea for the members of the committee in the St. James's rooms. There were speeches and toasts to the various people involved in the arrangements for what had proved to be a most successful event. The accounts were presented to the committee and Thomas Scott proposed a vote of thanks to the honorary secretaries. At 8.30pm that evening there was a grand ball at the hall put on by Mr. Bridges and the committee, which was attended by some 200 stall-holders and their friends. The ball continued until 5.30am the following morning.

The highlight of the Lynn Mart in 1897 was the demonstration of the new **'Cinematograph'** which was shown by Randall Williams, who placed a notice in the local newspapers advertising the event: **'IMPORTANT NOTICE. RANDALL WILLIAMS, THE KING OF SHOWMEN wishes to inform the inhabitants of King's Lynn and neighbourhood that he has bought the Latest and Most Scientific Invention of modern times, namely, THE CINEMATOGRAPH OR ANIMATED PHOTOGRAPHS, the same that had created the greatest furore ever known in the Agricultural Hall, London. These animated photographs will be exhibited in a large tent specially erected on the Tuesday Market during the Mart. A series of Performances will be given at a stated time on the outside of the building. Prices of Admission: Back seats and promenade; 3d; Front Seats 4d; and a few reserved seats, 6d. R.W. wishes to inform his patrons that these animated photographs are worked by a powerful electric light. The electric engine can be seen working free of charge on the outside'.**

Over the next three years, trade seems to have flourished in King's Lynn's High Street and the Christmas sales period in 1897 was probably the busiest that the town had ever witnessed. However, on Boxing Day, Monday 27th December, disaster struck with the destruction of many of the shops at the Saturday Market Place end of the street. A fire, which started in Jermyn & Perry's drapery store, spread to Jermyn & Sons' furniture shop and burned with such intensity that it ignited the shops on the opposite side of the street. The store had been due to remain closed on Boxing Day. At about seven o'clock that morning, a young lad named Bunton from Sedgeford Lane called to see the night watchman, Mr. Collins, and lit a taper so that he could find a watering can to dampen the sawdust for sweeping the floors. Almost immediately, Collins smelled burning and sent Bunton off to the police station. The fire brigade arrived at 7.40am, with second officer Oakley and fireman Goldsmith in command. Within ten minutes of starting work, the steam fire engine broke down and could not be used for the next three hours. The fire took hold quickly and the roof was ablaze even before the bells of St. Margaret's church could be sounded. The firemen could do nothing to save Jermyn & Perry's and soon Jermyn & Sons was also doomed. As they tried to contain the fire from spreading to the nearby shops, the whole of the huge High Street façade of Jermyn's 'Bon Marché' came crashing down, firstly the drapery department's frontage, soon followed by that of the furniture department. With no effective fire-fighting equipment available to them, the Fire Brigade could do nothing to stop the burning remains of the store setting fire to the shops opposite. One of the firemen, Richard Starling, was badly injured when another wall collapsed as the crew fought to save shops further up High Street.

The photograph below, taken looking towards the Saturday Market Place, shows the boarded-off site of Jermyn's former shop on the left and the devastation on the opposite side of the street.

Nine shops were razed to the ground. A further four were so seriously damaged that they had to be rebuilt and two more were temporarily put out of business. Scott & Son's furniture trading competitors, Jermyn & Sons, had to find alternative premises, which they did within a matter of a week or so, setting up temporary shop in Waterloo Street. Although Scotts may have seen some increase in trade at their end of High Street for a while, those shops affected by the fire were quickly rebuilt and were open again by the end of 1898. The fire was headlined as the 'Great High Street Fire' by the press, which devoted whole pages to its reporting. However, the widespread effects of the conflagration seem to have been very much underplayed in more recent books on Lynn which mention Jermyns but not the other businesses that were destroyed. The setting-back of the shops opposite to Jermyns was done during the rebuilding of the burned-out premises as part of the Town Council's street widening policy, which had become an imperative due to the fact that the fire had spread so easily from one side of the narrow street to the other.

By this date, it is probable that William Crawshay Scott was beginning to take the lead role in the Scott & Son partnership. He appears to have been just as astute a businessman as his father and he undertook the task of consolidating Scott & Son's position on the High Street with relish. There is evidence that he was very much involved in the acquisition of property and in the planning and execution of alterations and improvements. It may well be that he gave the instructions to Scott & Son's architects for all of the larger building contracts. In this regard, 1898 was a big year in more ways than one for Scott & Son, involving the acquisition of new premises, the planning of their redevelopment, and also dealing with an unforeseen disaster.

The first significant event was the purchase of two shops, Nos. 93 & 94, High Street, near to the one that they were currently occupying. On 6th August 1898 Scott & Son made the following announcement in their advertisement in the Lynn Advertiser: '**EXTENSION Of PREMISES - SCOTT & SON COMPLETE HOUSE FURNISHERS AND CABINET MAKERS, beg to announce that in addition to the large business carried on by them at 89 High Street, they will on SATURDAY NEXT, August 6th, Open Extensive New Show-Rooms on premises lately occupied by Messrs. Cox Bros., at 93 and 94 High Street, and will make a MAGNIFICENT DISPLAY OF FURNITURE, BEDSTEADS, AND BEDDING, Manufactured at their Steam Factory in St. James Street, in which new labour-saving machinery has lately been added.**'

They were clearly not content to let the business stagnate and were pursuing its expansion with vigour, not least of which involved upgrading the machinery and processes at the St. James Street factory. They were offering: '**A Large and Choice range of Drawing and Dining-Room Suites in Leather from 55/-, in Tapestry from 65/, and in Saddle-bags from £6/15. Bed-Room Suites; Painted and decorated from £3/18/6, in Satin Walnut, Birch, Walnut and other kinds of wood, finished with Plate Glass, from £8/8 the complete Suite.**'

The photograph on the previous page shows Scott & Son's shop at Nos. 93 & 94, High Street, taken soon after they moved in, circa August 1898. It would appear that No. 93 was a wide-fronted, timber-framed building, which formerly had a pair of bowed display windows. By the time that Scotts took it over, it had been altered, although it would be hard to say that it had been modernised. Indeed, it was clearly one of the least up-dated of High Street shops and had very low storey heights. On 12th August 1898 their advertisement read: **'SCOTT & SON'S EXTENSION. We have pleasure in announcing that business in our New Premises, 93 & 94 HIGH STREET, is now in full swing. Handsome and extensive Show-rooms have been added and refitted, in which we are exhibiting and selling the Best and Cheapest Stock of FURNITURE, BEDSTEADS, BEDDING, CARPETS, AND HOUSEHOLD REQUISITES IN THE DISTRICT'.** Scott & Son advertised a special display of drawing, dining and bedroom suites and went on to extend the following invitation: **'The tastes of all our clients have been catered for. All are invited to a free promenade of Inspection. We are offering a very tempting Suite in Blue and Gold or Crimson and Gold Tapestry, comprising well-made couch, two easy and four small chairs, for £3/6/0 the complete suite'.**

Later that year, on 18th November Scott & Son indicated in their advertisement in the Lynn Advertiser that their business was very buoyant and they invited their customers to visit their factory to see the furniture and bedding being made: **'Owing to the increased favour and patronage of the residents of this town and neighbourhood, we have lately extended our Show-room accommodation, and have now nearly doubled the number of large newly-fitted show-rooms, replete with a bigger stock than ever of genuine and reliable HOUSEHOLD FURNITURE and BEDDING, manufactured at our own Steam Factory in St. James Street, which is the busiest spot in the busy town of Lynn. We have had innumerable customers ask to see all round before buying, and we invite all to see not only the Largest, Cheapest and Best Stock of Finished Goods, but also Furniture and Bedding in all stages of production. We are proprietors of the only Steam Factory in Lynn or district and can furnish Cottage or Mansion throughout from stock'.**

Steam power was not without its dangers and there are frequent instances of Norfolk mills and works being burned down. Scott's factory suffered a similar fate and, on 10th December 1898 The Lynn News & County Press reported:

DESTRUCTIVE FIRE AT LYNN

About twenty minutes past one on Thursday afternoon a fire broke out in some buildings at the rear of St James's street, Lynn, which were used by Messrs. Scott and Son, house furnishers and cabinet makers, as a steam factory and for warehousing purposes.

The building comprised two storeys. Underneath was a mattress and bedding factory, together with stables, etc., the machinery comprising a steam engine, gas engine, and steam chaff cutter; overhead were rooms in which were carried on the various operations of cabinet making, polishing and upholstery. In the yard were piles of wood, consisting of mahogany, birch, walnut, etc. At half-past twelve o'clock, the workmen went to dinner, leaving everything apparently safe but in about another three quarters of an hour the discovery was made that the place was on fire. Word was immediately conveyed to the police station and information of the outbreak telephoned to the old Waterworks. As soon as possible the Fire Brigade turned  **out under Second-officer Oakley. The new and old fire engines were requisitioned, and the manual was also taken along although it was only used as a hose-carrier.**

When the firemen arrived it was pretty evident that the building was doomed for the flames had got a strong hold upon the building. A number of lengths of hose were run out, and water was obtained from the street main and poured on the burning building. The factory was situated in close proximity to a number of other buildings, but little space dividing it from Tower house (occupied by Messrs. Jermyn and Perry's young lady assistants) and premises occupied by Mr. T. H. Curson (draper), Mr. Sawyer (butcher) and Mr. Hildon (this being an oil

warehouse) as well as the Crown hotel stables. There is also a lot of cottage property in the immediate vicinity, and some of the property is very old. Every effort was made to preserve the surrounding buildings, and these endeavours were successful, for the fire was confined to the building in which it originated. This was, however, with its contents, completely destroyed, as was also the stock of wood in the yard.

At the time of the outbreak the warehouse and factory contained a large quantity of furniture in various stages of completeness, including a number of finished chairs, and piles of bedding. The contents were of a very inflammable nature, and the flames shot up to a great height, accompanied by volumes of smoke. The firemen had to mount all sorts of buildings, including out-houses, and their work was pursued amid in some instances considerable danger. One of them had a marvellous escape. Just before the roof fell in he was seated on a corner of it directing a stream of water to another part of the building, when a companion called out to him that he thought the roof was going. The fireman thus warned rose from his sitting position and stepped on to a ledge a foot or two lower, and not more than a second or two had elapsed when the roof fell in. Shortly before three o'clock a number of the Naval Reserve, under the direction of Instructor Budge, demolished the portions of the walls which still stood and smothered out the flames which were still burning. How the fire originated is a mystery. There was a fire in a stove in the polishing room, but the flames, it is stated, did not break out in that part of the premises. About 20 workpeople were employed at the factory. The building and its contents were insured, partly in each of three offices – in the "County" with Mr. G. W. Page for £1,100, in the "Norwich Union" with Mr. W. Hitchcock for £400 (stock and machinery), and in the "Alliance" with the late Mr. W. B. Whall for £300 (the building). When the fire broke out there were four horses in Messrs. Scott and Son's stable, but they were got out safely.

Unfortunately, therefore, in less than a month from Scott & Son issuing an open invitation to all their customers to visit the factory in St James Street, they were left without any manufacturing premises at all. They hurried to reassure their customers that there was sufficient stock to cater for demand held at their shop: 'MESSRS. SCOTT & SON Beg to inform their Customers and the public generally that the fire at their Steam Furniture and Bedding Factory in St. James Street on Thursday will in no way affect their business in High Street, where they always have an enormous stock of Finished Household Furniture, Bedsteads and Bedding ready to send out. Post orders punctually attended to as usual'.

Within less than ten days of the fire, Scott & Son had secured alternative premises in the town and their factory was up and running again. The speed with which they were able to do this seems to have been typical of any trader or manufacturer in those days. Indeed, after the great High Street fire of 27th December 1897 it was extraordinary to read that most traders were operating again from other, temporary, premises by the first week of January 1898. Only those with inadequate insurance, or without any cover, were unable to start up again quickly. One of those affected was Sidney Count, a chemist whose shop on the corner of Union Lane was destroyed. He moved into 97, High Street, as a tenant of John Ayton Nokes.

Scott & Son announced the re-commencement of their furniture and bedding manufacturing in the Lynn Advertiser on 16th December 1898: 'SCOTT & SON Have much pleasure in announcing that they have secured extensive and convenient new premises opposite the Railway Station, in Waterloo Street, which are being used, and will be fitted up as their new Steam Furniture and Bedding Factory in place of the works destroyed by fire last week. We are now able to execute any orders entrusted to us. Our men are all working full time and overtime, and in a few days our new engines and labour-saving steam machinery will be in full working order, which will give us facilities for prompt despatch and moderate charges enjoyed by no other house in this district. The fire has in no way interfered with the business carried on at: 89, 93 & 94 HIGH STREET where we always have an enormous stock of finished goods'.

It is clear that, with hardly a pause, the company were re-stocking their High Street shop with newly-made furniture and bedding fresh off the production lines at their Waterloo Street works. This seems quite an impressive achievement, occurring as it did at one of their busiest times of the year and within four months of expanding into new shop premises at 93 and 94, High Street. By the 27th January 1899 the company was able to include the following statement and invitation to their customers: 'We are the only genuine Manufacturers of Furniture and Bedding in King's Lynn or district. We (Scott & Son) are the sole retailers in this district who were apprenticed to the trade; we do not wish to have a finger in every pie; and our desire is to turn out sound and reliable Household Goods, at Lowest Possible Prices. We feel it our duty to caution the public against dealers who buy cheap London-made rubbish, patch and varnish it up, and then advertise 'Behold! Our Goods, finished in our own workshops.' We shall be pleased to show customers over our Factory. Buy of the Makers and save Dealers' Profits'.

PLAN of ST. JAMES' STREET. c1892 - 1898
SHOWING THE LOCATION OF
SCOTT & SON'S FURNITURE
& BEDDING FACTORY

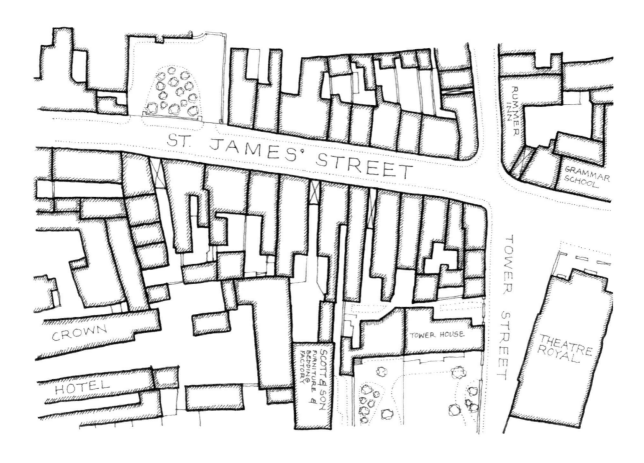

At about this date, Scott & Son leased a warehouse from the council on The Friars. Apparently, William Scott was somewhat dilatory in signing the lease. The council took action to pursue the matter through but it was resolved without recourse the courts.

> The Town Clerk reported that Mr. W. C. Scott had taken possession of the warehouse on the Friars, but had failed to sign the lease, and that consequently a summons for specific performance of the agreement and for damages had been taken out in the County Court, whereupon Mr. Scott expressed his readiness to sign the lease and pay all costs incurred.

It is quite possible that the Waterloo Street premises leased by Scott & Son were the very same ones that Jermyn & Sons took-over in the aftermath of the great High Street fire of 1897, which they would have vacated when their new store opened on 8th October 1898.

In January 1899 Scott & Son's annual stock taking sale had been underway for a week when they announced that it would be extended through until the end of March. In addition to offering the goods manufactured at their factory at sale prices, they made special purchases of other products, advertising in the Lynn Advertiser on 3rd February, 1899: **'GREAT FURNITURE SALE IN KING'S LYNN In connection with this Sale we have just received the LARGEST CONSIGNMENT OF BABIES' Carriages, Perambulators and Mail-carts, EVER BROUGHT INTO THE TOWN, Which will all be offered at Lowest Sale Prices. This will LET our customers have an opportunity of securing 'EM at unprecedentedly low prices. We guarantee them ALL good workmanship, and the large choice will suit all who COME and inspect our big purchase'.**

The work of clearing up after the fire at the factory in St. James Street was continuing and in the same advertisement on 3rd February, they offered some of the stock that had been saved: **'SALVAGE! SALVAGE! SALVAGE! In addition to our usual Stock, we shall include in this Sale the Salvage saved from the Fire in St. James Street. Several dozens of all kinds of CHAIRS will be Cleared at Less than Cost of Production'.**

Having announced on 12th August 1898 that they had refitted their new showrooms at 93 and 94, High Street, it may seem surprising, on the face of it, that Scott & Son would be planning to demolish and redevelop these two shops just seven months later, but that is exactly what happened. It is probable that they had always planned to do this but needed to use the extra showroom space for the Christmas and New Year sales rush and for their spring stocktaking sale. However, another possibility is that the opening of Jermyn and Sons' brand new shop on 8th October 1898 had left Scott & Son's shop looking very old fashioned, impacting adversely on their trade. It would seem certain that Jermyn's great new store would have been the big attraction in the High Street during the latter months of 1898 and early 1899 and that Scott & Son felt obliged to do something to bring the customers back to their half of the street. Perhaps it was a combination of reasons that led to their development plans. In any event, Scott & Son's proposals for rebuilding Nos. 93 and 94, High Street unintentionally stirred up a hornets' nest within the Town Council.

Building plans had to go before the council's Urban Sanitary Committee, where they were scrutinised for compliance with local bye-laws. The turn round was commendably quick, most being approved within a week and some being dealt with on the day they were received, if this coincided with a meeting. Few plans were 'disapproved' by the council, unless the proposals were deficient in, for example, the provision of space around the new building or in sanitary arrangements. There is nothing to suggest that Scott & Son's plans, which had been professionally drawn-up by local architect William Jarvis, were in any way non-compliant with the council's bye-laws, however the process of obtaining approval from the Town Council did not proceed smoothly and led to some frustrating delays for Thomas and William Scott.

The Council's Urban Sanitary Committee considered the plans on 6th April 1899 when they resolved: **'To approve them but it be recommended that a building line be prescribed on the West side of High Street and that the Borough Surveyor be instructed to prepare a Plan shewing such building line for submission to the next Meeting of the Committee'.**

The council had prescribed a building line for the southern end of High Street, where the shops affected by Jermyns' fire had been set back. There was no such line for the northern end of the street, however, and it seems unfortunate that Scott & Son's proposals should have prompted the committee to think of setting back some of these properties, too. It was doubly unfortunate that the councillors were not in any way unanimous in their thoughts on the benefits or otherwise of pursuing a policy of setting back more premises in High Street. The rebuilding of the properties opposite Jermyns' new store to a new building line did not please all the members, mainly because this still left other shops standing forward of the new line. Others considered that the cost of compensation payable by the council to the owners of the properties had not proved to be money well spent, especially in view of other priorities. The committee was at this time involved in the provision of new sewers and in upgrading the street lights by converting from gas to electric lamps and by extending the coverage. The renewal and upgrading of the Fire Brigade's equipment was another costly item.

On 20th April the Borough Surveyor submitted his proposed building line and the Urban Sanitary Committee resolved to pass this to the 'Hall' (a meeting of the full council), with the recommendation that they formally prescribe the new line. Then, on 4th May, Thomas Scott and William Jarvis attended the committee meeting when their proposals were again considered, this time in terms of compliance with the proposed new building line. Thomas Scott would not have been pleased to hear the debate over the level of compensation that the council were to offer. The minutes record that: **'It was moved by Mr. Alderman Jermyn, seconded by Mr. Councillor Brown: That the sum of £400 (i.e. £10 per square yard) be tendered to Messrs. Scott & Son as compensation for loss or damage sustained by them by the setting back of their premises Nos. 93 and 94 in High Street. Amendment moved by Mr. Councillor Bardell, seconded by Mr. Councillor Springall: That the sum of £300 be tendered to them as compensation.**

Upon the amendment being put, 2 voted for and 4 against it, and it was declared negatived, and the original motion was then put and carried'.

Although Thomas Scott would have been aware of the level of compensation paid to the shop owners affected by the Jermyn's fire, he would also have known that some owners, including Messrs. Trenowath Brothers, had challenged the amounts offered and that an arbitrator had been appointed to resolve the issue. It is no surprise, therefore, to learn that Scott & Son did not accept the offer of £400 immediately.

On 10th May, the full council considered the proposals for the new building line and for the rebuilding of Scott & Son's shop for the first time. Taking the minutes of the Urban Sanitary Committee's meeting of 20th April the council approved an amendment which deleted the reference to the building line. They then went on to consider the minutes of the meeting of 4th May, when again they approved an amendment, referring Scott & Son's application back to the committee. The minutes of the meeting fail to reveal the liveliness of the debate, which is related in the report of the council's meeting in the Lynn News of 12th May. Thomas Scott was at the meeting and witnessed first hand what was, in part, almost a farcical debate. Opposition to the proposed building line was led by Mr. W. Miles: **'Mr. W. MILES called attention to the proposal for prescribing a building line in High street. He said that as chairman of the committee he took no part in the discussion, but he supported the view of the two gentlemen who voted in the minority, and he now proposed that the paragraph be struck out. It would be a dangerous thing to prescribe a building line for the north end of High street, because they could not tell what the cost would come to, and to prescribe a line for 50 feet, whatever it cost would not be worth the money. The widening of that portion of the street where the fire occurred was an improvement, but to go to the further end of the street and prescribe a building line for every little gap would make it look very bad indeed. There was a suggestion to offer a certain sum of money, which to his mind was a very large sum indeed – (No! No!) – but the owners would not be satisfied with that even.**

Mr. FLOYD: There is nothing in the report pointing out any sum of money.

Mr. MILES: Well, it is in the next, and we shall take it later on.

Mr. PRIDGEON seconded the amendment. He said that they had had enough for a time of paying a large sum of money for an improvement that was not worth the price, and they could never make High street anything else than a narrow street. ("Oh!") If he (Mr. Pridgeon) were in the place of Messrs. Scott, he would set the council as defiance, and would not pull the place down at all.

Mr. BROWN: Is Mr. Pridgeon aware that Mr. Scott is present?

Mr. PRIDGEON: It makes not the slightest difference to me.

Mr. SMITH: It will go into print.

Mr. PRIDGEON: It may go into print or not, it makes no difference to me. I am glad Mr. Scott is present, so that he can hear what I say. This thing should not go on in the way we are doing it, because we can never make the improvement we should if the street were down. We could then decide to have a new building line, but here it would be just a little bit. I was asking a gentleman how long he thought it would be before they got the building line which has been prescribed at the south end of the street as far as Baker lane, and he said it might be done in about 150 years.

Mr. REAM supported the amendment.

The TOWN CLERK, replying to a question by Mr. F. MILES, said that if a building line were prescribed, that building line would of course be in existence, and the Council must set up to it; and directly a man pulled down his premises he must set them back to the prescribed line.

Mr. F. MILES: Then we should be preventing gentlemen from improving the fronts of their buildings, because they cannot improve them without pulling down the front.

The TOWN CLERK: there is nothing to prevent a man improving the front of his building, but he must not take it down.

Mr. SMITH hoped he had been consistent – (Mr. DEXTER: Ah! I hope so! – Laughter.) – as to the widening of High street, from beginning to finish, and he was not going to change to-day. They had had to pay a pretty good price for what they had done already, and if the building now in question were set back, they would have a projecting awkward corner, and no-one could say what the compensation would amount to.

Mr. ROSE thought that if a big fire had razed a lot of houses and shops to the ground, as happened at the other end of the street, the Council might fairly have considered the committee's recommendation favourably; but seeing this was not the case, and that only a comparatively small property was affected, he did not think they would be justified in going to any expense in the matter.

Mr. CHATTERTON also supported the amendment, saying that if the report were adopted they would simply be putting a premium on these alterations, because owners of property in High street would know that when they made alterations the Council would have to pay the cost'.

The most significant point raised in the debate was that made by Mr. Pridgeon, when he suggested that Messrs. Scott & Son should consider defying the council by leaving their building standing. Although they did redevelop Nos. 93 & 94, High Street and comply with the new building line, they were later to defy the council over the setting-back of Nos. 95 to 97 at the corner of Purfleet Street.

When the committee met again, on 18th May, they reconsidered the proposals for 93 & 94, High Street and the following letter was read from Scott & Son:

May 18th, 1899.

Gentlemen, - We are most anxious to begin building our new premises in High street; and if you had permitted us, we hoped to have them well on the way to completion by this time. It means a very serious loss to us, as our busy time is now coming on; we therefore respectfully beg you to come to some arrangement to-day.

We have been considering the matter, and to facilitate your decision we will accept £800 for the frontage you wish to take. We feel sure you do not wish us to be out of pocket through your indecision, but we assure you that each day's delay means a distinct loss to us. Anticipating your courteous consideration in this matter, - We are, &c., SCOTT & SON.

The committee once again made a meal of the matter and the minutes read as follows: 'After prolonged discussion and after various motions had been dealt with it was eventually resolved by 6 votes to 4 that the plan submitted by Messrs. Scott & Son be not approved but that if the existing buildings are taken down the building line recommended by the Borough Surveyor be approved and the Council requested to prescribe same and that Messrs. Scott and Son be required to set back their premises if taken down in accordance with the building line so prescribed and that the sum of £400 be tendered to them as full compensation'.

When this minute was put to the full council on 1st June, the debate over the pros and cons of widening the street through the imposition of a building line affecting new development kicked off once again. The debate was reported in some detail by the Lynn Advertiser on 2nd June. Although there was some measure of agreement within the council for the principle of setting back some properties in High Street, there was no accord on how this should be done.

The immediate past holder of the office of mayor, Alderman William Samuel Valentine Miles, led the debate in favour of approving Scott & Son's plans. He was the principal auctioneer and valuer in King's Lynn and would have known both Thomas and William Scott very well because they had bought several properties through his auction sales. It is tempting to think, therefore, that Thomas Scott had his supporters on the Council who did their best to force through his proposals. However, it is clear that those in favour of approving his plans had come to the conclusion that piecemeal setting back of properties was unlikely to

MR. WILLIAM SAMUEL VALENTINE MILES, C.C.
From a Photograph by Mr. Walter Dexter, King's Lynn.

achieve their aims for widening the street. They also believed that the cost would be unjustified. Another indication that Alderman Miles was not necessarily showing any favour towards Scott & Son was that he had said that it would be pointless trying to negotiate with them since they were holding out for too much money. The sketch, above right, of Mr. Miles appeared in the Lynn News & County Press on 11th February 1893. Alderman Miles, as chairman of the Urban Sanitary

Committee, found himself in the difficult position of proposing the minutes of the committee at the council meeting but then wishing to propose amendments to them.

The council had the benefit of hearing Scott & Son's case as set out in their letter of 18th May to the committee. This had the effect of complicating the issues under debate even further. Some councillors asserted that it would be a waste of time trying to agree a reasonable amount of compensation because Scott & Son were holding out for an unrealistic sum. Councillor Brown was one of the main proponents of the widening proposal and his views were reported as follows: '**Mr. BROWN hoped the council would not let this opportunity of widening High street go by. The Borough Surveyor was instructed to prepare a building line, which he did, and he (Mr. Brown) thought it was a very good one. He was surprised at gentlemen saying this would not be an improvement. The point in question was at the narrowest part of the street, and on Tuesdays when the carrier's cart sometimes stood against the Mayor's shop, people had to wait ten minutes or a quarter of an hour before they could get past. The cost would be only £400, for he was confident Mr. Scott would accept the offer proposed by the committee. Then the Corporation would have the opportunity of buying the property at the corner of Purfleet street and making a further improvement. He questioned whether Mr. Scott's plans could be legally passed, because he thought they provided for too high a building for so narrow a street**'.

The council's powers with regard to street widening enabled them to force any new development to comply with their requirements. This meant that Scott & Son's proposals, which had been submitted over eight weeks before the new building line was formally prescribed, would inevitably be caught should the council decide to extend their street widening policy to the northern end of High Street. Consequently, following the resolution of the Town

TO BUILDERS AND CONTRACTORS.

PERSONS desirous of tendering for the pulling-down of Nos. 93 and 94 High street, King's Lynn, and the erection of proposed New Shops and Show-rooms upon the same site, for Messrs. Scott and Son, are requested to send in their names to the undersigned not later than Friday the 16th inst.
Plans, &c., can be seen, and all further particulars obtained, at my office.
WILLIAM JARVIS, Architect.
Market square, Lynn.   [8912]

Council on 1st June, Scott & Son were compelled to comply with the setting back requirements if they wished to proceed with their redevelopment plans. They decided to go ahead with their planned new shop and, on 9th June 1899, a notice appeared in the Lynn Advertiser inviting tenders for the demolition of the two old shops and the erection of a new one (illus. above right). Mr. W. H. Brown, of London Road, won the contract.

At the meeting of the Urban Sanitary Committee on 15th June 1899 a letter was read from Messrs. Scott & Son. In this, they stated that they would accept the offer of £400 compensation. This was provided that the Corporation would allow them to use the blank gables of the two adjoining properties, Nos. 92 and 95, High Street, for advertising purposes until such time as they, too, were set back. The council agreed to this but sought a formal agreement to the use of the two gable walls. At the other end of the High Street, Messrs. Trenowath Bros. had been allowed to use a gable created by the setting back of their premises but at a cost of £5 per annum.

The shop redevelopment was announced in Scott & Son's advertisement in the Lynn Advertiser on 10th March 1899: '**SELL OR SPOIL - SCOTT & SON'S RECORD SALE WILL CONTINUE ANOTHER FORTNIGHT. Many Things Further Reduced. Stock must be Cleared. Nos. 93 & 94 High Street are to be pulled down previous to erection of New Premises. This has been the most successful sale of Furniture and Household Requisites ever held in King's Lynn, but to prevent any part of the immense stock being damaged by dust and dirt in course of razing the old shops, Still Greater Bargains will be Offered in all Departments**'.

The construction of the new shop was completed by November 1899 and on the 8th of that month, the following article appeared in the Lynn Advertiser:

'**A NEW SHOP: - Much was heard a few months ago of the proposal made in the Town Council to require Messrs. Scott and Son, who were pulling down some of their premises in High street, to set them back a certain number of feet so as to increase the width of the street at that point. This has now been done, and although the additional width in this particular place is not of much service at present, it is apparent that a great improvement will have been effected when the houses that intervene between Messrs. Scott's new shop and Purfleet street have been similarly treated. The new shop now under notice is on a site previously occupied by two small old houses which have done duty of late years for the carrying on of grocery and leather-selling businesses; they were recently acquired by Messrs. Scott and Son, who have now raised a building of rather imposing dimensions, in which to carry on those branches of their trade which are concerned principally with carpets, curtains and pianofortes, leaving their older establishment, a few doors away, to deal more particularly with the furniture**

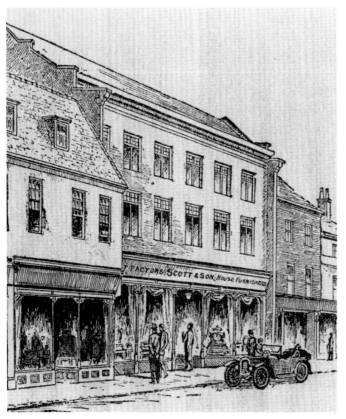

which is made at the firm's factory in Waterloo street. The new shop has a frontage of 50 feet and the depth of the strip of land which has been acquired by the Corporation varies from 9 feet at one end (that nearest Purfleet street) to 5 feet at the other, leaving a depth of 45 feet for the new premises. The building, which has three storeys, is faced with red brick and stone dressings. The ground floor has, of course, an ordinary shop front, and each of the other floors is well lighted by five French windows. The upper storeys are approached by a winding staircase rising from the centre of the shop, all three floors being intended for show purposes. The ground floor is lighted by three electric arc lamps, arranged in series, with a fourth, which is to be placed outside, and the other portions of the building are being supplied with 16 candle power incandescent lights. The new premises were built by Mr. W. H. Brown, in accordance with the plans of Mr. W. Jarvis, and the electric wiring has been done by Messrs. Rogers & Co.'

Following the rebuilding of Nos. 93 and 94, High Street, these two units became known to the staff of Scott & Son as the 'New Shop'.

Tuesday 1st August 1899 was unusual in many ways for the townspeople of Lynn. For one thing the shops were mostly closed, even though the streets were thronged with people; more than had ever gathered before for any carnival, procession or coronation parade. It was to be, without any exaggeration, the most exciting day that Lynn had experienced in the whole century. In the very early hours of the morning four huge trains started to pull into the station and straightway the crowds began gathering to watch the arrival of Barnum & Bailey's 'Greatest Show on Earth'. By 4.00am the first train was being unloaded with practised precision that would be hard to match today. Ramps were placed against the first truck of each train and as that was emptied, the vans in the

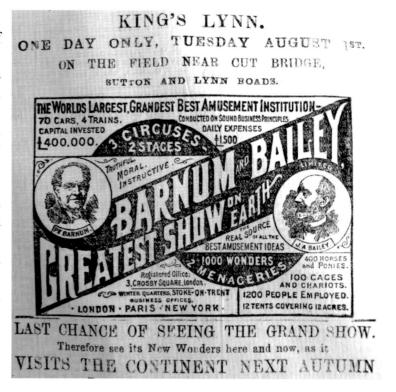

trucks behind, containing the animals and equipment, were wheeled forward towards the front. As each van rolled off the ramp, a team of eight horses was attached and set off to the field where the show was to take place. This was between the river and the West Lynn Road, near the Cut Bridge.

By eight o'clock, the four enormous tents had been erected and breakfast had already been served to the 850 people involved with the show. The main show tent was 590ft long and the menagerie tent over 400ft. It took four hours for all of the vans to reach the showground from the station. The greatest sights were the horses, one group being 56 strong, and the sixteen elephants. Meanwhile, the town had filled up with thousands and thousands of people who were lining the streets along the route of the procession: Wisbech Road; London Road; St. James Road; Blackfriars Road; Norfolk Street; Chapel Street; St. Nicholas Street; Tuesday Market Place; King Street; Queen Street; Saturday Market Place; and St. James Street; returning by London Road. People had been arriving from far and wide since before

8.00am, even though the discounts offered by the train companies did not take effect until the evening. The cavalcade set off from the show ground at 9.00am precisely. Following the police marshals, the first carriage was that of the grand show band, drawn by a team of forty horses, driven by one man. Next came the cages of wild animals, including lions, tigers, bears, wolves and leopards, each with its own trainer. Then the big tubular bells, automatically playing a series of tunes, the mounted riders, chariot drivers, a second band, teams of horses and miniature ponies, and

a caravan of camels and dromedaries. The only slight disappointment was the non-appearance of the elephants, who had proved problematic in other towns and who stayed at the show ground. After the camels came the decorated tableaux, the last one being a representation of the return of Columbus to Barcelona. The grand throne car of Ferdinand and Isabella was preceded by a troop of trumpeters and was followed by elegantly dressed courtiers and noblemen.

Bringing up the rear was the grand steam calliope (illus. left); a huge musical instrument consisting of steam whistles, operated by a piano-like keyboard. Not surprisingly, in view of the narrowness of some of the streets, there were some accidents; at Blackfriars Street corner a horse tripped and one of the handlers broke an ankle, and at the Norfolk Street / Chapel Street corner, part of the frontage of the 'Flower-pot Inn' was knocked off.

There were two performances, at 2.00pm and at 8.00pm. The grand tent could accommodate 15,000 people but was only two-thirds full for each performance.

The menagerie tent was open for an hour before each performance and animals and human 'prodigies' were paraded on a large platform. These included: the Egyptian giant 7ft 11in tall; the Indian dwarf, just 1ft 10in tall; the bearded lady; the 'moss-haired girl'; Morris the elastic skinned man; Rob Roy, the man who could dislocate his joints; Tomasse, the 'human pincushion'; and Billy Wells, the 'hard-headed man'. The

main tent contained three circus rings and a large platform. The entertainment was non-stop and presented on a lavish scale by massed performers, including battalions of clowns. There were three equestrian performances, five acrobatic events or two aerial displays happening at any one time, and the spectacle was quite breathtaking. Every circus act conceivable was included, each on a grand scale that was far bigger than anything seen in Lynn before. By all accounts, it lived up to its billing as 'The Greatest Show on Earth'. This had been a day for Lynn folk to remember and to talk about for years to come.

The photograph above shows Scott & Son's new shop at 93 & 94, High Street in about 1900.

CHAPTER THREE
A new Millennium
and the Great War:
Scott & Son
1901 – 1918

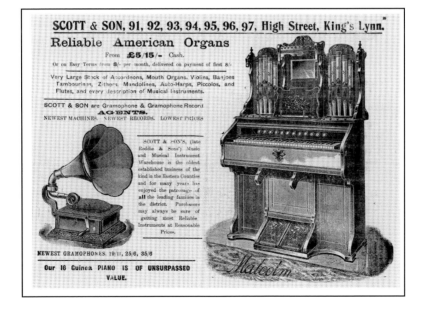

3. A new Millennium and the Great War: Scott & Son 1901 - 1918

Unlike the present generation, who celebrated the Millennium at the end of 1999, the Victorians knew when one century ended and another began. New Year 1901 was when they celebrated the start of the 20th Century and most advertisers reflected this - but not Scott & Son. Maybe they were too preoccupied with their building and redevelopment work but, for whatever reason, they did not place any special Christmas or New Year advertisements in December 1900 and January 1901.

On 21st January 1901 Queen Victoria died aged 81. She had been queen for 63 years, presiding over the industrialisation of Britain and the expansion of the Empire overseas. But she also had a lasting influence over the values of the time and the Victorian age became synonymous with prudish gentility and repression. Following Prince Albert's death in 1861, Victoria wore widow's mourning for the rest of her life. At her death, there was a nationwide outpouring of mourning, with all adults wearing black and shopkeepers draping black and purple banners from their windows. Fortunately, her son King Edward VII signalled a new era by limiting the period of mourning for his mother to three months.

There was much development and building work to be planned by Scott & Son at the start of the new century; their factory was operating from temporary premises in Waterloo Street and their High Street shops were not next door to each other.

William Scott was certainly the right man to take on the job of developing the property holding of the company on the High Street / Purfleet Street corner, at what had become, in spite of Alfred Jermyn's misgivings, the very heart of Lynn's shopping centre. He had already begun the task of merging the individual shops into a single store, undertaking improvements to the internal accommodation and to the front windows and fascias. Now he had to try to acquire additional shop units in order to create the sort of household furnishing store to effectively rival Jermyn & Sons and the other King's Lynn shops. However, he had another major task to accomplish first - to find a site where new premises could be erected to house Scott & Son's factory and warehouse.

Buying property was one of William Scott's particular interests and strengths. His son, William Crawshay jnr., would later say of his father that "he bought and sold property like other people do loaves of bread." He certainly proved himself to be more than capable of realising Scott & Son's ambitions by securing the property required for their factory and warehouse and for their shop expansion.

Scott & Son moved from their temporary factory in Waterloo Street into a new, purpose-built three-storey building on the South Quay in 1902. The site was a walled yard, 34ft 10in across the South Quay frontage and 45ft deep, backing onto William Scott's house, 29 Queen Street. This yard contained a small office fronting onto the South Quay and a greenhouse. The new works were closer to their shops in High Street. There may have been other reasons for moving, too, because the new location was undoubtedly more convenient for their transport requirements. The South Quay was directly linked to the rail network, with a track for goods wagons, and the new site provided stabling for the horses and plenty of loading and manoeuvring space for the vans. The new works and warehouse were designed to accommodate garaging for the furniture vans on the ground floor, with the factory works and warehouse on the two upper storeys. To enable the bulky materials and

SCOTT & SON'S FURNITURE and BEDDING FACTORY

furniture to be lifted and lowered to and from the upper levels, there were loading doors on each of the two upper floors with a hoist above.

In February 1902, tenders were invited '...**to erect the three storey warehouse on the South Quay King's Lynn in strict accordance with the plans and specifications prepared by your architect Mr E. E. Colman of King's Lynn ... within eight weeks from the date of commencing the works.**' Evidently, Scott & Son and their architect, Ernest Colman of 41, Railway Road, were keen to obtain the best possible price because they invited about a dozen local building firms to submit tenders. Eleven tenders were received, the highest being £553 10s 0d and the lowest £453. However, the contract was offered not to the lowest tenderer, W. F. Smith, but to Tash Langley & Co., whose works were at 45, London Road and at Guanock Terrace. They had submitted a price of £497 10s 0d but it seems that this was negotiated down to £433. The new works were completed by June 1902 at a total cost, inclusive of extras, of £501 18s 8d.

The photograph, left (courtesy of Brian Howling), shows the South Quay soon after the construction of Scott & Son's new factory, which can be seen to the right of centre, opposite the sailing vessel and between the first and second lamp standards.

Completion of the new steam factory occurred in the same month that the Coronation of King Edward VII was scheduled to take place. Public holidays had been declared for 25th and 26th June, when all the shops would be shut. Scott & Son did not announce any special arrangements or displays in the weeks running up to the date set for the Coronation, although other shops in the town did. However, the King fell seriously ill and had to undergo an abdominal operation. On 28th June, it was announced that the Coronation had been indefinitely postponed. The ceremony went ahead on 9th August and special displays were again announced, with Jermyn & Perry advertising bunting, flags, flagpoles and many other items for sale.

Although Scott & Son had still not extended their premises in High Street, they were making the best of what they had through the internal layout of their showrooms and by maximising their window display space. On 19th July 1902 their advertisement in the Lynn News included the address of their new steam factory for the first time. In their summer sale that year they offered perambulators and mail carts at half price and discounts of three shillings in the pound (15%) on everything-else. At No. 89, High Street they stocked second-hand furniture, including bedsteads from 5/6.

SCOTT & SON,
89, 93 and 94, HIGH STREET,
KING'S LYNN.
Steam Factory:—SOUTH QUAY. ..

Carpets and floor coverings were a speciality of Scott & Son and they advertised '**CORK, LINO and FLOOR CLOTH SQUARES can be fitted to any sized rooms without joining. All kinds of LINOLEUM & FLOOR CLOTHS in any width. LARGEST STOCK. LOWEST PRICES. Rugs and Slips to match all carpets. COMPETENT MEN to Measure, Fit and Lay all Floor Coverings**'. They also offered to take up existing carpets, beat and relay them. Window blinds were made to measure.

In early 1903, Scott & Son acquired the music business of J. H. Reddie & Sons at No. 42, High Street. Josiah Henry Reddie had fallen ill (he died in 1905, aged 83) and his sons Ferdinand and Percy decided to sell the business. The following notice appeared in the Lynn Advertiser on 9th January, 1903: '**Messrs. Reddie & Sons beg to inform their customers and the public generally that, owing to the illness of the senior partner, they have disposed of their business as a going concern to Messrs. Scott & Son, the well-known House Furnishers, and in gratefully thanking their friends for the favours liberally bestowed for so many years, beg to assure them of Messrs. Scott's ability to carry on the business as satisfactorily as heretofore**'. It must have seemed to Scott & Son that this acquisition would provide the ideal opportunity to expand their music department. Reddie's shop was exactly opposite Scott's at No.

High Street c1908 - Copyright the Francis Frith Collection.

89, so there would have been little problem in managing the shop. At the same time, it would have released much needed space to increase their display of furniture at Nos. 93 and 94. Scott & Son took on David Dey, who had been working as a tuner for J. H. Reddie & Sons for about three years. They also retained the services of both Ferdinand and Percy Reddie for a time. Ferdinand continued to give piano lessons at No. 42. William Scott engaged W. Jarvis & Son to design a new shop front for the music department. The frontage was 18ft 6in and the proposal was to insert a large new plate glass window, 12ft 3in wide and 10ft tall, with a glazed shop door to the left, with a fanlight over. This was set under a new fascia bearing Scott & Son's name. The photograph above shows Scott & Son's music department c1908 on the far right, next door to Boots the Cash Chemists. The advertisement (below right) appeared in the Lynn Advertiser on 30th March 1906.

William Scott had by this time bought the freehold of other premises in the block which became their big store at 91 to 97, High Street, but these were subject to existing tenancies and he had to wait for them to become vacant. However, he did own other shops and was able to relocate some of his tenants. At some time in 1904, it appears that Scott & Son bought Nos. 95, 96 and 97, High Street, along with property in Purfleet Street. In March of 1904 they received approval to plans submitted by E. E. Colman for a new shop front to No. 96. The proposal involved setting back to the council's new building line but this was never done. Scott & Son's china department was moved into these premises, but it was separated from their main shop at Nos. 93 & 94. The Maypole Dairy Company was in occupation of No. 95 but Scott & Son held the freehold. In December of 1904 they received approval from the Council for alterations to the Purfleet Street property, the plans having been prepared by Jarvis & Son.

Sometime about August, 1904, Scott & Son vacated No. 89, which was taken over by Alfred Speed, a gold and silver smith, watchmaker and jeweller, who moved from premises in Railway Road.

On Monday 12th March 1906, there was another High Street fire. On this occasion, fortunately, the Lynn Fire Brigade was able to get the

flames under control and prevent it from spreading too far. The outbreak started at No. 90, which was called 'Handel House', being occupied by Messrs. Pamment & Smith's music shop, a partnership between Robert W. Pamment and Thomas Henry Meadows Smith. Thomas Smith was blind but had pursued a successful career for many years as a piano teacher and tuner whilst living with his family at No. 50, High Street. He married Robert's sister, Charlotte Pamment, in 1896 and they were living on the premises at No. 90 on the night of the fire. Thomas was about to go to bed at 11.30pm when he heard a crackling sound and alerted his wife, who discovered that the house was on fire. They made their escape and met Alfred Speed, who had smelt the fire, in the street outside. The Fire Brigade arrived within about twelve minutes but could not stop the fire from destroying Pamment & Smith's completely. The music shop stock of gramophone and phonograph records and pianoforte varnish, was highly inflammable and created clouds of toxic smoke that made fighting the fire difficult. The heat was intense and soon the shops opposite, Ladymans at Nos. 39 to 41 and Scott & Son at No. 42, were threatened, so the firemen doused these shop fronts to prevent them from igniting. Nevertheless, Scott's window was cracked by the heat and the records in their display were melted.

It was after this fire that the front of No. 90 was set back to the council's building line. No. 91 was owned by Mr. J. H. Love and he asked the council if they would compensate him if he set back to this line as well. The council offered him the same rate that they had previously agreed with Scott & Son.

On 30th March 1907 Scott & Son included illustrations in their advertisements for the first time (illus. right). These were taken, presumably, from their catalogue, which was still being advertised annually. Sketches of carpets, drawing room suites (from £7/15/-), dining tables (from 21/-), wooden high-back armchairs (from 3/11), solid satin walnut suites (from £5/12/6), go cars (from 8/11) and bedroom suites (from £9/18/6, complete) were included. Similar illustrated advertisements appeared over the next four months before they reverted to single-column adverts with no pictures. Other prices included: convertible mail carts **'For one to lay – one to sit – or two to sit'** from 29/6; strong perambulators from 27/6 **'May be purchased on easy terms,'** strong kitchen chairs from 2/3 and high chairs from 3/3.

> "89, 93 and 94 High street, King's Lynn,
> "18th March, 1907.
> "To Mr. Woolstencroft.
> "Dear Sir,—*Re* proposed new shop window, 96 High street.—This shop cannot be set back to new building line until the whole corner is dealt with, but the new window will not add to the compensation required by me when the alteration takes place. — Yours truly, WM. CRAWSHAY SCOTT."
> The plan was approved.

On 12th April 1907 it was reported in the Lynn Advertiser (illus. above) that the council had approved an application from Scott & Son to fit a new display window to No. 96. William Scott had written to the Town Clerk explaining that the shop could not be redeveloped and the front set back, in accordance with the council's previous approval, in isolation from the corner property, No. 97. The firm had started their final push to consolidate their block of property at the corner of High Street and Purfleet Street. In 1900, the occupants of No. 97 were Frost & West (Late Glenny), Tailors & Outfitters. The acquisition of No. 97 was to be the last piece in the jigsaw for Scott & Son in assembling the corner block.

On 8th June, they advertised their new china and glass department which was established in No. 96, High Street. They were now occupying 42, High Street (J. H. Reddie & Sons' old shop) where they displayed music, instruments and furniture, 93 and 94, High Street (furniture and bedding), a warehouse in Purfleet Street displaying carpet and cork lino, and 96, High Street. On 5th July 1907 they placed a notice in the Lynn Advertiser announcing that they had bought the entire stock of Messrs. Collins Clayton's china and glass shop, at No. 5, High Street and that they were selling it off. The agreement between Scott & Son and Collins Clayton & Co. was dated 13th May, 1907 and reads: 'This Agreement Certifies that Messrs Collins Clayton & Co. China & Glass Merchants of Market Place, Wisbech and 5, High St. Lynn agrees to sell all the stock of China, Glass and earthenware and all the fixtures and fittings (excepting those scheduled in the lease) and all trade utensils, for the sum of Two Hundred and Sixty Five Pounds, this price to include the use of the premises to the end of June, 1907. The name of Collins not to be used by Scott & Son after the end of June '07. Messrs Collins Clayton & Co. also agree not to open another shop in the Borough of King's Lynn as China, Glass or Earthenware Merchants'.

VALUABLE FREEHOLD BUSINESS PREMISES.
92 HIGH STREET, KING'S LYNN.

Messrs. MILES & SON

ARE instructed to Sell by Auction at the Globe hotel, King's Lynn, on Thursday 5th September, 1907, at 7 o'clock in the evening. All that well-placed commodious

SHOP AND PREMISES,

No. 92, on the west side of High street, King's Lynn, and containing well-arranged shop, sitting and drawing-rooms, 3 bed-rooms, kitchen, yard and outbuildings, together with a 3-storied warehouse in the rear, with back entrance into Gibson yard, Purfleet street, occupier Mr. Alfred Spinks. Annual rent £45.

Particulars and conditions may be had of the Auctioneers, Broad Street Chambers, King's Lynn; or of

Messrs. BELOE & BELOE.
28008]   Solicitors, King's Lynn.

In September 1907 William Scott purchased 92, High Street for £700 (illus. left - sale particulars). Interestingly, William Scott, in signing the Sale and Purchase Agreement, gave his occupation as 'Furniture Warehouseman' (illus. below right). In those days, a large shop or grand retail display area was referred to as a warehouse. Taking the modern use of the term warehouseman, it would be tempting to imagine William Scott strolling into the auction room wearing brown overalls in a ploy to convince the other bidders that he was no threat.

Evidently, William Scott was able to obtain vacant possession of the shop within a short space of time. Mr. Spinks, a confectioner occupying No. 92, may have been planning to consolidate the business at his Tower Street premises. However, there was still a tenant,

Messrs. Love Bros., occupying the next door shop, 91, High Street. It was necessary, therefore, for Scott & Son to undertake some temporary alterations to 92, High Street and to wait until they had vacant possession of 91, at which time they would be able to undertake a more comprehensive rebuilding of these shops. It was also necessary to satisfy the council's requirements to set back the front of the shop to a new building line in order to widen this part of the street.

Mr. Ernest E. Colman produced plans that showed the setting back of the new shop front some 4ft 7in from the existing line. The frontage of No. 92 was very narrow, with a small shop window and an entrance door to the left hand side. The proposals did away with a separate shop entrance to No. 92, with customers gaining access to this part of the shop via the existing door at No. 93. The new shop front had two plate glass windows, each 6ft 9in wide and 7ft tall. Internally, a large chimney breast was removed and the wall taken down to link up with number 93, referred to as 'Scott's Furniture Emporium' on the plans. Two small stores and an old bake oven at the back of 92, in Gibson's Yard, were also incorporated into the 'Furniture Emporium'.

At the time of their application to the council, Scott & Son's proposed use of No. 92 was as an extension to their carpet and floor covering department. It seems, however, that they changed their plans and decided to establish their expanded household linen and drapery department in the new premises.

On 24th January 1908 they advertised in the Lynn Advertiser that they were holding a sale for one month, starting on the following Tuesday. They had ordered new lines for the coming spring season and were clearing out all their current stock.

It was Scott & Son's practice to include the individual numbers of the shop units that they were occupying in their advertisements and to list their separate retail departments, but it was not until 25th July that they included No. 92. Then, on 8th August, they announced the establishment of their expanded drapery department:

'Messrs. SCOTT & SON'S HOUSEHOLD DRAPERY DEPARTMENT has developed and expanded most amazingly, mainly owing to the large selection and splendid value always offered, these goods being sold at prices quite 25 per. Cent lower than Drapers' prices.

Sheets and Sheetings, Blankets, White and Colored Quilts and Bed-Spreads, Toilet Covers, Turkish, Huckaback, Honeycomb and other Towels, Damask Cloths, Lace Curtains, Table Covers, etc., etc. Choice Display in the LARGE NEW SHOW WINDOW, 92 HIGH STREET.'

SCOTT & SON.
FURNITURE, BEDDING & BEDSTEADS, 42, 92, 93, 94, 96 & 97, HIGH STREET.
PIANOFORTES & MUSIC (late J. H. Reddie & Sons), 42, HIGH-STREET.
CARPET AND CORK LINO WAREHOUSE, PURFLEET-STREET.
HOUSEHOLD DRAPERY & LINEN DEPARTMENT (92, HIGH-STREET).
CHINA AND GLASS DEPARTMENT 96, HIGH-STREET.
STEAM FURNITURE AND BEDDING FACTORY, SOUTH QUAY.
KING'S LYNN.

Later that year, Scott & Son took over No. 97, High Street and, on 19th December 1908, listed all their departments in the Lynn News (illus. right).

At this date Scott & Son were occupying all of their 91 to 97, High Street block apart from numbers 91 (Messrs. Love Bros.) and 95 (the Maypole Dairy Co.). The carpet store in Purfleet Street was in Gibson's Yard, at the back of the Oddfellows Hall.

In January 1909, as part of the continuing push to improve and update their expanding estate of small premises and turn them into a single, coherent shop unit, William Scott commissioned the services of William Jarvis & Son, Architects & Surveyors of Paradise Road, King's Lynn. They prepared plans and specifications for '...work in carrying out certain alterations to Shop and premises situated in Purfleet Street, King's Lynn, for Messrs. Scott & Son.' The application was submitted to the Borough Council on 27th January and related to the corner shop, 97, High Street, and the next door property, No. 1, Purfleet Street.

It is not clear when William Scott bought this property. After John Ayton Nokes, who had a shoe shop there in the late 1890's, the premises were occupied by a succession of businesses including, temporarily, Sidney Count, whose chemist's shop at No. 17 had been burnt down in the 1897 fire. Frederick Glenny, who had another shop in Wisbech, opened a Ladies and Gentlemen's Tailors there on 24th March 1899, but he retired the following year and his businesses at Wisbech and Lynn were taken over by Frost & West. Charles West announced that he had sold the premises (implying the freehold) in October 1901 and the business then became John Kirk's tailors. William Scott seems to have acquired the freehold sometime between 1901 and 1904 and John Kirk may have been his tenant.

The shop was accessed by a door in the splay, on the corner of High Street and Purfleet Street. The ground floor of the shop was overall about 16ft by 27ft deep but there was a staircase which took up some of the space. Through the shop was a former sitting room 15ft by 12ft, with a fireplace, and at the back was a lobby with a second set of stairs leading up to a landing and three bedrooms with windows over Purfleet Street. At the very back, giving the only direct access onto Purfleet Street, was a small store and a narrow passage. The alterations involved the removal of internal walls to enable the whole ground floor area to be used as a shop. The front wall onto Purfleet Street at ground floor level was removed and steel columns and beams inserted to support the upper floor. Three new plate glass windows were fitted under a fascia which lined up with that on the corner shop. One of the staircases was removed and the other was repositioned to give access to store rooms on the first floor.

There was a rather sad history attached to No. 97, concerning the Nokes family. In 1897, both Alfred Nokes and his wife Ida became ill with typhoid fever, which was prevalent in the town. The following year Ida began to recover slowly and was convalescing, although Alfred was still bedridden. However, she was troubled by headaches and an inability to concentrate enough to get anything done about the house. On Friday 18th March 1898, Ida dressed her baby son after breakfast, kissed him and told her servant, Agnes Morton, to look after him and not to go into the hall. Agnes thought that she had gone out and it was not until about 1.30pm that it was discovered that Ida had hanged herself in the lumber room at the back of the shop. Many years later, some of

Scott & Son's staff would insist that part of the old shop was haunted, although apparently they did not know about this tragic event.

In July 1909 William Scott submitted an application to insert a new shop front at 68, High Street. It seems that he bought this shop either to enable him to relocate one of the tenants in his block of properties on the corner of Purfleet Street and High Street, or to let as part of his increasing property portfolio. The new front had a central doorway, set back six feet from the pavement, with curved plate glass windows on either side.

A year later, on 30th April 1910, the lease to the Maypole Dairy Company expired and they announced that they were vacating No. 95, High Street: 'EXPIRATION OF LEASE!!!- MAYPOLE DAIRY CO., LTD. Beg to notify their Lynn customers that they are transferring their business from 95, High Street to 38a, HIGH STREET on Thursday next.'

SCOTT & SON
ARE ABOUT TO ADD TO THEIR
HUGE PILE OF BUSINESS BUILDINGS
The Shop and Premises lately occupied by
THE MAYPOLE DAIRY CO.

On 14th May 1910 the town was in mourning for King Edward VII and the shops were closed on Friday 20th May for his funeral.

Scott & Son took over No. 95 on the expiration of Maypole Dairy's lease and announced in July (illus. above) that 'SCOTT & SON are about to add to their MAMMOTH PILE OF BUSINESS BUILDINGS The Shop and Premises Lately Occupied by THE MAYPOLE DAIRY CO.' They extended their glass and china department, along with part of their furniture sales, into their new premises. On 20th August, 1910, they advertised: 'PERAMBULATORS AND MAILCARTS are being shown in the New Window, 95 High Street GO-CARS FROM 5/11.'

Bedroom suites in satin walnut were advertised, with illustrations, by Scotts on 7th January 1911 in the Lynn News and County Press. The dressing table and wardrobe were fitted with best bevelled plate glass mirrors and the washstand had a marble top and a tiled back. The three pieces were for sale at £5 7s 6d complete. The following week their 'Great Winter Sale' was announced, starting on Saturday 21st January. Bedroom suites were again the special offers. Already, however, the shop was getting ready for spring and was promoting its prams and baby carriages. They had purchased a special order of over 100 perambulators which were priced at 29/6 upwards and Go-cars started at 5/11, whilst 'beautifully upholstered and carriage-painted Mail Carts' (illus. left) cost from 28/11.

The big event that year was the Coronation of King George V on 22nd June. On the 24th June, the Lynn News carried a big article with a photograph of the King in his Coronation robes.

Local events included a 'great service of praise for the people' held at the Lynn Central Hall on Sunday 26th June. The mayor gave an address on the theme of 'God Save the King, God Save the Queen, God Save the People'. He spoke about the King and social reform. The mayor was Mr. C. W. Perry, the man brought to the town by Alfred Jermyn in 1890 as his partner in the drapery department; another

indication of the good judgement shown by Alfred Jermyn in choosing his partner.

Many people travelled to London to see the Coronation parade and to join in the festivities in the Capital but most had to make do by celebrating nearer to home. Lynn put on a big civic procession and the crowds came out to watch. The day's events started with a huge gathering in the Tuesday Market Place (illustrated on the previous page), which was followed by a great procession around the town, reported as follows:

THE CIVIC PROCESSION: A Representative Gathering.

The proceedings at Lynn opened with a monster procession, formed up on the Tuesday Market-place at ten o'clock. The square was gaily bedecked, and for the large crowd of onlookers there was a pretty spectacle with the various uniforms, regalia and banners. A platform, tastefully decorated, had been erected near the lamp in the centre of the square and facing the south side, and here, just before the procession started, representatives of the various public bodies, with public officials, took their stand with the Mayor.

The arrangement for the assembling of the processionists was an exceedingly good one. On the programme numbers had been given to show where the different sections were to come in, and number boards had been erected to show where on the Market-place the people who were to compose the sections should take their stand.

When the general assembly was complete, the Mayor, stepping to the front of the platform, said: "This is a unique occasion. Most of us have never taken part in a similar gathering before, and many of us will never take part in another. I invite you all, at the lead of the band, to sing from your hearts and with all your voice, *God save the King*."

Two other processions formed; one, with the mayor, for the service at St. Margaret's Church and the other for the United Free Church service at the Wesleyan Church in Tower Street. Other services were held at All Saints, St. Nicholas, St. John's and the Roman Catholic Church. After the service at St. Margaret's, a special meeting of the Lynn Town Council was held at which the seal was affixed to an address which was sent to the King. In the afternoon, the children of the town gathered in the Tuesday Market Place before processing to the Walks for tea. Children's entertainments and activities were arranged at the Red Mount field and the recreation ground. The Town Band was joined by the bands of the Royal Navy Reserve and the Salvation Army to provide music throughout the afternoon. The events ended with a fireworks display. Every school child in the town received a special commemoration card designed and printed by the local firm of Messrs. Barton Bros. The card, printed in green, blue, brown and gold, bore the royal arms and portraits of the King and Queen, together with photographs around the border showing views of the town: the Walks; Greyfriars' Tower; the Town Hall; South Gates; Custom House; the quay with St. Margaret's Church, and the Red Mount. The card was printed with the words: '**Borough of King's Lynn. Presented to ……. As a souvenir of Their Most Gracious Majesties King George V and the Queen.**' The cards bore the signature of the mayor.

On 8th July 1911 Scott & Son announced the expansion of their second-hand furniture department:

'**Another Enormous Addition. Messrs. Scott & Son have pleasure in announcing that they have opened most commodious premises for the Sale of Second-hand Furniture, Bedsteads & Bedding, and are now offering a very large and Clean Stock at Low Prices Any Quantity of Furniture Bought for Cash. All communications to be addressed to 93 & 94 HIGH STREET.**'

It seems that this announcement was linked to William Scott achieving his aim of consolidating Scott & Son's retailing business into one big store at the corner of High Street and Purfleet Street. The final piece in the assembly of Scott & Son's big block of High Street property fell into place during July 1911, when No 91 was added to their other shops. However, it was not until the end of the year that the new property featured in their list of furniture departments. Their summer sale that year started on 29th July and floor coverings

INLAID LINOLEUMS, FROM 1/11¼ PER SQUARE YARD. OVER 50 PIECES OF SCOTT'S LYNNLINO TO SELECT FROM. The Pattern goes right through to the back, therefore it Cannot Wear Off. Made in 3 qualities only, 2/7 per square yard, 3/3 per square yard, and the best at 3/10½ per square yard.

were their headline items: '**Unusually heavy stocks of Carpets, Carpet Squares, Rugs, Mats, Linoleums, Floorcloths, Linoleum and Floorcloth Squares Etc. etc. will be offered at Enormously reduced Prices. Several Tons of Floorcloth Remnants. Useful lengths of two to ten yards will be sold REGARDLESS OF COST. Buyers should be early on the scene to inspect this unparalleled lot.**'

Scott & Son's wide range of furnishing items for sale in their various departments was summarised in the advertisement in the Lynn News on 7th October 1911:

SCOTT & SON: make the Furniture Displayed in their Windows and Showrooms at: 42, 92, 93, 94 96 & 97, HIGH STREET, & PURFLEET STREET – Customers therefore secure Dependable Furniture at FIRST COST.
SCOTT & SON: have been famous for fifty years for their PURE BEDDING, made at their Steam Bedding Factory on South Quay and on show at: 93 & 94, High Street.
SCOTT & SON: are the Largest Buyers and Sellers in the Eastern Counties of CARPETS, INLAID LINOS, CORK LINOS, & FLOOR CLOTHS. Exhibited in their: CARPET SALOON, PURFLEET STREET.
SCOTT & SON: Have a Special Assortment of ALL BRASS & BLACK & BRASS BEDSTEADS at: 93 & 94, HIGH STREET.
SCOTT & SON: Always have on hand a Splendid Stock of PIANOFORTES, ORGANS, & MUSICAL INSTRUMENTS at: 42, HIGH STREET (Late Reddie & Sons.)
SCOTT & SON'S CHINA & GLASS DEPARTMENT contains every requisite for Hotels and Private Houses: 95 & 96, HIGH STREET.
SCOTT & SON'S HIGH-CLASS ENAMEL WARE. Popular Prices. Splendid Assortment: 92, HIGH STREET.
SCOTT & SON'S HOUSEHOLD LINENS & DRAPERY: Largest Stock. Best Value. Lowest Prices: 92, HIGH STREET.
SCOTT & SON'S BABY CARRIAGES are noted for Durability & Lowness of Price. See the Stock at: 93 & 94, HIGH STREET.
SCOTT & SON always have a Splendid Selection of SAUCEPANS, KETTLES, FENDERS, BRASSES, IRONS, & IRONMONGERY at: 95, HIGH STREET.
SCOTT & SON'S Show & Sell Range of BRUSHES, BROOMS &c at: 95, HIGH STREET.
SCOTT & SON REPAIR RENOVATE & RECOVER FURNITURE & RE-MAKE BEDDING in: THEIR STEAM FACTORY: SOUTH QUAY.
SCOTT & SON Send Tuners and Repairers anywhere within a radius of 30 miles: 42, HIGH STREET

Floor coverings were always a speciality of Scott & Son and their 'Lynnlino' appears to have been a popular line. 'Floor cloth' (sometimes 'floorcloth' or 'oilcloth'), was simply a cloth material, usually canvas, painted with oil paint. Originally, the canvas would have been from ships' sails. It was quite tough in normal use but would not stand the tread of hobnailed boots! Even if it was damaged, it could be repaired easily by touching-up with oil paint. Companies that sold the really expensive oilcloths would repaint them for their customers as part of the sale agreement. Floorcloth was laid on top of newspaper to protect it from protruding nails or splinters in the wood floor or uneven surfaces below. Linoleum was a hard, smooth flooring made from a solidified mixture of linseed oil and ground cork, laid on a backing of canvas or burlap – a strong, coarsely-woven cloth made from jute, flax or hemp fibres. Linoleum was more durable than the canvas floorcloths and easier to keep clean. Linoleum was pioneered by Michael Nairn of Kirkcaldy in Scotland in the mid-nineteenth century. The Nairns moved to America in the 1880s and continued to manufacture linoleum throughout the early 1900s. In the early 1920s, they joined forces with another company and became Congoleum-Nairn (now the Congoleum Corporation). They started manufacturing 'Congoleum', an asphalt-based material that was produced up to the late 1930s. Then vinyl materials started to be developed, although their introduction was interrupted by the outbreak of the Second World War. Congoleum was so named because the asphalt came from the Belgian Congo.

By December 1911 Scott's new shop, No 91, High Street was ready for use, having been fitted with a new shop window. On 2nd December, their advertisement in the Lynn News included the announcement 'SPECIAL SHOW OF NEW BEDSTEADS AND BEDDING In the New Show Window, 91, High Street.'

For spring 1912, Scott & Son made a big push to promote specially-made patterns of lino which they advertised as 'Scott's Lynnlino'. Their advertisements read: 'OVER 50 PIECES OF SCOTT'S LYNNLINO TO SELECT   FROM. The Pattern goes right through to the back, therefore cannot Wear Off. Made in 3 qualities only, 2/7 per square yard, 3/3 per square yard, and the best at 3/10 per square yard.'

Although Scott & Son now had a run of seven shops in High Street, the frontage was by no means uniform and the properties at either end projected forward of the central ones, which had been rebuilt to the Borough Council's new building line. This left two 'wing walls' where the set-backs occurred. In March 1912 an agreement was drawn up between 'The Mayor, Aldermen and Burgesses of the Borough of King's Lynn' and William Crawshay Scott for the continued use of the wing walls in High Street for advertising purposes. This was a simple agreement that made it clear that the wing walls were on land acquired by the Corporation for widening the street and that the walls would have to be demolished if and when they acquired the adjacent land to complete the street works.

This was a time of change in the High Street. Ladymans moved their retail department into No. 41 so that their premises at 39 and 40 could be rebuilt. The music department of Scott & Son moved out of No. 42 and went across the road into No. 91, High Street, an announcement being placed in the Lynn News on 8th June (illustrated on the previous page). They had occupied the shop for the past seven years following their purchase of the business of J. H. Reddie & Sons. On 22nd June, there was an advertisement in the Lynn News announcing the impending arrival of a business that would bring a '**Revolution in Tailoring'** to King's Lynn. On 6th July, it was revealed that this new shop was to be Hipps Ltd., and that they were opening up their Lynn branch in 42, High Street. Scott & Son retained the freehold of No 42, leasing it to Hipps for many years. Hipps were a huge national chain, advertising over 54 branches throughout Scotland, Wales, Northern Ireland and England. Their advertisement set out their approach to bringing affordable clothing to the people of Lynn: '**Revolution in Tailoring. Direct from Loom to Wearer. HIPPS Ltd., THE PUBLIC BENEFIT TAILORS, have Come to King's Lynn. No fit, no pay is our way. We have a huge turnover. No Middleman's profit. Up-to-date methods. 42 High St.'**

A month later, Scott & Son announced a sale of the stock of their music department (illus. above), so that they could clear the shop for further alterations. They were arranging to accommodate all of their departments in their block of buildings from No. 91 to No. 97, on the corner of Purfleet Street. Although they were maintaining a music department, it was on a smaller scale than their shop at No. 42; consequently, they had a significant amount of stock to clear before they could move across the street. A few of the instruments that had been hired out were sold at '**Ridiculous Prices'**, while all other instruments were to be sold at half price and all their sheet music and albums were greatly reduced for clearance.

The most significant event in 1912 for Scott & Son was the retirement of the founder, Thomas William Scott. He had been taking a back seat role in the running of the business for several years. Now well into his seventies, he finally withdrew completely and the father and son partnership was formally dissolved, with a notice being placed in the Lynn Advertiser on 10th August 1912 (illus. above left).

The shop alterations were completed in time for the Christmas sales push and Scott & Son decked out their store for their '**GRAND CHRISTMAS BAZAAR.'** This was, they claimed, '**The most charming Christmas display in the entire District – No visitor to Lynn should miss this novel Exhibition.'** The shop was filled with artificial palms, ferns and flowers '**1d, 6 ½d, and 1s the Spray.'** Among the goods on offer were '**Large stock of Chesterfield Settees & Lounge Chairs. Dainty Drawing-room suites. Fancy Cabinets &**

Handsome Sideboards. Splendid assortment of Eiderdown Quilts & Blankets, from 2/11 each. Wicker Chairs in great variety. Useful show of Draught screens from 12/6. CHINA and GLASS DEPARTMENT: Special preparations have been made for Christmas Trade. Dinner, Dessert, Breakfast and Tea Services in Excellent and Tasty Designs. PIANOFORTE & MUSIC DEPARTMENTS: See Stock of Reliable Instruments. See the new Stanley Brinsmead Pianoforte, Prices from 16 Guineas, Fully Warranted.'

Scott & Son, like many of Lynn's traders, made the most of the influx of visitors to the town coming to enjoy the pleasures of the Mart. This provided a welcome boost to sales in February when trade would otherwise be expected to be slack, during that cold winter period between Christmas and spring. On 1st February 1913 Scott & Son proclaimed: 'In KING'S LYNN The Two Great Popular Events Of the Year 1913: SCOTT & SON'S SALE and THE MART Will both commence on the same day: February 14th.' They advertised that their entire stock had to be cleared and that all linen, calico sheeting, lace curtains and blankets would be offered with one penny in the shilling discount.

The national news in 1913, as reflected in the pages of the Lynn News and County Press, was preoccupied with the 'Irish Question' and the prevarication of the government over the introduction of women's suffrage. Meanwhile, closer to home, the headlines on 5th February 1913 reflected concern throughout the town over the Town Council's proposals for a new road that would affect the Walks: 'WALKS DEFACEMENT AVOIDED – Victory of Petitioners'.

The debate in the council chamber concerned a petition signed by a number of local residents who were incensed at the recently-taken decision of the council to proceed with proposals for a road to link Tennyson Avenue with the Blackfriars Road / St John's Terrace corner, beside the church. The petitioners were outraged at the impact that the road would have on 'the beautiful Walks, the boast and pride of the residents of the borough.' There was a long and lively discussion by the councillors before a vote was taken and they resolved to reverse their previous decision. Petitions against decisions of the Town Council at this time seem to have been fairly common and this is not the only instance of a decision being reversed.

Another current local issue was what the newspaper referred to as 'Thinning Lynn's Inns.' The Balfour Act of 1904 required the breweries to re-apply for their licences and made provision for compensation to be paid in cases where the authority decided that the licence should not be renewed. During the preceding seven years 43 licences lapsed, with one brewery losing a third of its original total in the town and another losing half. However, the paper reported that there was still one licence for every 142 people resident in Lynn. In February 1913 four licences were referred to the Norfolk Compensation Authority: the King's Head in Queen Street; the Carpenters Arms, Norfolk Street; the Duke William, Norfolk Street, and the Duck, Pilot Street.

Scott & Son put on a spring display of baby carriages and

perambulators, advertising: 'Scott & Son's BABYLAND' in the Lynn Advertiser on 21st February, 1913 (illus. above right). Their latest carriage was 'Very Stylish, Splendidly Made, With 1/2in. Wired-on Tyres and Safety Chain Brakes. ONLY 35/11'.

An incomplete Scott & Son catalogue survives from c1912/13 and, together with a list of all their departments that appeared in the Lynn Advertiser in April 1913 gives a clear picture of the range of goods that they sold. At this date almost all of the furniture that they sold was made in Lynn. On the following pages, copies from this catalogue are reproduced, together with extracts from the April 1913 advertisement. The range of services and furniture are: Pianos & Organs; China, Glass & Earthenware; Hardware, Cutlery & Ironmongery; Household Drapery & Linens; Curtains & Blinds; Dining & Drawing Room Suites; Recovering & Renovation; Perambulators & Mail Carts; Bedroom Suites; Bedsteads & Bedding; Carpets, and Linoleums & Floorcloths

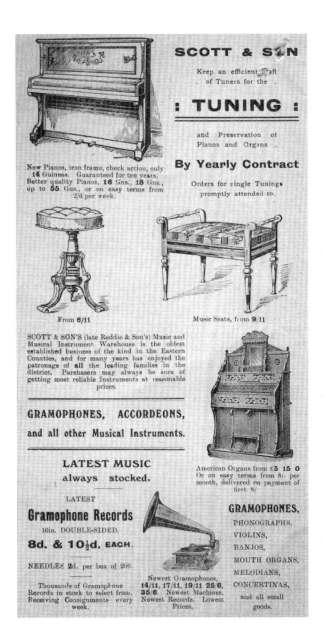

Pianos & Organs.

We have a splendid stock of very fine instruments which are, without doubt, the best in the district at the price, being very carefully selected from the best makers, with keenest regard to tone, touch and durability. Prices from 16 to 40 guineas, or can be had on easy terms from 2/6 per week. Every instrument guaranteed for 10 years. Experienced staff of tuners sent to any part. Repairs of every description. Latest music and newest albums. Gramophones and records. Violins, banjos and every kind of musical instrument.

China, Glass & Earthenware.

Our showrooms are crowded with an exquisite stock of these goods which for variety and value cannot be equalled. Every item

for household use is here in lavish profusion at exceedingly reasonable prices. Clubs, Hotels, and Publics supplied. Pots and pans and all kinds of earthenware and stoneware. Fireproof ware.

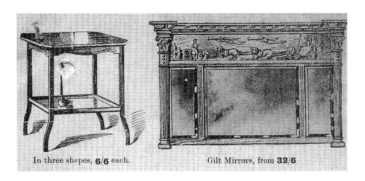

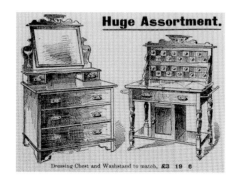

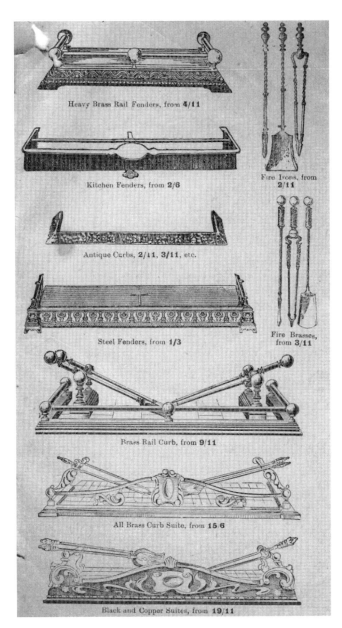

Heavy Brass Rail Fenders, from **4/11**

Kitchen Fenders, from **2/6**

Fire Irons, from **2/11**

Antique Curbs, **2/11, 3/11**, etc.

Steel Fenders, from **1/3**

Fire Brasses, from **3/11**

Brass Rail Curb, from **9/11**

All Brass Curb Suite, from **15/6**

Black and Copper Suites, from **19/11**

Hardware, Cutlery & Ironmongery.

Our usual method of supplying the best goods at moderate prices is especially evident in this department. Our prices are chosen to meet every requirement in domestic economy, and offer an extraordinary range and variety for selection. We stock warranted cutlery from best Sheffield makers. Fine selection of ironmongery, including a variety of every article necessary for the home. Brooms and brushes. Tin and enamel goods of every description.

Household Drapery & Linens.

The satisfactory increase in the bulk of business transacted in these departments is proof that the quality is good & the prices right. We supply every article for the complete outfit of this portion of house furnishing. Details of the items are impossible in this space, so we ask you to call and we shall be proud to exhibit the grand value offered in these departments.

Curtains, Blinds, Etc.

Our new stock of fabrics for the season includes an unrivalled stock of lace curtains, direct from the looms, at prices varying from 1/6 to 39/6 per pair. Curtains and hangings, just those that will give an artistic tone and the touch of good taste to your home. Blinds of every design, color and texture made to order. Casement and cornice poles and fittings.

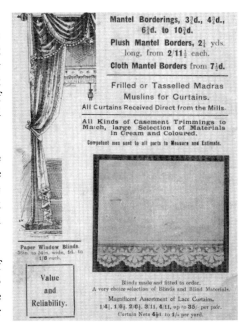

6-piece Solid Oak Suite, beautifully finished, upholstered in pegamoid, prices complete, from £4 7 6   Child's High Chair, 3/3

FIRST CLASS MAKE & FINISH.

Lowest Possible Prices.

Patent Screw Dining Table, with extra leaves, dual top,
4ft. 6in. by 3ft., 25/6 ; 5ft. by 3ft. 3in., 29/6 ;
5ft. by 3ft. 6in., 35/- ; 6ft. by 4ft., 39/6
Also made in solid mahogany, walnut or oak.

Acknowledged by all to be the Cheapest in the Trade.

Handsome Suite in saddlebags, comprising couch, 2 easy chairs, and 4 small chairs, **£5 15 0**

Dining & Drawing Room Suites.

We have a wonderful display of suites of various designs that will stand hard wear. These are made in our steam factory and are marked at amazingly low prices. We have leather suites from 55/- complete. Saddlebag suites from £3 15/- and lounge suites in velvet from £7 1/6. Easy chairs that are really easy at all prices. Cabinets, Sideboards, Cheffoniers & Overmantles in great variety.

HIGH STREET, KING'S LYNN. 7

This handsome Suite in velvet or moquette, £11 15 0 complete.

Chesterfield Settees in great variety, from 58/6

EVERY-THING MARKED IN PLAIN FIGURES.

Suite, comprising couch, 2 easy chairs and 4 small chairs, in moquette, £11 11 0 complete.

The Furniture we sell is noted for its *good value*, good quality, design and the strict integrity of its manufacture.

Easy Chairs in saddlebags, from 32/6   Easy Chair, in tapestry, 27/6

Drawing and Dining Room Suites.

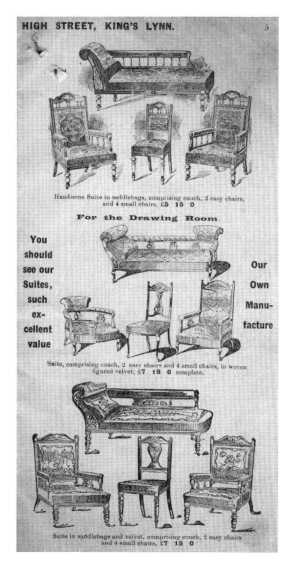

HIGH STREET, KING'S LYNN. 5

Handsome Suite in saddlebags, comprising couch, 2 easy chairs, and 4 small chairs, £5 15 0

For the Drawing Room

You should see our Suites, such excellent value

Our Own Manu-facture

Suite, comprising couch, 2 easy chairs and 4 small chairs, in woven figured velvet, £7 18 6 complete.

Suite in saddlebags and velvet, comprising couch, 2 easy chairs and 4 small chairs, £7 15 0

All Carriages Fitted with Wired-on Tyres.

Easy Payments can be arranged.

As design, 39/11

All Carriages are fitted with chain brake and wheels with Hughes' wired-on tyres. Splendid Assortment of Alpaca Canopies and Covers, in all Colours.

Best Value in the Trade.

Strong Folding Go-Cars, as design, 6/11

Mail Carts from 32/6 to £5 5 0

Perambulators and Mail Carts may be purchased on our **EASY PAYMENT SYSTEM.**

We hold a large stock of the very highest grade Cars, as well as those of a lower quality.

As design, from 8/11

Better qualities, 11/9 to 21/-

Special Machinery for fixing Wired-on Tyres.
Comparison of Quality and Price Invited.
Special Catalogue of Perambulators and Mail Carts on application.

Painted Washstands, from 3/11, 5/11, 7/11

Dressing Tables, from 3/11

Painted Chests, 16/6

Painted Chests, 22/6

We Provide Everything for the Complete Equipment of the Home.

All sizes, from 1/11½

Commode Chair, 22/6

Cane Seat Chairs, 2/3

Birch or mahogany Commode, patent pan, 12/6 Cheaper make, 7/11½

Solid Satin Walnut Chest, 63/-

Mahogany Chests, from 32/6

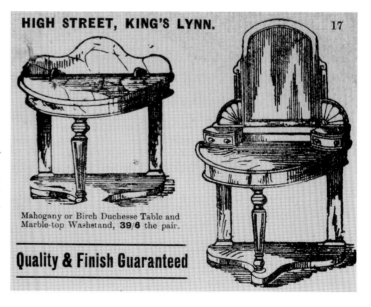

Mahogany or Birch Duchesse Table and Marble-top Washstand, **39/6** the pair.

Quality & Finish Guaranteed

Perambulators & Mail Carts.
Our stock of baby carriages is more varied this year than ever. We have many that are ideals of beauty and comfort, at quite low prices. Our latest carriage is very stylish, splendidly made and comfortable, with ½ inch wired-on tyres and safety chain brakes. We sell it at 35/11. Better qualities 39/11, 45/-, 49/6 &c. Latest designs in Mailcarts from 32/6. New Go Cars 5/6, 6/11, 7/11 &c. Canopies in coverings of alpaca, silk & muslin, water-proof and white fancy aprons.

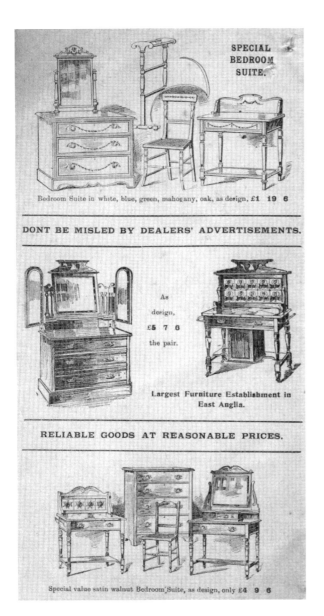

Bedroom Suite in white, blue, green, mahogany, oak, as design, £1 19 6

DONT BE MISLED BY DEALERS' ADVERTISEMENTS.

As design, £5 7 6 the pair.

Largest Furniture Establishment in East Anglia.

RELIABLE GOODS AT REASONABLE PRICES.

Special value satin walnut Bedroom Suite, as design, only £4 9 6

SPECIAL BEDROOM SUITE.

Very smart satin walnut Bedroom Suite, as design, £5 17 6 complete.

NOTE OUR LOW PRICES FOR GOODS OF DEPENDABLE VALUE.

Box Ottoman in cretonne, 17/11

Very fine satin walnut Bedroom Suite, as design, £6 18 6 complete.

Bedroom Suites.

In satin and black walnut, oak or mahogany, beautifully made and of artistic design. We sell a solid walnut bedroom suite consisting of wardrobe with plate glass door, dressing chest and marble top tile-back washstand at £5 17/6 complete, a marvel of value. Come and see the many designs we have to show you. We shall be pleased to send designs and prices on application.

Quality and Finish Guaranteed.

Leather Chairs, from **12/6**

Leather Seated Chairs, **3/6**

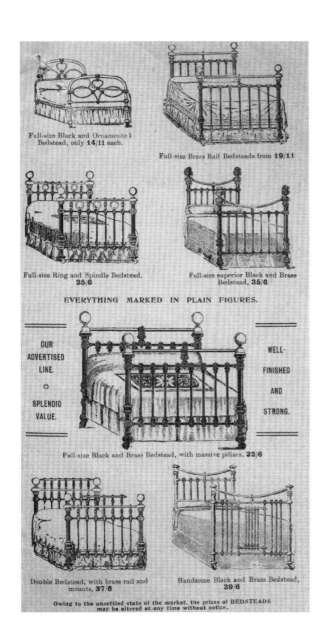

Full-size Black and Ornamental Bedstead, only **14/11** each.

Full-size Brass Rail Bedsteads from **19/11**

Full-size Ring and Spindle Bedstead, **25/6**

Full-size superior Black and Brass Bedstead, **35/6**

EVERYTHING MARKED IN PLAIN FIGURES.

OUR ADVERTISED LINE.

SPLENDID VALUE.

WELL-FINISHED AND STRONG.

Full-size Black and Brass Bedstead, with massive pillars, **22/6**

Double Bedstead, with brass rail and mounts, **37/6**

Handsome Black and Brass Bedstead, **39/6**

Owing to the unsettled state of the market, the prices of BEDSTEADS may be altered at any time without notice.

BEDDING.

We have special Steam Machinery for making our noted Pure Bedding.

WOVEN WIRE MATTRESSES.

Full-size Spring Mattresses, from **9/11** to **35/-**

All our Bedding is Sterilized and Guaranteed of the Government Standard of Purity.

Full-size Feather Beds, bolster and 2 pillows, **39/6, 45/-, 55/-** and **70/-** the set. Flock Bed, bolster and 2 pillows, **12/11** and **15/6** the set. Straw Palliasses, **7/11, 8/11** and **9/11** the pair. Flock Pillows, **1/3** each. Flock Bolsters, **2/6**. Feather Pillows from **2/11**. Feather Bolsters from **4/11**. Hair and Wool Mattresses from **39/6**. All Hair Mattresses from **50/-**. Special machinery for re-carding mattresses and cleaning feather beds, etc.

Scott & Son's Home-made Bedding is always of dependable quality.

Patent Airduct Bedding our Speciality.

This Bedding is divided into sections, with air passages between each section. The top, bottom and ends are perforated. The air enters in at the bottom and ends and out through the top row of eyelets to the body of the sleeper.

Sterilized full-size mattresses, from **15/11**

These Chair-Bedsteads are most convenient, as they can be used as a Chair at day-time and Bedstead at night, same as design.

From **12/11**

Combination Bedstead with Wire Spring Mattress, **14/11**

Best Materials only used. All mattresses made with good clean filling and strong ticks.

Bedsteads & Bedding.

Our stock of bedsteads is comprehensive. We have full size iron bedsteads from 14/11. Iron and brass and all brass up to £12/12/-. The most unique & original are the wood bedsteads, which are made in oak, walnut, satin walnut and mahogany, in really artistic designs to match all kinds of bedroom suites. **Bedding:** the most perfect in the world. Guaranteed pure and hygienic. Made at our own works. Full size bed-sets from 12/11. Full size mattresses from 13/11. Full size feather bed-sets from 37/6. Customers may always see beds and bedding in the course of construction at our works.

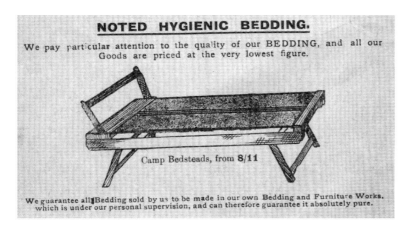

NOTED HYGIENIC BEDDING.

We pay particular attention to the quality of our BEDDING, and all our Goods are priced at the very lowest figure.

Camp Bedsteads, from **8/11**

We guarantee all Bedding sold by us to be made in our own Bedding and Furniture Works, which is under our personal supervision, and can therefore guarantee it absolutely pure.

Children's Cots, from **12/6**

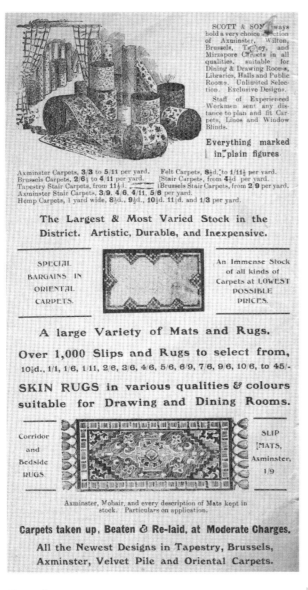
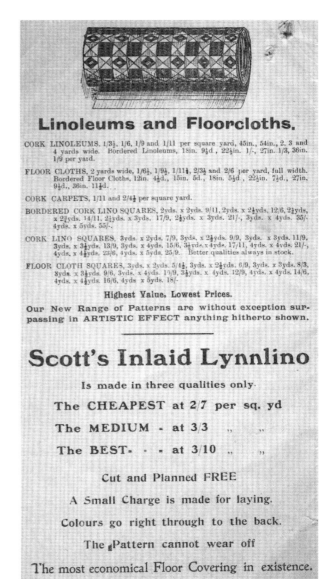
Carpets.

We are making a very choice exhibition of all kinds of newest Carpets including: Axminster, Wilton, Brussels, Turkey, Tapestry, & Kidderminster. We stock these by the yard or in bordered squares in the following sizes: 2½ x 3, 3 x 3, 3 x 3½, 3 x 4, 3½ x 4, 4 x 4, 4 x 4½, 4 x 5, and 4½ x 5, at prices ranging from 18/6 to 10Gns. Hemp Squares in sizes as above from 5/11. Striped & Floral Hemp Carpets; from 7½d. per yard. These Carpets have been selected with great care from the best makers, and in quality, design, colorings, and reasonable prices are "second to none" in the County. Hearthrugs to match all Carpets. Unlimited choice. Stair Carpets of every Make. In charming variety at lowest prices.

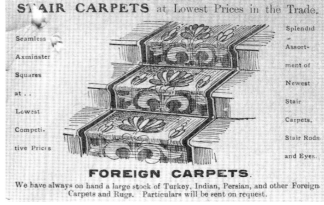
Linoleums and Floor Cloths.

We hold a huge stock, representing most of the best manufacturers, and we are selling at the lowest prices in the trade. THE FAMOUS Scott's Lynnlino. Colors right through to the back, patterns cannot wear off. Made in 3 qualities, only 2/7, 3/3, and 3/10 the square yard. CORK LINOLEUM, 1s 3½d, 1s 4½d, 1/6 and 1/9 the square yard. BORDERED CORK LINO SQUARES, in all sizes at lowest prices. Bordered Linoleums, 18in, 22½in, and 34in wide, in various designs. FLOOR CLOTHS, 2 yards wide, 1s 6½d, 1s 9½d, 1s 11½d, and 2/3 per yard, full width. Bordered Floor Cloths. All widths. All prices. We have always a very large stock of Mats and Mattings, at prices which defy competition.

As part of their summer sale promotion in 1913, Scott & Son celebrated their 21st birthday. This confirms the fact that the 1874 date refers to the first upholstery and cabinet-making workshop opened by Thomas William Scott in Church Street. They advertised in the Lynn Advertiser on 11th July 1913 (illus. above) that they would be giving every customer spending 20/- or more 'a handsome souvenir'. Unfortunately, it is not recorded what these were. Perhaps, as with some of today's special offers and 'free gifts', the size and value of the souvenir depended on how much you spent at the shop. Bedding was the special promotion in October of that year: 'WE HAVE SPECIAL STEAM MACHINERY FOR MAKING OUR NOTED PURE BEDDING. We Specialise in Hygienic Bedding, Which is Guaranteed of Government Standard of Purity. PATENT AIRDUCT BEDDING. The Bedding is divided into Sections, with air passages between each Section. The top, bottom and ends are Perforated, the air enters in at the bottom and ends, and out through the top row of eyelets, to the body of the sleeper. 4ft. 6in. SOFT MATTRESSES, 16/6, 18/6, 21/-, &c., &c., HAIR AND WOOL MATTRESSES from 39/6. ALL HAIR MATTRESSES from 50/-.'

Although the firm appears to have still had some horse-drawn vans at this date, they were now advertising: 'SMART DELIVERY OF GOODS IN UP-TO-DATE STYLE BY OUR FLEET OF MOTOR-VANS.'

For the year ending 31st January 1914, the accounts show that they were still paying out £126 13s 6d to maintain the horses. They may have maintained one or two of the large, horse-drawn pantechnicons for storage purposes and for emergency use, should the new motor vans let them down. They may well have found that this was very useful to them during the war years when petrol would have been in short supply. William never drove himself, although he had a private car from an early date. In the days before the arrival of the motorcar, he was driven around in a small horse-drawn trap. The photograph above, taken on the South Quay outside Scott & Son's works c1914, shows William Scott standing, with Messrs. Whincop, Dodson and Walter Hart (driving). The horses are 'Tommy' & 'Charlie'. After purchasing a car, William began employing a private chauffeur. For family outings his son, William Crawshay jnr., became the driver and may well have advised his father on all matters to do with motor transport.

The same accounts for 1913/14, show Scott & Son's trading balance to be a total of £17,768 1s 9d, made up of stock valued at £8,134 11s 0d and sales of £9,633 10s 9d. William Crawshay Scott had invested some £6,592 of his own capital into the company which was shown as a liability alongside £2,000 owed to the bank. Thomas William Scott was being paid an annuity of £208.

The year of 1913 ended for Scott & Son with a big display of Christmas goods (illus. right). A furniture store does not, perhaps, easily lend itself to the promotion of items that are best suited to be exchanged as Christmas presents. Nevertheless, Scott & Son made every effort to make their windows and showrooms as seasonal as possible, with the emphasis on the useful and practical gift. As in previous years, artificial palms and flowers were the most decorative items on sale and they seem to have bought these in quantity to form a central display. Their claim was that Scott & Son **'is the Cheeriest, most Christmas-like Place in East Anglia, and you can get there the widest choice of Christmas Presents, both Artistic and Useful, at the Very Lowest Prices'.** They devoted their two central windows and the adjoining showrooms to their Christmas display.

The following year, 1914, started normally enough, with the newspapers still preoccupied with the Irish Question and the issue of women's suffrage. The rumblings of war from across the channel were yet to monopolise the main headlines. Scott & Son held their annual stock-taking sale in February. They advertised £10,000 worth of furniture, carpets, cork linos, bedsteads, and bedding at sale prices. In their drapery department, they offered 1d in the 1/- discount.

On Saturday 8th August, the headlines changed dramatically, with the Lynn News reporting: **THE MOST TERRIBLE WAR IN THE WORLD'S HISTORY: FIRST DAYS OF WAR: HISTORIC SCENES IN LYNN AND NORFOLK.**

Reporting on the declaration of war made by Germany at seven o'clock on the previous Tuesday, 4th August, the paper gave details of how the news had been received at King's Lynn. The town had to wait for the news to arrive by telegram at the Post Office and for it to be conveyed by messenger to the Purfleet Street offices of the Lynn News and County Press, where it was posted in their window. At 1.45am on the Wednesday morning, a crowd of several hundred saw the messenger leave the Post Office and they followed him to Purfleet Street, where the message was posted in the windows, which were specially illuminated for the purpose. However, the news was not what the crowd expected. The notice read: **'Reported action in North Sea denied'.** The actual message from the Foreign Office reporting the declaration of war did not get to Lynn until 2.31am, when it was posted in the Purfleet Street window. Throughout the duration of the war, the staff of Scott & Son must have witnessed the extraordinary sight of Purfleet Street acting as the information hub of the town, with people thronging down the narrow road and gathering outside the offices of the Lynn News to read the latest messages.

The earliest complete Scott & Son catalogue to have survived dates from around the time of the outbreak of the 1914/18 War (front cover illus. right). Printed by J.C. Bird & Sons of King's Lynn, the catalogue features items for sale from every department of the store, together with information about the services offered. Customers did not even have to come to the shop to see what was on display in the **'Forty enormous showrooms'.** Scott & Son advertised that **'ON RECEIPT OF REQUEST a Customer can at any time be waited upon by a Representative of the Firm**

at their own residence'. Their newspaper advertisements invited people to send for a copy of this illustrated catalogue: **'Send for our Free Furnishing Guide. It will show the working man how to furnish his cottage in the cosiest and most lasting way at the smallest outlay of money.'**

The manufacturing of furniture and bedding at the South Quay factory continued to be a major selling point. The staff there included cabinet makers, upholsterers and French polishers and **'with the aid of the latest Labour Saving Machinery, SCOTT & SON are enabled to make Good Sound Furniture and Bedding at lowest possible Prices. Any article made to Customer's own design'.** They were also making, renovating, re-covering, relining and repairing perambulators and mail carts and had special machinery for fixing wired-on wheels. All purchases to the value of £5 or more were delivered free, without limit on the distance, and there was an 'Easy Payment System' with one third being paid down and the balance being paid by monthly instalments. In addition to supplying the requirements of the home, Scott & Son provided a service to commercial establishments, such as clubs and hotels, making seats, bar room chairs and iron-framed bar tables with wood or marble tops. These could be made to any size required by the client.

SCOTT & SON

The Largest, Best, and Cheapest Complete House Furnishers.

☞ **IMPORTANT NOTICE.**—SCOTT & SON respectfully intimate that it is a matter of impossibility in so small a compass, to give anything like a fair representation of their **IMMENSE STOCKS**, they therefore invite all those about to Furnish to pay their Establishment a visit, and allow them the pleasure of showing their many different makes of Furniture, and various Classes of Goods, as displayed in **40** enormous Showrooms.

ON RECEIPT OF REQUEST a Customer can at any time be waited upon by a Representative of the Firm at their own residence.

FURNITURE MANUFACTURING.—At SCOTT & SON'S Steam Furniture and Bedding Factory, South Quay, King's Lynn (which is the only one within 40 miles), is kept an experienced Staff of Cabinet Makers, Upholsterers and French Polishers, and with the aid of the latest Labour Saving Machinery SCOTT & SON are enabled to make Good Sound Furniture and Bedding at lowest possible Prices. Any article made to Customer's own design.

SPECIAL ATTENTION is called to the fact that one visit only is needed to our Establishment to completely furnish a house to the smallest detail, as SCOTT & SON supply everything necessary, and deliver in one consignment.

A GREAT CONSIDERATION.—All Purchases of the value of £5 and upwards made by Customers in our Establishments, are Delivered Free, any distance, in our own Vans. All Goods are marked in *Plain Figures* at the lowest possible NETT CASH PRICES.

EASY PAYMENT SYSTEM, Strictly Private.—Goods of the value of £5 and upwards will be delivered Free, on payment of ONE-THIRD of the value down, the balance being paid by small Monthly Instalments. Full particulars on inquiry.

THE DAILY INCREASING NUMBER OF NEW CUSTOMERS generally express their astonishment at the magnitude of our Show Rooms, the large and varied character of the Stock, its Style and Finish, and the wonderfully Low Prices quoted.

HOURS OF BUSINESS.—9 a.m. to 8 p.m.   Wednesdays 9 a.m. to 1 p.m.   Saturdays 9 a.m. to 10 p.m.

Cheques and Postal Orders should be made payable to SCOTT & SON, KING'S LYNN, and all Letters fully addressed, SCOTT & SON, House Furnishers, 91/97, HIGH STREET, KING'S LYNN.

Special attention given to Renovating, Repairing, Re-covering, and Re-polishing old Furniture.
ESTIMATES FREE.

Their factory and workshop facility enabled the firm to offer a service renovating, re-covering and re-polishing old furniture. They also had one showroom devoted to the sale of second-hand furniture and would buy and sell any quantity for cash. In an age when beds and bedding were expected to last a lifetime, there was a constant demand for dressing and re-making mattresses, bolsters and pillows. At their factory, they had a patent steam process installed to dress the feather infill and advertised that they would guarantee them free from smell or dirt following treatment. All their new bedding was similarly guaranteed and they made great play of the fact that they could do this because they were supervising the work throughout.

Having moved out of Reddie & Sons' former music shop at 42, High Street, Scotts now maintained a well-stocked department in No. 91. There they sold pianos, American organs, accordions, mouth organs, violins, banjos, tambourines, zithers, mandolins, auto-harps, piccolos, flutes and other instruments, together with the latest gramophones and records (illus.

SCOTT & SON, 91, 92, 93, 94, 95, 96, 97, High Street, King's Lynn.

Reliable American Organs

From £5/15/- Cash.

Or on Easy Terms from 8/- per month, delivered on payment of first 8/-

Very Large Stock of Accordeons, Mouth Organs, Violins, Banjoes, Tambourines, Zithers, Mandolines, Auto-Harps, Piccolos, and Flutes, and every description of Musical Instruments.

SCOTT & SON are Gramophone & Gramophone Record
AGENTS.
NEWEST MACHINES.   NEWEST RECORDS.   LOWEST PRICES.

SCOTT & SON'S, (late Reddie & Sons') Music and Musical Instrument Warehouse is the oldest established business of the kind in the Eastern Counties and for many years has enjoyed the patronage of all the leading families in the district. Purchasers may always be sure of getting most Reliable Instruments at Reasonable Prices.

NEWEST GRAMOPHONES. 19/11, 25/6, 35/6

Our 16 Guinea PIANO IS OF UNSURPASSED VALUE.

above right). In addition to their music department sales staff, Scott & Son employed experienced piano tuners and were able to undertake repairs. They took orders for individual tuning and servicing requirements as well as offering yearly contracts.

On display in 95 and 96, High Street was the glass, china and enamel ware (illus. left). All the basic needs for the kitchen and the dining room were catered for there. The drapery and linen department at 92, High Street was stocked with a full range of household requirements including: **sheets; pillow-cases; white counterpanes; coloured quilts; eiderdown quilts; bed-spreads; blankets; linens and sheetings; coloured rugs and blankets; toilet covers; glass cloths; white damask cloths; afternoon tea cloths; tray cloths; sideboard cloths; piano covers; unbleached damask cloths and towels.**

Scott's '**Carpet Saloon**' was situated in Purfleet Street. Their workmen were prepared to travel any distance to measure, plan and fit carpets, linoleum and both inside and outside window blinds. At the shop they held a large stock of Axminster, Wilton, Brussels, Turkish and Mirzapore carpets in a wide variety of patterns. Curtain poles were made to measure and they stocked curtain and blind materials and all the necessary trim and fittings.

Distance was also no trouble to them for conducting funerals and they were prepared to travel to any part of the country.

In terms of the range of departments, services provided and the number of staff employed, it may well be that the period immediately prior to the outbreak of the Great War was the one when Scott & Son were at their peak. However, the war had a dramatic effect upon every aspect of their retailing and manufacturing business. During the war, the impact included, of course, their evening opening hours. The blackout requirements were rigorously imposed and it must have been especially difficult for shopkeepers to comply. There were severe shortages in the supply of goods and raw materials for furniture making. This was, therefore, a period of upheaval and uncertainty for traders such as Scott & Son. As with every other large employer, their greatest problem was the loss of their male employees through volunteering or conscription to serve in the armed forces. Shopkeepers relied on the replacement of their male assistants by engaging female staff. Scott & Son's greatest loss of personnel through enlistment was in their factory, where all the staff were men. Whilst there may have been the

opportunity to employ some boys who were too young to volunteer, and some girls to do stitching work in the upholstery workshop, the factory could only have been ticking over, at best, during the war years.

On 12th September 1914 the newspaper published a list of recruits from King's Lynn who had responded to the appeal. There were 96 who had volunteered for Kitchener's Army and another 160 who had joined the Territorials. The recruitment notice, right, also appeared in the papers.

The dangers that were faced by the soldiers serving at the front were soon brought to the attention of the people of Lynn, firstly through the publication of lists of local men who had been killed or injured and, secondly, by the arrival of a dozen wounded soldiers at King's Lynn in November 1914. They were brought by train from Cambridge to be cared for at the West Norfolk and Lynn

Hospital. They arrived at about 7.00pm and were driven to the hospital in cars provided by notable Lynn residents and traders, the latter including W. H. Johnson, the motor company, who volunteered their services.

Considerable pressure was put on the male population to enlist and it would have been very hard for any man of eligible age to have resisted. The Lynn News set it out clearly in their paper on 2nd January 1915, with the wording: **THE GREAT RESOLUTION FOR THE NEW YEAR – "I will be a man and enlist today."** (illus. left).

Meanwhile, life went on as near to usual as it was possible in these extraordinarily difficult conditions. In January 1915 Scott & Son held a **'SPECIAL SHOW FOR THE NEW YEAR'**. They advertised a large selection of **'Fancy Goods at Lowest Prices'**. These consisted mainly of the type of goods that they had bought in for their 1914 Christmas displays, including their stocks of artificial ferns and flowers, as well as their pictures, vases, toy prams and go-cars. Although sales had remained buoyant throughout 1914, they were significantly down during the first half of 1915. Doubtless, people felt reluctant to commit to anything other than essential expenditure in view of the uncertainty over what lay ahead for them. During the night of 19th January, 1915, the people of King's Lynn were rudely awakened to the full horrors of war when a German Zeppelin dropped bombs and incendiaries on the town.

There was outrage throughout the country to these attacks, which involved two airships targeting Norfolk towns and villages, the first aerial bombing raid in history. It was a while before there was general acceptance that modern warfare inevitably put the civilian population at risk of being killed and injured. The Lynn News and County Press responded in typical fashion with this heavily sarcastic headline: **'SPLENDID NEWS FOR GERMANY! SUCCESSFUL AIRSHIP RAID ON HEAVILY FORTIFIED LYNN, SNETTISHAM AND HEACHAM. SOLDIER'S WIDOW AND LAD OF FOURTEEN GLORIOUSLY MURDERED. LINNET KILLED ALTHOUGH IN ITS FORTIFIED CAGE. MANY WINDOWS SMASHED AND HUNDREDS OF CHILDREN ALARMED. VILLAGE CHURCH DAMAGED: QUITE CLOSE TO THAT IN WHICH OUR HEAVENLY EMPEROR HAS PRAYED. THE GOOD OLD GOD DELIGHTED WITH OUR LATEST HEROIC FEAT OF ARMS'.**

The young lad referred to in this headline was Percy Goate. He lived in Bentinck Street, one of the tightly-knit terraces of houses located between St. James Road and Tower Street, near to where the town's swimming pool and multi-storey car park are now situated. Percy was an errand boy at Le Grice's shop in the High Street and had been a school pal of William Crawshay Scott jnr. His death was a great personal shock to young William who, at times throughout the rest of his life, would sometimes recall the tragic death that befell his former chum. It seems certain that the impact of this Zeppelin raid was felt particularly keenly in the Scott household, both because of the loss of William's friend and because the family formerly lived in the area of the town where Bentinck Street was situated.

The death of Scott & Son's founder, Thomas William Scott, was announced in the newspaper on Saturday 13th February 1915 (illus. right). Amongst those attending the funeral were some of the staff of Scott & Son, including Mr. H. H. Styles, the shop manager, Mr. David Dey, from the music department, and Mr. Albert Smith, the foreman at the works on the South Quay. The floral tributes from the staff included: **'In loving memory of our late master, from *employés* at works, South Quay'. 'With deepest sympathy, from Mr. Herbert Styles'. 'With Mr. and Mrs. David Dey's deepest sympathy'. 'With sincere sympathy and deepest regret, from the young lady assistants at High-street'.**

DEATH OF MR. T. W. SCOTT,
ONE OF LYNN'S BUSINESS PIONEERS,
HEAD OF THE FAMOUS FURNISHING FIRM OF SCOTT AND SON.

One of Lynn's most successful business men, Mr. Thomas William Scott, died at his house on London-road on Friday in his 81st year. His death will be greatly deplored in the district by the large circle who are familiar with the well-known firm of Scott and Son, whose growth has been chiefly due to the untiring efforts and great business abilities of Mr. T. W. Scott.

The last of these is particularly significant because it indicates that the male assistants were away fighting for their King and Country.

The pressure on men assistants in Lynn's shops to enlist was increased by the publication of a cartoon in the newspaper on Saturday 20th February, showing a young shop assistant, with the caption: '**TO THE SHOPKEEPERS OF ENGLAND** - **Have you any young men serving at your counter who ought to be serving your Country?**' (illus. below left).

Have you any young men serving at your counter who ought to be serving your Country?

The summer sale at Scott & Son went ahead as usual, starting on Saturday 17th July 1915. There was little scope for a furniture store to relate its advertisements either to the privations, or to the necessities, of wartime Britain. Nevertheless, Scott & Son sought to reflect the difficulties that people faced with the following slogan advertising their sale: '**PRACTISE ECONOMY. SCOTT & SON'S SALE is the greatest money-saving opportunity of the year. All goods marked in plain figures at HEAVY REDUCTIONS, as the huge stocks must be cleared**'.

The local police and the magistrates were cracking down hard on anyone contravening the lighting regulations. Nobody was exempt and the newspapers reported several cases each week. On 18th September 1915 the headline read: '**THE LIGHTS OF LYNN - NEGLECT OF ESSENTIAL PRECAUTIONS - POLICE WARNING TO THE PUBLIC**'. Those prosecuted included Sir Edward Barry, of Raynham House, Tennyson Avenue, who was a Lt-Colonel in the Berkshire Regiment. Other serving soldiers, who should certainly have known of the need to observe the regulations, included a Lieutenant and a Trooper. A High Street trader was fined, together with the manager of the Dukes Head and the licensees of the Maids Head and the London Porter House. Motorists, motor cyclists, drivers of commercial vehicles and even the occasional bicyclist, were fined for having lights that were too bright.

September 1915 was not a good month for William Crawshay Scott snr. On Monday 20th, he seems to have spent too much time in one of the local public houses, possibly in Purfleet Street and, on staggering back to his shop, he attracted the attention of a large crowd. It is more than likely that there was already a big throng in Purfleet Street looking at the latest news of the war in the window of the Lynn News. Whatever the cause, he started shouting at the crowd and at his staff, who were trying to calm him down and encourage him to go home. After a shop window had been broken, the police were called and eventually he was arrested and suffered the indignity of being marched to the police station, where he spent a night in the cells. The magistrates fined him 20/- the following day. None of this was likely to have improved staff morale, which must have been very strained by the extra work that they had to put in to help run a large store with a reduced number of assistants.

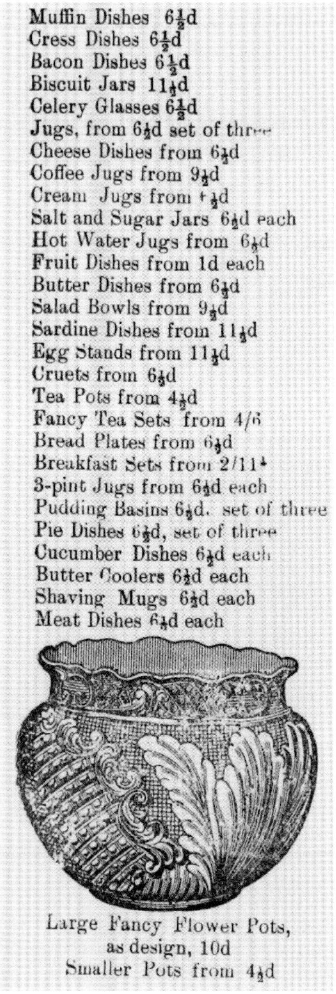

For six months, from October 1915 to April 1916, no advertisements were placed by Scott & Son in the Lynn News. However, there was a special Christmas shopping feature in the newspaper on 4th December 1915 which included a paragraph promoting the shop. The introduction to this feature emphasised the difficulties that the shopkeepers were facing in trying to maintain a normal service: '**EARLIER CHRISTMAS SHOPPING PREPARATIONS AT LYNN. The Labour Shortage. TRADESMEN MEETING THE PUBLIC HALFWAY. Preparations by Lynn tradesmen for supplying the wants of their customers at Christmas are being made this year earlier than usual. Prevailing conditions not only suggest but demand this. With a population which, including our khaki friends, is about as big as usual, there are fewer men and youths to deal locally with the Christmas trade. This depletion of staff, with so many away with the Colours, is quite understood. Then the restricted hours of shopping is**

Muffin Dishes 6½d
Cress Dishes 6½d
Bacon Dishes 6½d
Biscuit Jars 11¼d
Celery Glasses 6½d
Jugs, from 6½d set of three
Cheese Dishes from 6½d
Coffee Jugs from 9¼d
Cream Jugs from ⅞d
Salt and Sugar Jars 6½d each
Hot Water Jugs from 6½d
Fruit Dishes from 1d each
Butter Dishes from 6½d
Salad Bowls from 9¼d
Sardine Dishes from 11¼d
Egg Stands from 11¼d
Cruets from 6½d
Tea Pots from 4¼d
Fancy Tea Sets from 4/6
Bread Plates from 6½d
Breakfast Sets from 2/11¼
3-pint Jugs from 6½d each
Pudding Basins 6½d. set of three
Pie Dishes 6½d, set of three
Cucumber Dishes 6½d each
Butter Coolers 6½d each
Shaving Mugs 6½d each
Meat Dishes 6½d each

Large Fancy Flower Pots,
as design, 10d
Smaller Pots from 4¼d

another consideration. One of the prominent traders in the town pointed out to one of our representatives that the conditions surrounding us at present seem to suggest that shopping should be done much earlier in the month of December than usual, that this business should be attended to much earlier in the day than a good many people seem to think necessary and that as far as possible local people with purchases to make them on days other than market days. "We are glad, of course," said this gentleman, "to see our Patrons, and to oblige them at any hour of any day so long as the shops are open. But if they come in when country people are about, and if, as many of them do, they drop in with orders only an hour or two before closing time, it becomes difficult to deal with them and to oblige them as we should like to do – this because of our depleted staffs". Undoubtedly, too, it would be as well for those who have Presents to send away – and there will be many sent away in spite of the times in which we live – to purchase them sooner than usual. Our Christmas Shopper has been round to some of the tradesmen as usual and chatted with them about their displays.

FURNITURE ON THE GRAND SCALE

Messrs. Scott and Son, High-street, in their extensive range of premises, cater for the public in different directions and do it well. If you want furniture or fittings for mansion, hotel or cottage you can find it here. You can get anything and everything for all departments from the basement to the attic, in all kinds of designs and to suit every purse. A speciality is being made this year of leather suites from £5 5s. and saddlebag suites from £6 18s. 6d. Eiderdowns, blankets and bedding of all descriptions find a place in another department; in a third you can get pianos, gramophones and musical instruments of all kinds, together with sheet and book music; and in a fourth your china and glassware for Christmas'.

Scott & Son commenced advertising again on Saturday 8th April 1916. In the same edition of the Lynn News the Theatre Royal announced its current programme, from which it can be seen that the public were being offered variety acts of all descriptions to help keep their spirits up: 'THEATRE ROYAL AND HIPPODROME KING'S LYNN ONCE NIGHTLY AT 7.30 Monday, May 22nd for Six Nights Only, Capt. De Villiers' WIRELESS AIRSHIP THE ZEPPELIN DESTROYER, A Real Dirigible, 18ft by 6ft., which sails round the Auditorium. ARTHUR CLARKE, COMEDY DANCER. PYNKIE WHITE, the Californian Comedy Girl in

Walnut Sideboards
from £4/15/0

"Studies From Life", THE KLEEN TWINS in a Comedy Boxing Act. LITTLE MARY, the star of Lilliputians, in a Serpentine Globe and Wire-walking Act. DORIS DELMAR, the Brilliant Young Violinist. CHAS. & LES. GLADWELL, Potpourri Comedians. "Where's the Porter?" 8 IRIS GIRLS, in a Medley of Song, Dance & Harmony.'

The staff shortages, especially at the senior assistant and department manager levels, may have led to Scott & Son's decision to close for the whole of the Bank Holiday week in August 1916. However, having announced this on 8th July, they appear to have found that they had sufficient cover to be able to open on two days that week, making the following announcement on 22nd July: 'SCOTT & SON POSTPONEMENT OF HOLIDAYS. BUSINESS AS USUAL. Monday and Tuesday, August 7th and 8th'.

Later that year, on Sunday 3rd September, Scott & Son suffered a serious fire at their High Street shop, as reported in the Lynn News and County Press the following Saturday:

A SERIOUS FIRE AT LYNN
IMPORTANT PREMISES DAMAGED
A LIGHTING (sic) FLASH THE CAUSE

A serious fire was caused by lightning at King's Lynn on Sunday, the premises of Messrs. Scott & Son, the well-known house furnishers, being involved and considerable damage resulting. Serious as it was, at one time the outbreak threatened to be disastrous, but thanks to extremely good work by the fire brigade danger of the fire spreading was soon averted and it was confined to the portion of the premises where it originated.

The thunderstorm, which was accompanied by extremely heavy rain, passed over Lynn shortly after noon. About 12.30, there was a particularly vivid flash of lightning, accompanied almost simultaneously by a terrific crash of thunder, and it was soon afterwards found that Messrs. Scott & Son's premises had been struck on the roof, the lightning passing through and causing an outbreak of fire in the upper part of what is known as the new shop – the portion of the establishment built in 1899 for Messrs. Scott & Son by Ald. W. H. L. Brown and which was set back in accordance with the High Street widening plan. One or two residents near assert that they saw the roof struck by the brilliant shaft of lightning, but some few minutes elapsed before the fire was noticed.

When the alarm was raised to summon the fire brigade, the upper portion of the premises – two floors, one in the roof, and both full of furniture, etc. – were one mass of flames, these then being particularly noticeable at the rear, with smoke pouring from the front into High-street. The brigade turned out smartly and very quickly the escape was in position to enable the hose to be taken up so that the fire-fighters could get to work with greater power. Fireman Pearman sustained a badly burned hand (necessitating surgical treatment) in carrying out his duties at the top of the escape soon after the brigade had arrived with hose pipes, tender and the engine, but he did excellent work, while another hose was very successfully used at the bottom of the staircase on the first floor. Others soon were busy from the roofs of adjoining buildings in High-street and Purfleet-street, and six or eight deliveries of water were in action in a short time. The water main in High-street is one of the best in the town, and full use of the hydrants, with the steamer working at high pressure, enabled the firemen to get the mastery in an incredibly short time.

As indicated, before Capt. Shaw and his men got working, the fire had got a strong hold and was blazing furiously. Tongues of flame were bursting through the roof, and gusts of wind took them right across the street several times, severely blistering the premises opposite and placing these in danger. Police, soldiers and civilians lent valuable aid to the firemen with the hose and in other ways, though in this there was an element of danger, by reason of the falling slates and flying fragments of fiery material.

In half-an-hour the fire was well under control. There are, fortunately, very good gables to the premises, and the joists of the second floor proved to be excellent. These circumstances, combined with the efficient work of the brigade, greatly assisted in keeping the outbreak to the narrow limits in which it was confined. By three o'clock some of the firemen left, but for a day or two watchers were on duty.

The two top rooms, of course, and their contents were entirely destroyed, while in the showroom underneath and in the shop on the ground floor everything suffered severely from water. The premises were unusually crowded with furniture, bedding, crockery, etc., in readiness for the Michaelmas sales, and the loss, of course, is the greater in view of the difficulty of replacing stock in the present times. Messrs. Scott are insured.

Almost needless to say, the fire and the work of the firemen were witnessed by a large number of townspeople, to whom additional excitement was provided by the falling of first one and then the other of the horses attached to the tender when they were pulled up on the wet and slippery wood-paving in High-street.

The problem encountered by the horses happened very frequently, especially at the turn from the Tuesday Market Place into High Street and the High Street / Norfolk Street corner. The horses would be taken at quite a speed by the firemen as they raced to get to a fire quickly but this was dangerous in wet and, especially, icy weather. At the premises of James H. Martin, florist and seedsman, at 66, High Street, some coconut mats were kept, hanging in the yard at the side of the shop. James Martin and his assistants would rush out with these to put under the horses to help them stand up whenever they slipped over at these corners.

Rather surprisingly, there was no mention of the fire causing damage to the stock and premises in any advertisements placed by Scott & Son later that month. There were no 'Business as Usual, during Rebuilding' notices, nor any offers of damaged furniture for sale. Perhaps they took it all in their stride, although clearly there was serious disruption to their business operations.

In their Christmas advertisements, Scott & Son were offering furniture, bedsteads and bedding 'at Pre-War Prices'. On 16th December 1916, the Lynn News again published a feature on local shops and their Christmas promotions:

THE THIRD WAR CHRISTMAS
Sensible Presents in Lynn Shops
HOW AND WHERE MONEY MAY BE WISELY SPENT
The Christmas of 1916, like its two immediate predecessors will pass amid oppressive conditions. One may be fairly cheerful, but at any rate temporary gaps, caused by the absence of the boys on active service, and, worse than all, the absent places that can never be filled, will have their sobering effects. It is sad to think that three years in succession the advent of the Prince of Peace will be celebrated during the progress of a world-wide war. Naturally the traders at home will not do so much business as when we had a normal population at home, nor will they be so busy – save through the shortage of labour – as twelve months ago, when the soldiers were in our

midst. Still, many of them have been, and yet are, receiving orders for things for our soldier boys away, and they are doing their best amid the trying conditions of the times to make a brave show for what, in ordinary times would have been a truly festive season. We give herewith an account of what some of the leading tradesmen are showing.

Messrs. Scott & Son's extensive establishments in High-street are packed with good things in many a department. When one remembers that the firm cater, and cater successfully, for complete house furnishing, including the china and crockery, and will find you pianofortes, American organs and other musical instruments, with music ready to hand for the choosing, one realises that here one's requirements can be met in many different directions.

It is not known how many men from Scott & Son enlisted but we can see from the Roll of Honour that at least two members of staff tragically lost their lives and another former employee was also killed.

Prior to 1907, Albert Little was employed as a cabinet maker at Scott & Son's factory on the South Quay. He served with the 6th Norfolk Regiment from 1907 to 1910 before emigrating to Canada, where he worked in the same trade in Montreal until enlisting with the 5th Canadian Mounted Rifles in 1915. He was killed on the Somme in September 1916.

William Edward Carter, of Windsor Road, was an upholsterer with Scott & Son when he enlisted at King's Lynn as a Private in the Royal West Kent Regiment in June 1916. He was sent to the Western Front in November that year and was wounded on 11th April 1917. He died in the Canadian Hospital four days later. William left a widow, Lucy Irene Carter, and five children, including a son, Graham Edward, who later worked at Scott & Son.

Frederick William West, a young lad of just eighteen, who was a driver for Scott & Son, was killed soon after he enlisted.

Scott & Son may have lost other staff because they moved into other jobs on their return from the war.

Two casualties of the war who came to work at Scott & Son were driver Joe Dixon and upholsterer Percy Hall.

One of the members of staff who came back to Scott & Son at the end of the war was Arthur Meggitt. He was taken on as an apprentice cabinet maker on 1st February 1899. He joined the Royal Naval Air Service at the start of the war, as a rigger in the kite balloon section. He transferred to the newly formed Royal Air Force in 1918, where he helped to maintain the wooden-framed aircraft, including the polishing of the propellers.

The advertisement, above left, appeared in the Lynn News on 6th January, 1917.

After the war, the firm found themselves having to face up to other inevitable changes, including the advances made in the mechanisation of manufacturing processes and in road transport. Whether Scott & Son's 'Modern Steam Factory' was still up to date by the end of the Great War is not certain but it is probable that new machinery was required to keep up with the times and to remain competitive. William Crawshay Scott snr. seems to have wholeheartedly embraced new technology, both in the conduct of his business and by providing the latest labour-saving goods for sale to the public.

In 1916, at the age of 15, William Crawshay Scott jnr. had to leave school to help fill the gaps in Scott & Son's work force. He joined his father's business as an apprentice cabinet maker and upholsterer. It was at this time that he suffered a serious injury to his left hand in the workshop on the South Quay at Lynn. He received a skin graft with tissue from his mother – quite an unusual operation at that time and one which was being developed by pioneering surgeons treating the burnt and scarred soldiers from the Great War. The operation was a success, leaving him with a shiny area of skin on his hand that was hardly noticeable. After his apprenticeship in upholstery and cabinet making, William Crawshay Scott jnr. gained experience in every department of his father's business, including sales and shop management, becoming thoroughly adept in all aspects of the running of a large house-furnishing store.

The advertisement, below, appeared in the Lynn Advertiser on 6th September 1918 and lists some of the main items of furniture and furnishings that Scott & Son sold at that date.

SCOTT & SON
FOR
COMPLETE HOUSE FURNISHING.

HUGE STOCK to Select From.

BEDROOM SUITES
in Oak, Walnut and Mahogany.

DINING ROOM & DRAWING ROOM SUITES
of the Latest Styles.

BEDSTEADS AND BEDDING.
Straw Palliasses.
Spring Mattresses.
Flock Bed Sets.
Soft Mattresses.
And Feather Beds.

Kitchen Tables.
Dining Tables.
Occasional Tables.

Carpets, Floorcloths.
Linoleum and Matting.

Fenders, Kerbs and Fireirons.

Sheets, Blankets and Quilts.

Perambulators and Mailcarts.

Glass, China and Earthenware.
Music and Musical Instruments.

EVERYTHING
IN STOCK
for Complete House Furnishing
AT
SCOTT & SON'S,
91—97 HIGH STREET, KING'S LYNN.
WRITE FOR CATALOGUE AND PRICE LIST.

PLAN of HIGH St. & PURFLEET St. c1890
SHOWING PREMISES OCCUPIED by SCOTT & SON

High Street premises:

1892 – 1904	No. 89 (rented)
1898 – 1971	Nos. 93 & 94
1903 – 1912	No. 42 (sold 1959)
1904 – 1971	No. 96
1907 – 1971	No. 92
1908 – 1971	No. 97
1910 – 1971	No. 95
1911 – 1971	No. 91

Purfleet Street premises:

c1898 – 1971	No. 24
c1902 – 1971	Nos. 2 & 3
1927 – 1971	No. 4 (Oddfellows' Hall)
1935 – 1971	Nos. 21-23 & 25-28
1955 – 1968	Nos. 6, 7 & 7a
1959 – 1971	No. 5 (Central Hotel)
1959 – 1968	No. 8
1959 – 1960	No. 9

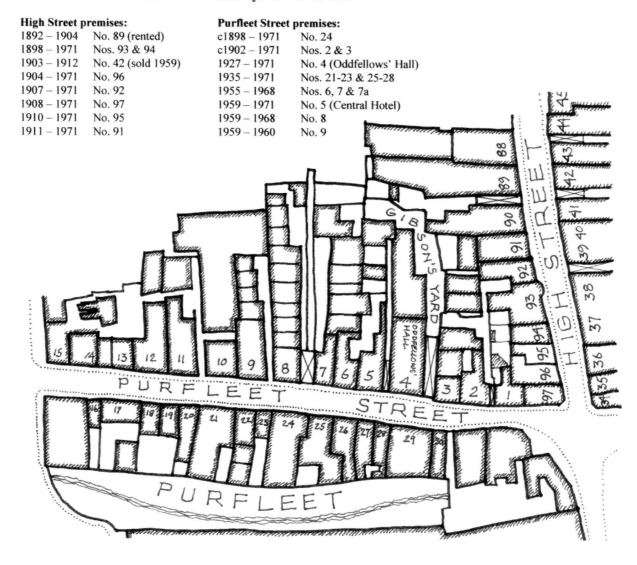

CHAPTER FOUR
The Depression
and the Second World War
Scott & Son: 1919 - 1945

4. The Depression and the Second World War: SCOTT & SON 1919 – 1945

At the end of the war, the town made preparations to welcome home its brave soldiers and sailors following their demobilisation. The Lynn Mart was back in February 1919, heralded as the 'Peace Mart'. The Theatre Royal put on plenty of uplifting performances to bring some cheer back to the town, such as:- **'Direct from the Savoy Theatre, London, Mr. Charles Hawtrey's Famous Farcical Comedy, The Private Secretary'.**

The tailors of the town were the first to advertise their wares to the homecoming troops, offering 'civvy' (or sometimes 'civvi') suits. Ernest Sadler's of 23, Tuesday Market Place headlined their advertisement **'MUFTI AGAIN'**, and offered lounge suits for £7/7/- and a special blue cloth lounge suit for £5/5/-. A great fireworks display was held in the Walks, where a huge illuminated sign read **'Peace and Victory – thanks to Our Lads'.** The same wording was used on a banner strung up in the Town Hall, where the mayor, Mr. P. T. Chatterton, held a series of great welcome home feasts. Four of these feasts were held during August and William Crawshay Scott snr. was one of many townspeople invited to attend the third one, on the 9th of that month.

At the start of 1919 there was no way of telling from Scott & Son's advertisements that the Great War had just ended. Life appeared to be continuing smoothly along without any dramatic interruption. On 4th January, they advertised:- **'LEATHER SUITES, from £10/10/- SUITES IN SADDLEBAGS, from £15/18/6 SUITES IN TAPESTRY, from £15/15/- Special offer of BLANKETS, for full-sized Beds, 16/11, 18/11, 21/6 per pair. Perambulators and Mail Carts. GLASS, CHINA & EARTHENWARE. MUSIC & MUSICAL INSTRUMENTS. EVERYTHING IN STOCK FOR COMPLETE HOUSE FURNISHING'.**

However, on 1st March 1919 the wording of their advertisement in the Lynn News and County Press (illus. right) indicated to what extent they had missed their workers who had been fighting in the war: **'SCOTT & SON For COMPLETE HOUSE FURNISHING. Having received the greater proportion of our workmen from His Majesty's Forces, our Works are now in full swing, and are producing a Large Quantity of Dining Room, Drawing Room, And Bedroom Furniture OF THE VERY LATEST DESIGNS'.**

The use of the word 'Works' in this advertisement is interesting. In the latter years of the firm, the South Quay operation was always referred to as the 'Works', rather than the 'Factory' and it would appear that this change of name came into use at about this time.

One sunny day in October 1919 the Mayor of Lynn, accompanied by members and officials of the Corporation, gathered at the railway station to welcome a most unusual gift – one that was soon to become a rather unwelcome embarrassment to the town. The gift was a Mark IV tank, No. 284, weighing in at 28 tons and powered by a 105 h.p. Daimler engine which gave it a maximum speed of 4 mph. Having served in France in 1917, it was deployed at the battle of Cambrai, when 450 tanks were used. After that, it was used for training purposes at the depot at Wool in Dorset. When operating, the tank was equipped with six machine guns and was referred to in Army terms as a 'female' tank – its 'male' equivalent sporting two six-pounder Hotchkiss guns and four machine-guns. In battle, the 'male' tanks would go in first to clear up the concrete emplacements, with the 'female' tanks following behind, raking the enemy trenches with machine gun fire.

The tank was presented to the town by the National Savings Committee in recognition of the money raised by the townspeople in response to the local War Loans appeal. It was the 26th tank to be given to a municipality in the country and, apparently, these gifts were already creating some vigorous debate amongst the residents of the towns that had received them. Very soon, a similar debate was raging within the council chamber at Lynn's Town Hall, as the townspeople started to complain that this was a most inappropriate and unwelcome gift. Sited on a concrete base in St James's Park, the tank was a rusting and uncomfortable reminder of the war, especially to those who had lost family and friends. Those living nearby complained that the tank was unsightly and was causing a nuisance and danger as it was a magnet to local children. It was not until November 1928 that the tank was dismantled and taken away for scrap by Mr. Palmer of Great Massingham, who had paid £15 for the privilege. The photograph, above left, of the tank in St. James Park in 1919 was taken by Miss Ivy Martin, daughter of James Henry Martin the High Street florist, who was later to marry William Crawshay Scott jnr.

The interwar period was one of modernisation and consolidation for the firm of Scott & Son. In order to advertise its services and goods, the company were now producing their illustrated catalogues on a regular, annual basis, augmented in some years by spring catalogues, too. These catalogues were quite comprehensive, usually containing forty pages, illustrating items from almost every department of the store. They were available at the store or by post and were also delivered by Scott & Son's staff to existing and potential customers around the town.

SCOTT & SON
FOR
COMPLETE HOUSE FURNISHING

AN APOLOGY.

Such a demand was made for our well known HOME-MADE FURNITURE AND BEDDING during the past year, it was utterly impossible to execute all the orders entrusted with us.

Having made an extensive alteration at our Works and with the addition of extra machinery, we hope to double the output for the year 1920.

On 16th January 1920 they placed a notice in the Lynn Advertiser (illus. right), apologising for their inability to satisfy demand for their own make of furniture and bedding. They announced that they had made extensive alterations to their works and that they were hoping to double their output in 1920.

It is not unfair to say that Scott & Son were never at the forefront of modern design in the furniture that they produced, relying on sturdy, practical items at reasonable prices. However, it is evident from their advertisements and catalogues that they were producing contemporary designs. Their quality guarantee was backed-up by their ability to rectify promptly any defects in their own workshops, collecting and delivering the furniture in their own vans at no cost. Although their early post-war catalogues illustrate that some of the goods that they stocked appear to be somewhat old-fashioned, they were not alone in this. Indeed, immediately after the Great War there was a rush throughout the country to produce new goods for the civilian market and, to satisfy the demand, most items were produced to old pre-war designs.

After the end of the war, William Scott's eldest daughter, Florrie (Florence Elizabeth), became engaged to Percy Frederick Cox. Percy's elder brother had been engaged to Florrie but he died towards the end of the war. Percy was a driver for the Royal Flying Corps during the war and after his discharge was taken on by Scott & Son as the manager of their hardware department. Florrie and Percy were married in 1924. The photograph, above left, shows Percy sitting in his Leyland lorry, which he has named 'Flo'. Percy was the son of

James Cox, a chair manufacturer from High Wycombe. This was the centre of chair making in England and Scott & Son bought from some of manufacturers there, the families becoming friends. When Scott & Son were due to re-stock, they would take an empty furniture van to Wycombe and it would be completely filled with chairs before returning.

William Crawshay Scott jnr. was taking-on an increasing role in assisting his father in running the shop. His notebook for 1919/1920 indicates his particular interest in motor transport, recording the prices of some new cars, possibly prior to his father purchasing a 16HP Sunbeam tourer in 1919, including:- an Austin at £595; a Maxwell at £500; a car 'in window' at £700; and a Scootomotor for £51. At the start of 1920, he kept a list of the amounts of petrol bought (by number of cans), together with parts, maintenance and repairs, including a hood envelope (presumably for the Sunbeam). When the Sunbeam tourer ceased to be used as a family car, it was relegated to delivering Scott & Son's catalogues around the town and the locality.

Situated in Gibson's Yard, which gave access from Purfleet Street to the back of Scott & Son's premises, were some small old cottages, used for storage. At a time when brown glazed earthenware was the most commonly used everyday crockery, William Scott had a stock of it in one of these cottages. He was approached one day by a salesman who had acquired a huge amount of this crockery as bankrupt stock and was trying to offload it all in one lot. "Well", said William, "I've got one room full of it, so I might as well have a whole cottage full!"

The photograph below shows Scott & Son's shop at the corner of Purfleet Street and the constriction that it created at this junction with High Street. It was taken in about 1920.

In 1922, Ernest E. Colman drew up plans for Scott & Son to replace four small cottages in Gibson's Yard with a purpose-built, two-storey warehouse, 32ft deep by 54ft long. The ground floor was to be 12ft high with seven windows in the west elevation, facing into the yard. The second floor was to be 10ft high, lit by nine windows overlooking the yard. There were no windows in the other elevations. The roof was to be pitched and slated.

15 High Street, King's Lynn

Scott & Son advertised a sale commencing on Saturday 1st July 1922 for three weeks. They included a special notice (illus. below) in their advertisement explaining that they were aiming to reduce their stock, to enable them to carry-out their expansion plans. This was the first of a series of alteration plans that were submitted to the Town Council in 1922 and 1923 for further improvements to Nos. 95, 96 and 97, High Street. Not all of these were to be approved and it was not until 1924 that there was a final resolution to the problem. The difficulty arose because of the need to satisfy the Borough Council's requirements to set the building back to a new line to provide for the widening of High Street. The council already owned the strip in front of Nos. 91 to 94 High Street and this included the flanking wall to that part of No. 95 that jutted forward some 14ft 6in or so. The plans

SPECIAL NOTICE.

——:o:——

We are having Part of our Premises Rebuilt, and are determined to Clear Stock previous to the Opening of the New Extension ; therefore the Prices will be cut down irrespective of cost, and Customers will find Wonderful and Phenomenal Bargains. In fact, no reasonable offer will be refused.

approved by the council on 14th February 1923 show a new window and doorway in this piece of wall. Approval was granted on payment of an acknowledgement rent of £1 per annum and subject to a formal agreement to be prepared by the Town Clerk.

Internally, the small shop units were to be merged into one by the removal of partition walls and by building a new staircase. This required the insertion of large steel joists, supported on columns, to take the weight of the upper floor. It is not clear whether this was a temporary measure agreed by the council in the expectation that the whole of the frontage of Nos. 95 to 97 would later be set back. What is certain is that William Scott was not one to agree to giving-up land that he owned, however narrow the strip, without receiving sufficient benefit, as he saw it, in return. His architect, Ernest E. Colman, attempted on his behalf to obtain permission from the council for a scheme to modernise the ground floor shop windows of 95 to 97 without setting back the whole façade of these three shops. The council were not persuaded and refused the scheme, on the grounds that:- **'Council considers a direct attempt has been made to evade the Building Line which architect knew was fixed for High Street'.** The plans were turned down at a meeting of the full council on 10th October 1923. On 28th November 1923 a letter from Mr. Colman was read out at a meeting of the council's Streets, Buildings & Markets Committee, requesting that he and his client be invited to address the committee. This was agreed and William Scott and Ernest Colman attended the meeting on 2nd January 1924. This did no good and the committee resolved not to depart from their previous decision. This was confirmed by the full council on 9th January.

This seems to be the last occasion on which this particular matter appeared before the council. William Scott appears to have gone away and to have decided to spite the council by developing a plan that enabled him to operate without having to set back the properties on the corner of High Street and Purfleet Street. Of all the shops in High Street, the ones that the council most wanted to set back were Nos. 96 and 97, but they were never able to achieve this aim.

William Scott's solution involved taking advantage of the council's February 1923 approval to making a doorway in the wing wall. By doing this, he created a new pedestrian way, or arcade, in line with the set-back pavement, but which retained part of the old shop front on the street side as lock-up display windows. Whatever the council may have thought of this at the time, the result was a distinctive and attractive piece of townscape that is reflected today by the jutting forward of the modern shops at the High Street / Purfleet Street corner. Scott & Son never relinquished the ownership of the projecting part of their premises and the pedestrian way through the arcade was always a permissive path, never a public right of way. At night and when the shop was shut on Wednesday afternoons and on Sundays, the arcade was closed by locked steel folding shutters.

The catalogue for 1924/25 contains an illustration of a motor-driven furniture van (above left), confirming that the horse-drawn pantechnicon vans had been superseded by this date. The photograph (above, right) was taken c1920 and shows two early motor vans in the ground floor garage at the South Quay works, the one on the left being similar to that depicted in the sketch.

In an introduction to this 1924/25 catalogue, Scott & Son emphasised that they were **'...practical Furniture and Bedding Manufacturers, and our Steam Factory is the only one within 40 miles of King's Lynn'.**

Further on inside the catalogue, the company again emphasises its reputation and gives a brief description of its store, illustrated below.

The company was still playing on what it saw as its main strengths; manufacturing its own furniture and bedding and being able to guarantee its quality. Their promise was 'ANYTHING NOT APPROVED CAN ALWAYS BE EXCHANGED'. They also emphasised the convenience to customers who were furnishing several rooms or whole houses of being able to purchase everything from one shop. These strengths were to be gradually challenged and eroded by the changes that were to come about in later years, through the mass-production of furniture and the proliferation of outlets for goods for the home, including furniture and furnishings.

Full size bedsteads were being offered at prices from 39/6 to 12 guineas, being made in oak, mahogany, walnut and satin walnut. They carried hundreds of bedsteads in stock, ready for immediate delivery and could match them to any bedroom suite and prided themselves in the quality of their Lynn-made bedding (illus. below). This gives some idea of the scale of the factory output and the sales and warehouse storage areas required to hold such a large amount of stock. It is perfectly possible to accept the claims that the company made about the size of its business.

Shop hours were now a little shorter than they had been ten years earlier:- Weekdays 9am to 6pm; Wednesdays 9am to 1pm; Saturdays 9am to 8pm. Scott & Son were advertising their own baby carriage catalogue, indicating that this was a department that was doing

Large variety of Oak, Mahogany, Walnut and Satin Walnut full size BEDSTEADS, prices from 39/6 to 12 Guineas. Every Bedstead is guaranteed to give entire satisfaction. Hundreds of Bedsteads in stock ready for immediate delivery.

These Wood Bedsteads are well made and fitted with good reliable fittings.

3ft. solid oak Combination Bedstead, from 32/6

Satin walnut Bedstead, full size, price £4/19/6

Full size oak Bedstead, price £4/8/6 Other makes from 39/6

3ft. fumed oak or Jacobean oak Combination Bedstead, 49/6

SATISFACTION IS GUARANTEED.

good trade. Their range of Lynn-made furniture remained comprehensive, including tables, sideboards, hat and coat stands, wardrobes, and three-piece suites.

The great event of 1925 for the townspeople of Lynn was the completion and opening of the new 'Free Bridge' to West Lynn over the River Ouse. The alternative name for the crossing was the 'Cut Bridge' – so named because it spanned the cut made in about 1821 to widen and straighten the course of the river between King's Lynn and West Lynn – and this soon became the usual way of referring to the road bridge.

The first bridge over the New Cut had been built entirely of wood and had an opening span to allow for the passage of river traffic. Shortly after that bridge had been built, however, a railway bridge was constructed nearby and the opening facility became redundant.

The wooden bridge was replaced in 1873 by the Ouse Outfall Commissioners but this one began to suffer rapid deterioration, due to the huge increase in heavy motor vehicle traffic that was using it during and after the First World War. The Ouse Drainage Board, in succession to the Commissioners, maintained that it was not their duty to strengthen the bridge to take this increase in heavy traffic. The County Council eventually agreed to take on the responsibility for replacing the bridge, at an estimated cost of £27,000, subject to their contribution being limited to £4,450. The other contributors were to be the Ouse Board (£4,000), Lynn Corporation (£1,000), and the Ministry of Transport (£17,550).

The bridge would never have been built without the large grant from the MoT. Local feeling was that this was the least that should be expected from the Ministry, because the Government was gathering enormous sums of money from the Road Fund Tax on cars but spending very little on new roads.

It had been decided to build the new bridge only after considerable debate at local, county and national level that had been very heated at times. The main point of controversy had been whether the old bridge should be closed and rebuilt in its original position or whether a new one should be built alongside it, so that traffic across the river would be uninterrupted during the construction process.

The new Cut Bridge was opened on Tuesday 3rd November, the ceremony being performed by Sir Thomas Hare in his capacity as Chairman of the Western Highways Committee of the Norfolk County Council. The dignitaries gathered on the Lynn side and outnumbered the very small crowd that gathered to listen to the speeches and watch the tape being cut – apparently few people knew when the opening was going to take place.

After Sir Thomas Hare had cut the tape, the official party walked across the bridge and then it was open to normal road traffic. Although it had been designed for heavy motorised vehicles, the first traffic to cross in both directions were horse drawn – a milk float and a governess cart. The first motor car to cross from the Lynn direction was driven by William Crawshay Scott jnr., with his father as passenger. On leaving Scott & Son's shop for lunch, William snr. had remarked that the new bridge should have been opened by then and he suggested that they drove over it. The bridge, which eventually cost £29,000 to build, is shown below in a photograph taken soon after it had been completed. The old bridge can be seen next to the new one.

The year of 1927 was a notable one in the development of Scott & Son as one of King's Lynn's premier shops. At the other end of High Street, Jermyns remained the most modern department store in the town, even though it was some 30 years since it had been completely rebuilt after their second disastrous fire. Compared to Jermyns' purpose-built store, Scott & Son's premises were far from ideal. Notwithstanding the rebuilding of Nos. 93 and 94, High Street in 1899, they were still making do with a jumble of older, smallish shops combined into one department store. They had now acquired the Oddfellows Hall in Purfleet Street and this needed adaptation to make it suitable for retail purposes. Also, the High Street frontage still had relatively small shop windows, unsuitable for showing off the latest furniture. William Crawshay Scott snr. decided, therefore, that while he was having the Oddfellows Hall altered, he should up-date part of the main frontage to provide a new shop front to display Scott & Son's wares to the High Street shoppers and to draw them in to look around the store. He turned once again to the Lynn architect, Ernest E. Colman, to prepare the designs, both for his new shop front to numbers 91 and 92, High Street and for the work in Purfleet Street.

Obtaining approval from the council for the rebuilding of Nos. 91 & 92 once again involved negotiating with them over the setting-back of the façade to comply with their street widening requirements. William Scott offered £250 for the land proposed to be added to the street. However, the council once again set their sights on widening the Purfleet Street corner as well. They appointed a sub-committee of five, including the mayor and the chairman of the Streets Committee to inspect the site and to report back to the next meeting. The Sub-Committee met on 13th July and resolved to offer William Scott £800 for setting back, to include the Purfleet Street corner. At their next meeting, on 27th July, Ernest Colman attended and a letter from William Scott was read out. In this, he explained that he was unable to accept the offer for the setting back at Purfleet Street corner. The Sub-Committee therefore accepted his offer of £250 for setting back Nos. 91 & 92. The following article appeared in the Lynn Advertiser on the 21st October 1927 and in the Lynn News on the18th October 1927:-

ANCIENT AND MODERN
A HIGH-STREET DEVELOPMENT SCHEME
MESSRS. SCOTT & SONS' ENTERPRISE

Hidden away in the passage at the side of the old Oddfellows' Hall, in Purfleet-st., is a portion of an old wall containing a fine doorway, of which we reproduce a photograph. There appears to be no record of its origin, but judging by its architecture, it is of considerable antiquity. That it formed no part of the monastic buildings of Lynn is almost certain, as the sites of these are pretty well known and the assumption, therefore, is that it a fragment of domestic architecture, possibly dating from the 13th or 14th centuries.

This interesting fragment forms part of the old Oddfellows' Hall estate which was acquired by Messrs. Scott & Son for the extension of their premises when the Oddfellows moved into their new club premises in Railway-rd.

Messrs. Scott & Sons' business has been established 53 years, and has been carried on in High-st. for 35 years, shop having been added to shop as the business developed until they now occupy seven shops in High-st. and three in Purfleet-st. The High-st. shops were formerly in the occupation of Messrs. Love, Bros., tailors: Messrs. Spinks, confectioners; Messrs. Noakes (sic), boot and shoe dealers; Messrs. Plowrights, tinsmiths; the Misses Weston, baby-linen shop; Messrs. Cox, Bros., grocers; and Messrs. Towlers, leather curriers. To this extensive range is now being added the old Oddfellows Hall, to which a new frontage is being provided, and the premises at the back of the hall extending back as far as Messrs. Bagge's brewery.

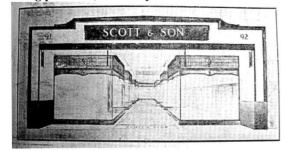

Important alterations are also being made to the High-st portion of the premises, and when these are completed the new building will consist of three storeys, built mainly of brick, with steel girders [two of which weigh over five tons each], with no columns, and roofed with slates. The ground floor will consist of an arcade 9ft. 6in wide and 60ft. long, paved with Terrazo mosaic in panels, and will be lighted by domes glazed with ornamental lead glazing. The shops will be entered by three main entrances on the south side of the arcade and the north side of the arcade will be show windows averaging 9ft. deep. In all there will be about 140ft. of show windows. The windows will have a polished blue granite curb and will consist of bronze metal framing with bronze metal transome rail and ventilator, glazed with plate glass below the transome, and ornamental lead glazing with the firms initials let in ornamental panels. The entrance doors and other woodwork will be of American brown walnut. The shop front next the street will be one of the latest picture frame designs, and will consist of blue polished granite bases with white marmorite pilasters and facia, the whole surrounded by a bold bronze moulding with bronze panels containing the firm's name. The whole of the frontage from the pavement level to the underside of the facia will be enclosed with steel collapsible gates fastening back into recesses during the day time behind walnut panelled doors. The front wall over the shop front will be built to match the existing furniture shop with Bawsey bricks relieved with cement architraves and heads to windows, and surmounted by a gable with cement moulded coping.

No additional floor space will be gained by these alterations, the object being to modernise the premises and to have as much show window space as possible.

The contract for the structural part of the building has been entrusted to Messrs. R. W. Fayers and Sons, of Lynn, and the shop front and fittings to Messrs. E. Pollard and Co., Ltd., of Clerkenwell, London. The electric lighting will be installed in the most modern manner by Mr. A. W. Crowther of Lynn. The building and shop fronts are being erected from the designs and under the supervision of Mr. Ernest E. Colman, F.I.A.A., architect, Lynn.

Our pictures show the old doorway referred to in the earlier part of this article, and the new High-st. frontage of Messrs. Scott and Sons' premises as it will appear when the alterations now in progress are completed.

The alterations to the Oddfellows Hall involved inserting a new shop doorway and three showroom windows in the ground floor frontage. Internally, the space was increased by the removal of a partition wall.

The new front to Nos. 91 and 92, High Street was conservative in design but quite stylish. The stepped gable, peaking 48ft above street level, with its oriole window at attic level, was a most distinctive feature. The rebuilding gave the opportunity to increase the internal floor to ceiling heights:- 13ft 6in on the ground floor; 11ft on the first floor; and 9ft on the second floor. The architect's main challenge was to bring light down to the internal arcade, which ran from front to back. This he did by the provision of a large roof light 12ft by 14ft, with corresponding light wells below, in the second and first floors. These light wells were covered by the glazed domes mentioned in the press write-up. In later years, when more sophisticated interior lighting was available, the light wells were rather an encumbrance, taking up useful display space, and were eventually dispensed with altogether.

These alterations were completed in time for the Christmas sales drive, their advertisements in the Lynn Advertiser, Wisbech Constitutional Gazette, and Norfolk and Cambridgeshire Herald proclaiming: 'SEE OUR NEW ARCADE WINDOWS SHOWING ALL THE VERY LATEST'. The photograph below shows the front of Nos. 91 & 92 soon after the new shop had been opened in 1927.

By this date, there were new labour-saving devices coming onto the market at regular intervals. Scott & Son took every opportunity available to them to secure sole agency rights to sell these and thereby keep one step ahead of their competitors in the town. Taking advantage of their frontage display windows, Scotts advertised these new products and had representatives of the manufacturers on hand to display them in use:- 'SCOTT & SON are the SOLE AGENTS in KING'S LYNN and DISTRICT FOR THE FAMOUS "Florence" Wickless Oil Range, as shown in the illustration. This wonderful stove burns paraffin the modern way, by first converting it into gas. NO WICKS, NO PRIMING. The flame can be regulated for fast or slow cooking, and will NOT CREEP, SMOKE OR SMELL. This heat is focused right on the cooking Safe, Sturdy and Handsome, the "FLORENCE" OIL RANGE is a credit to any Kitchen. You can prepare meals in comfort on the warmest day. To prove these Stoves will do all we claim for them, we shall display in one of our prominent Show Windows the various types of stoves, and during the period between MONDAY, FEB. 14th and

SATURDAY, FEB. 26th, we shall give Cooking Demonstrations Twice Daily, from 11a.m. until 1p.m., and from 3 to 5pm." It seems extraordinary now, but Scott & Son were even prepared to take their demonstrations of the stoves to the customers' homes: **'WE ARE ALWAYS PLEASED TO ARRANGE DEMONSTRATIONS OF "FLORENCE" STOVES AT CUSTOMERS' HOMES, at any time.'**

This heat is focused right on the cooking

Another of the innovations that was selling particularly well was the suction carpet sweeper. Scott & Son did not sell electric machines at this date and were promoting the non-electric models. In 1926 they were selling **'The Whirlwind'** suction sweeper for £4/19/6, complete with all accessories (illus. below). They advertised its principal merits as:- **'NOT ELECTRIC. No Wires. No Sparks. And British made by British Workpeople.'** The sourcing of goods from foreign manufacturers was a sensitive issue in the years following the Great War, especially

because of the overall lack of employment, particularly for disabled soldiers and war veterans.

The extent of the casualties suffered during the Great War may be judged by the appeal printed in the Lynn News on 3rd January 1928 from Lord Haig. This was a national New Year appeal to all employers to consider engaging injured ex-servicemen. The King's Roll National Council was working to find employment for men disabled while fighting. By 1928 they had placed about 350,000 disabled men but some 21,000 were still seeking employment.

It is not known whether Scott & Son responded directly to this appeal but they did employ at least two ex-servicemen who had suffered severe injuries during the war. Mr Percy Hall lost a leg during the war and had an aluminium prosthetic replacement limb. He was employed for many years as an upholsterer at Scott & Son's works on the South Quay. In later years, he was engaged in stitching and seaming-up carpets. The carpets came in one width and had to be seamed together to provide the necessary dimension for the client's requirements. Edges were similarly seamed. This work was carried out on one of the floors of the huge Purfleet Street warehouse, built in 1935. Percy Hall's party trick, performed to shock the unwary visitor, was to 'accidentally' push one of the long upholstery needles through his false leg! Mr Joe Dixon also carried a war wound, having been struck on the head by shrapnel, and had a metal plate attached to his skull. Although he always suffered from headaches, this in no way impaired his working ability and he became one of the longest serving and most faithful of Scott & Son's employees. For many years he was the head delivery van driver.

Sometime during 1928, Scott & Son received two new delivery vans that they had ordered from the local Ford dealer, J. F. Davy, whose garage was at the South Gates. These were the first two new 30cwt Ford standard chassis vans sold in the district. The photograph (above right) shows the two new vans on the South Quay in front of Scott & Son's works. The drivers are believed to be Joe Dixon, in the van on the left, and William Crawshay Scott jnr. in the other one.

The weather at the end of 1927 and the start of 1928 was very severe and there were photographs in the newspapers of huge ice floes on the River Ouse. This cold weather was followed by severe gales which led to the shipping disaster that befell the yawl 'Mystery', lost with all hands on Friday 6th January. The boat had set sail from the Fleet in the morning to drop anchor off Snettisham for cockle fishing. There were four on board, including three brothers. The 'Mystery' did not return and on the following day, Saturday, wreckage was washed up on Snettisham beach. Deep shock was felt throughout the town, but especially in the North End area and the mayor set up a relief fund to help the families affected.

Another disaster occurred on Monday 12th March when most of the townsfolk were woken at 3.18am by a huge explosion. The explosion, at the Distillers Company's experimental factory at Lynn Docks, was followed by a fire and three workmen were killed.

Fortunately, it was not just bad news that made it into the local papers that year and in March it was reported that William Scott jnr. had married Miss Ivy Martin on the 7th of the month. Ivy was the only daughter of James Henry Martin, a florist of 66, High Street, Lynn. Scott & Son's shop assistants gave them a wedding present of a silver cake basket and the staff at the works gave a silver tea set. In spite of the cold weather and snow, they took a touring honeymoon in the 1919 Sunbeam tourer that William snr. now 'gave' to his son. William jnr. apparently suffered a cut in his salary to pay for the Sunbeam. However, he was given a partnership in the business alongside his father and two William Crawshay Scotts now appeared on the company's headed paper.

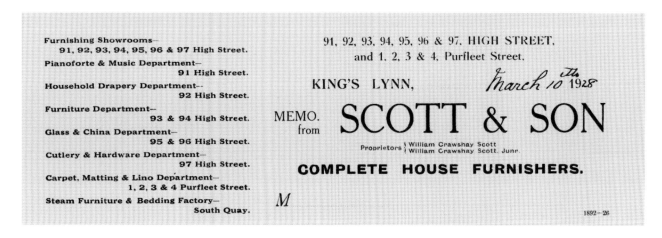

There was also some good news on the entertainment front in Lynn. On 22nd May, there was a big spread in the Lynn News featuring the opening of the Majestic **'Lynn's new Super-Kinema'**. The grand opening ceremony was to be on Wednesday 23rd May at 2.30pm with the mayor, Councillor J. W. Raby, members of the Corporation and **'other prominent Ladies and Gentlemen of the Town and District'** present. What was hailed to be the **'Greatest of all Films'** was to be shown; **'Ben Hur'**. The new 'Kinema' advertised **'cosy and comfortable seating'** and an **'orchestra second to none'**. Prices were:- 5d, 6d, 8d, 1/-, 1/3, 2/4, and 2/9. Later in the year, on 3rd October, the new ballroom at the Majestic was opened. The oak floor cost £1,000 and the walls were decorated with mirrors from the old Empire Theatre at Leicester Square. There was a roof garden for summer dancing.

King's Lynn's traders held another exhibition, at the Central Hall, from 16th to 20th October 1928, but Scott & Son appear to have been absent, relying on their central position in the High Street to command the attention of shoppers. Advertising that year's 'Ideal Home Exhibition', The Eastern Radio Co., of 28, Broad Street, proclaimed: **'TELEVISION IS COMING'**.

Later that year, Scott & Son commenced modernising their South Quay works and it may be that this was when they replaced the old steam engine with a single-cylinder gas engine. Much of the bedding and upholstery that they sold was still being made in Lynn and there was a strong demand for the renovation of customers' own furniture. It proved difficult for them to continue their output from the works while undertaking the upgrading of the machinery and in December they published an apology (illus. right).

Labour saving devices for the home were still very cumbersome by today's standards and those sold by Scott & Son relied upon manual power. It is clear that the lady of the house was expected to be the one exerting the power to operate these 'labour saving' devices. Retailers like Scott & Son saw themselves as offering husbands the opportunity to select an acceptable gift for their wives by advertising these aids to domestic drudgery. Two examples from 1928 were the 'Acme' wringer (illus. below left) and the 'Goblin' non-electric suction sweeper (illus

AN APOLOGY.

Owing to an exceptionally heavy demand for our

Noted Upholstery and Bedding,

this last six weeks, it has been impossible to give the prompt attention and delivery which we usually give.

We are making alterations at our works and installing new machinery, which will enable us to cope with the extra demand in the New Year.

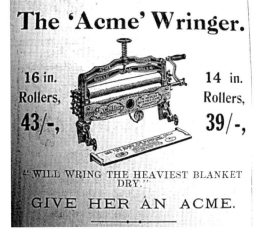

The 'Acme' Wringer.

16 in. Rollers, 43/-,

14 in. Rollers, 39/-,

"WILL WRING THE HEAVIEST BLANKET DRY."

GIVE HER AN ACME.

below right). Illustrations were becoming a regular feature of Scott & Son's advertisements by this date and throughout the first half of 1929 they adopted the approach of promoting particular items on a monthly basis. In January, the theme was wringing and mangling machines; February was brushes, buckets and mops, including the 'self-wringing' mop, followed in the latter half of the month by baby carriages 'built like cars – with steel bodies'; in March it was back to wringing machines; in April cooking stoves were offered, with bedroom suites later in the month; May saw a 'WHITSUN COMFORT' advertisement for hammock chairs, deck chairs, garden shelters and tables, with bedsteads and bedding at the end of the month; and in June the promotion was for fire screens.

The range of furniture made by Scott & Son at their Lynn works on the South Quay was declining, although they were still manufacturing much of the bedding sold at their shop. Chair frames were now being bought in more and more and these were made up for sale by Scotts' upholsterers. Lynn-made furniture was now giving way to suites and individual items purchased from the big national manufacturers. None came bigger than the Tottenham-based Lebus company, founded in the middle of the 19th Century. Scott & Son were buying furniture made by Lebus and other London companies, as well as from manufacturers in the midlands. In order to keep abreast of the latest designs, the retailers had to travel to the manufacturers' factories to inspect their products. The big exhibitions put on at Olympia and other venues were helpful, therefore, in providing the opportunity to compare different designs

The "GOBLIN" Non-Electric Suction Sweeper.

EASY TO USE.

No Sparks or Shocks.

COME IN AND SEE IT DEMONSTRATED.

Price £3/3/0

Price £3/3/0

See our Windows for Special Show of these Machines.

on display under one roof. In early 1929, William Crawshay Scott made one of many annual trips to the capital to select furniture from the new ranges on offer at the Furniture Exhibition at Olympia.

There was strong competition amongst the local and regional furniture suppliers. Customers could easily be tempted to take their business elsewhere if they knew they could get what they wanted cheaper or more quickly. It was essential, therefore, for Scott & Son to carry stock of their most popular furniture and this required having considerable warehouse and storage facility available to them. In addition to the storage at their High Street premises and at their South Quay works, they had further facilities across the road in Purfleet Street and at Guanock Terrace, on the southern edge of the town. There is evidence that these stores were used to capacity to hold a wide range of items in significant quantities. In May 1929 they advertised that they could supply bedsteads and bedding from stock.

There must have been considerable excitement amongst the staff of Scott & Son on Tuesday, 14th May, 1929, especially those working in the hardware department with windows fronting onto Purfleet Street. Doubtless there was some jealousy between those who could get out to see what was going on and those who had to stay inside the shop. Crowds were flocking down the street to watch a most spectacular display of daring by Murray, the Australian escapologist. The steamship 'River Witham' was moored close to the Custom House and over one thousand people gathered to see Murray escape from a straitjacket when suspended by his heels from the ship's derrick over the Purfleet creek. Evidently, Murray had performed a similar feat over Piccadilly Circus a year or so earlier and had then been challenged to do it over the smelly and muddy waters of the Purfleet. He escaped within six minutes and threw the straitjacket onto the ship to the cheers of the Lynn crowd. This was not the only exciting event on the riverfront that summer. On 4th June an RAF seaplane alighted on the River Ouse, close to the ferry steps, again watched by a good crowd. In true RAF style, the pilot and his crew nonchalantly came ashore for lunch in the town before flying back to Felixstowe, just before 3.00pm.

The illustration below shows Scott & Son's premises, as depicted on their catalogue c1930. The appearance of the shop changed little after this date and this sketch was used in advertisements for several years.

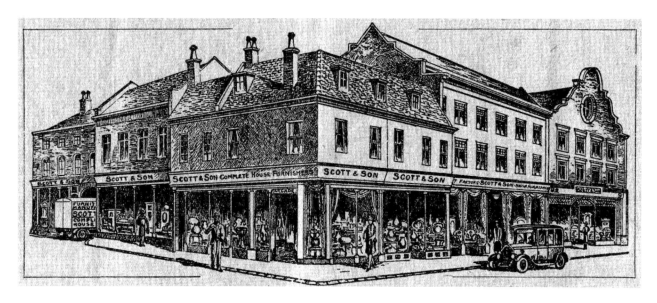

An indication of the absence of what, today, would be considered basic household amenities is provided by the range of galvanised items sold by Scott & Son in the late 1920s. These included:- 'Bungalow baths' - 48inch at 11/6, 54 inch at 12/11 and 60inch at 15/11; and strong linen boilers – 4 gallon at 5/- and 7 gallon at 7/0.

In 1929, Scott & Son advertised a series of demonstrations at their High Street shop of the **'Housewife's Darling Washer'**. The proud boast was **'A Week's Washing done in One Hour!'** This certainly did not sound like the great labour-saving device that the advertisements would have you believe, and it involved a fair degree of manual effort to operate. This was an all-British product **'Sound in Construction, Simple in Operation and a Marvel of Efficiency. No complicated Mechanism – only one moving part. This washer will wash a pair of blankets Absolutely Clean in 3 minutes using hot water and ordinary soap'**. The washer retailed at £4/17/6 on its own and £7/0/0 complete with an 'Acme' wringer. The main mechanism was a hand-operated paddle that was plunged up and down through the lid of the washer. It sounds as though it was hard work to operate! An illustration, above left, from Scott & Son's 1930 catalogue shows the 'Housewife's Darling' washer.

The Royal Norfolk Show did not have a permanent venue in those days and did the rounds of Norfolk's towns, in between displays at Norwich. The show had been to Lynn on nine occasions already when' on 19th and 20th June 1929, it returned to the town's Walks recreation ground. More and more traders of non-agricultural wares were being encouraged to take space at the show. Indeed, the recurrence of foot and mouth disease in recent years had meant that the number of animals entered was severely depleted and there was pressure on the show committee to increase the interest of these trade displays. Scott & Son were one of more than 160 traders who took space at the 1929 show in Lynn and they were allocated a very prominent pitch adjacent to the Railway Road entrance to the Show. Stand No 2 was the second to be seen by the visitors who had travelled by train to the show. The main display on Scott & Son's stand was of the 'Florence' wickless stoves and they had cookery demonstrations throughout the two days of the Show. In the photograph above, the corner of St. John's Church can just be seen on the right. Percy Cox, manager of the hardware department, is standing second left. Wm. C. Scott jnr. is on the far right, behind the Florence wickless stove display.

On the morning of Tuesday 1st November 1929 there was a great sight in the skies over Lynn as the new airship R101 circled overhead on its third proving flight. It had left its base at Cardington in Bedfordshire to travel more than 200 miles over Norfolk. In the afternoon, the great airship circled over Sandringham, before returning to its base. After twelve of these proving flights it was evident that the craft did not have sufficient lift for its intended cross-Atlantic flights. At Cardington, an extra mid-section was added, together with additional gas bags, and the modified airship undertook further trials during 1930, embarking on its last, fateful, flight on 4th October, less than a year after its Norfolk flight. The photograph, above right, shows the R101 over Lynn on 1st November 1929 taken from 31, Gaywood Road, looking towards Dodman's Bridge. The photographer was Mrs. Ivy Scott, wife of Wm. Crawshay jnr.

In their advertisement on Tuesday 10th December 1929 Scott & Son announced the opening of their Christmas toy bazaar:- 'THE TOY BAZAAR IS SHOWING Dolls, Toy Prams, Horses, Tricycles, Fairy Cycles, Teddy Bears, Motors, Engines, Treasure Cots, Metal and Wood Toys.'

The local news was dominated by the financial crisis faced by the hospital. The Lynn News reported that 'there are two waiting lists: those waiting to come out and those waiting to come in'. Funds were

Gifts that Children will Appreciate.

DOLLS, 5½d., 9½d., 1/6, 1/11, 2/6, 2/11, 3/11, 4/11, 5/11, up
TOY HORSES, 5½d., 6d., 7½d., 9d., 1/-, 1/3, 1/6, 1/11, 2/11 up.
ROCKING-HORSES, 12/11, 15/11 to 39/6.
TRICYCLE HORSES from 35/6.
FAIRY CYCLES, 37/6, 42/6, 49/6.
FAIRY KARS, 6/11, 9/11, 15/11.
TOY PRAMS, 4/11, 9/11, 11/6, 12/11, 14/11, 15/11 up.
TOY ENGINES, 1/6, 1/11, 2/11, 3/11, 4/11, 5/11, 6/11 up.
TOY MOTORS, 12/11, 16/11, 19/6, 25/6, 29/6 up.
TEDDY BEARS, 10½d., 1/11, 3/11, 4/11, 5/6, etc.
CHILDREN'S TEA-SETS, 5½d., 9½d., 1/-, 1/6, 1/11, 2/6 up.
WHEEL-BARROWS, 1/11, 2/11, 3/11, 4/11, 6/11 up.
DOLLS' CRADLES, 1/-, 1/6, 1/11, 2/6, 2/11.
BLACKBOARD AND EASELS, 1/6, 1/11, 2/11, 3/11, 5/6....
BOXES OF BRICKS, 5½d., 9½d., 1/6, 1/11, 2/11, 3/11.
TOY CRANES, 2/11, 5/6, 8/11.
FANCY WORK-BASKETS. METAL TOYS. DOLLS' COTS, 9/11.
TREASURE COTS, 7/11, 8/11, 9/11, 12/11, 14/11, 16/11.

desperately needed to expand the hospital and the newspaper carried an appeal for more donations.

Scott & Son were still banking with Lloyds Bank Ltd., in succession to the Capital & Counties Bank, who opened their new premises at 1, Tuesday Market Place, on the Surrey Street corner, on Monday 16th December 1929. Designed by Messrs Cautley & Barefoot of Ipswich, the new bank was faced with Portland stone.

The output from the South Quay works of upholstered suites was increased at the start of 1930:-

'SPECIAL NOTICE - Increased production consequent on a bigger demand has enabled us to further reduce our Upholstered Suites. Although the cuts in prices are considerable, the strength and durability are maintained, the suites being manufactured at our own factory, under our personal supervision, and every suite carries our usual guarantee.'

There was a special Lynn shopping week in the town in May, opened by Lady Elizabeth Townshend at the Saturday Market Place. At the opening ceremony there were costume dances and songs, performed by the girls of the St James's School.

On the 17th June 1930 the editor of the Lynn News expressed surprise at having to report that some councillors did not realise that houses in Purfleet Street still discharged raw sewage straight into the river:-

Work on the Purfleet
The minutes of the Health Committee, which were confirmed, contained an interesting reference to the Purfleet.

'The Borough Surveyor reported that during the past month the work of sloping the mud bank and flushing the bed of the Purfleet has been proceeded with; he suggested the provision of a pipe attached to the wall to take the sewage from some of the houses in Purfleet-st.'

Incredible though it may seem, there were members and officials of the Corporation who did not know that any sewage from the Purfleet-st. houses discharged direct into the Purfleet.

Indeed, we have been informed that members of the Health Committee were told that there was no such direct discharge.

Members of the Lynn News staff who some time ago explored the Purfleet in a boat could have told a different story!

After Wednesday's meeting of the Council a representative of this journal, with two members of the Town Council, inspected the Purfleet.

As they looked down upon the mud, one of the councillors remarked: "Phew! And they said it didn't smell! I don't smoke but you've got your pipe on; for heaven's sake puff up!"

Our representative did his best, but all the smokers in Norfolk, smoking strong twist in the rankest of pipes, could make no impression on the perfume of the Purfleet when it is going 'all out'!

The photograph (above, right), courtesy of True's Yard, shows the Purfleet, looking west towards the Custom House, prior to the demolition of the Purfleet Street buildings on the right, to make way for the construction of Scott & Son's warehouse.

Later that month saw the launch of the 'Lydia Eva' at the West Lynn shipyard. This was the 57th and, it proved, the last to be built at the yard. Commissioned by Mr. Harry Eastwick of Great

Yarmouth and launched by his wife, who broke a bottle of champagne over the bows of the new ship, and their daughter, Miss Lydia Eva Eastwick. The 'Lydia Eva' had a relatively short working life herring fishing, because by then the industry was in decline. However, after being sold by Mr. Eastwick in 1939, she was altered for Air Ministry contract work, servicing buoys around the west coast. In 1966, she was transferred to the marine services division of the Royal Navy. Having been purchased by the Maritime Trust in 1971 for preservation as the last remaining example of that particular type, she is now in the care of the Lydia Eva Charitable Trust.

The Scott & Son catalogue for 1930/31 displays a change in style that reflected the age. The furniture had a simpler look but was still made from solid oak, walnut and mahogany. Washstands came with marble tops and tiled backs. They offered a range of bentwood chairs, hall stands and tables. In the music department, they stocked the latest portable gramophones and stocked hundreds of records. 'Hygena' kitchen cabinets had become increasingly popular since their inception in 1926 and Scott & Son advertised them in various designs and sizes. 'Pyrex', another relatively new product, was also featured in the catalogue.

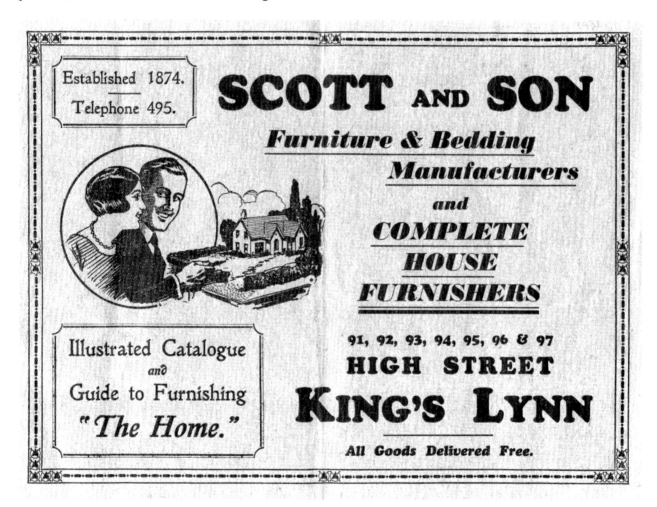

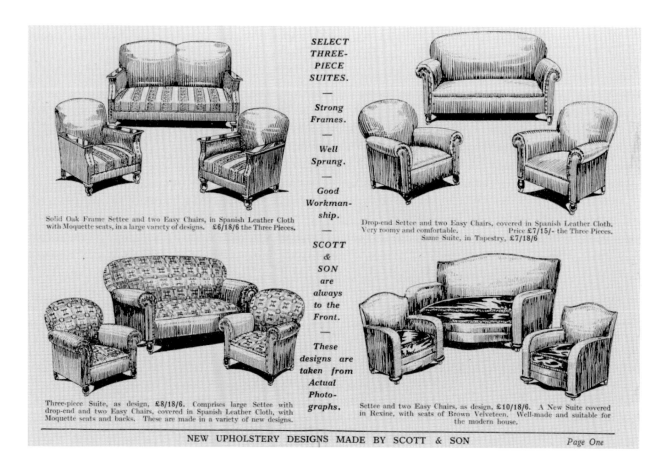

SELECT THREE-PIECE SUITES.

—

Strong Frames.

—

Well Sprung.

—

Good Workmanship.

—

SCOTT & SON are always to the Front.

—

These designs are taken from Actual Photographs.

Solid Oak Frame Settee and two Easy Chairs, in Spanish Leather Cloth with Moquette seats, in a large variety of designs. £6/18/6 the Three Pieces.

Drop-end Settee and two Easy Chairs, covered in Spanish Leather Cloth. Very roomy and comfortable. Price £7/15/- the Three Pieces. Same Suite, in Tapestry, £7/18/6

Three-piece Suite, as design, £8/18/6. Comprises large Settee with drop-end and two Easy Chairs, covered in Spanish Leather Cloth, with Moquette seats and backs. These are made in a variety of new designs.

Settee and two Easy Chairs, as design, £10/18/6. A New Suite covered in Rexine, with seats of Brown Velveteen. Well-made and suitable for the modern house.

NEW UPHOLSTERY DESIGNS MADE BY SCOTT & SON   Page One

SCOTT & SON, 91, 92, 93, 94, 95, 96, 97, High Street, KING'S LYNN.

Dressing Chest and Washstand, finished in Dark Oak colour, 2ft. 6in. Dressing Chest with three drawers and bevel-plate swing mirror ; 2ft. 6in. Washstand, with cupboard, marble-top tiled back and fitted with towel rails. Price only £3/19/6 complete.

Well Seasoned Materials.

—

Careful Finish.

—

Choice Designs and Very Moderate Prices.

Style, Quality and Finish Guaranteed.

2ft. 6 ins. Solid Oak Dressing Chest and Washstand as design. Dressing Chest has two drawers and frameless plate-glass swing mirror ; Washstand with marble top, tiled back and towel rail fitted. Price £4/19/6 the Pair.

THESE DRESSING CHESTS and WASHSTANDS are Beautifully Finished and Polished.

Marble Top and Tiled Back to Washstands and Bevel Mirror in Dressing Chest.

Dressing Chest and Washstand, in Oak or Satin Walnut comprises 2 ft. 9 in. Dressing Chest, with three drawers and bevel-plate mirror ; 2 ft. 6 in. Washstand, with cupboard, marble top, tiled back and towel rails, fitted. Price £5/9/6 the Pair.

2 ft. 6 ins. Oak Dressing Chest and Washstand, as design, £4/9/6 the Pair. Dressing Chest has three drawers and oval bevel-plate mirror ; Washstand with large cupboard, marble-top, tiled back and towel rails.

Page Ten.   ALL GOODS DELIVERED FREE IN OUR OWN MOTOR VANS.

100

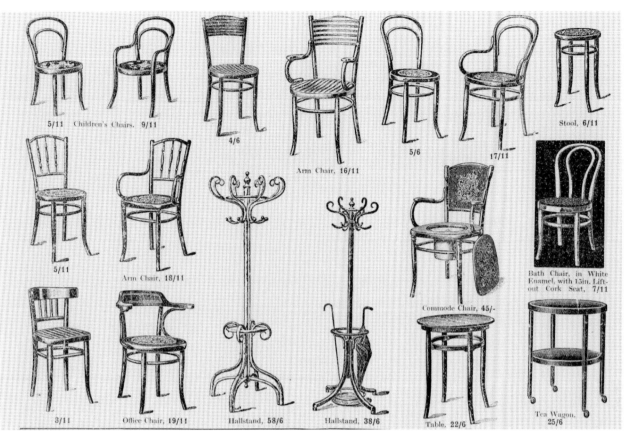

5/11 Children's Chairs. 9/11

4/6

5/6

17/11

Stool, 6/11

Arm Chair, 16/11

5/11

Arm Chair, 18/11

Bath Chair, in White Enamel, with 15in. Lift-out Cork Seat, 7/11

Commode Chair, 45/-

3/11

Office Chair, 19/11

Hallstand, 58/6

Hallstand, 38/6

Table, 22/6

Tea Wagon, 25/6

"HYGENA" KITCHEN CABINETS
The Ideal Method for Storing.

KITCHEN CABINET, as design. "JUNIOR" Model. White Enamelled Interior. 5 Spice Jars, 6 two-pound Glass Containers, Metal Egg Rack. Food Chart. Sliding Steel Porcelain Top Table, 33 × 24 ins. Cupboard and 3 Drawers. Towel Rail. Chopping Board, and Mincing Block. £9/9/-

KITCHEN CABINET, as design. Model "A." 3ft. 6in. wide Enamelled Interior. 2 Flour Bins. 12 half-pound Spice Jars. 12 two-pound Food Jars. Sliding Table, 3ft. 6in. × 2ft. Cupboard, Cutlery Drawer and 3 large Drawers. £14/14/-

KITCHEN CABINET, as design. "Vauxhall" Model. Enamelled Interior. 7 Spice Jars. Glass Liquid and Dry Measures. Metal Egg Rack. Sliding Table. Porcelain top. 3ft. × 2ft. Large Cupboard, 3 drawers. £10/10/-

KITCHEN CABINET, as design. "Olympia" Model. Enamelled Interior. Metal Flour Bin. 6 half-pound Spice Jars. 6 two-pound Store Jars. Food Chart. Steel Porcelain Enamel Table, 30 24 ins. Cutlery Drawer. Large Cupboard, lined Galvanised Steel. £7/7/-
Similar Model, 3ft. wide, with 3 drawers. £8/15/-

THE NEW KITCHEN TABLE with White Porcelain Steel Top. Ideal for Cooking and other Kitchen Purposes where Cleanliness is essential. No Scrubbing required : Cleaned Instantly with a Wet Cloth.

Size 2ft. 6in. × 1ft. 6in.	Price 19/6	Size 3ft. × 2ft. 6in.	Price 35/-
,, 3ft. × 1ft. 6in.	22/6	,, 3ft. 6in. × 2ft. 6in.	39/6
,, 3ft. × 2ft.	25/-	,, 3ft. 6in. × 3ft.	45/-
,, 3ft. 6in. × 2ft.	29/6	,, 4ft. × 3ft.	49/6

Scullery Tables, 9/11, 11/6, 12/6

ALWAYS A GOOD ASSORTMENT TO SELECT FROM.

Kitchen Tables, with leaves, 18/6 and 22/6, etc.
STATIONARY KITCHEN TABLES.

Size 3ft. × 2ft.	14/6	Size 3ft. 6in. × 3ft.	22/6
,, 3ft. × 3ft.	18/6	,, 4ft. × 3ft.	25/6

First-class Make and Finish. Lowest Possible Prices.
Patent Screw Dining Table, with extra leaves, Deal top. £2/18/6, £3/15/-, £4/18/6

COMPARISON OF QUALITY AND PRICE INVITED.

Competition for the furniture trade in Lynn and the surrounding district was increased considerably when, in September 1930, Jays' Furnishing Stores took the Blackfriars Hall in the town for a two week period. This encroachment onto Scott & Son's and Jermyn & Sons' patch must have caused both firms some concern at the time. Jays, of 31, St Stephen's Street, Norwich, called themselves **'The Largest Furnishing Stores in the World.'** They placed large advertisements in the Lynn newspapers, heralding a **'Great Furnishing Exhibition.'** Their initial run at the Blackfriars Hall was extended by another week and afterwards they continued to take advertising space in the local papers. Neither of the two main furnishing stores in the town appears to have responded to this incursion onto their patch by any special advertising or promotions, so perhaps no significant damage was done to their trade.

In the Lynn News of Tuesday 7th October 1930 Scott & Son placed the following announcement:- **'Norfolk and Norwich 33rd Triennial Musical Festival in St Andrew's Hall, Norwich: Wed., Thur., Fri., and Sat. 22nd, 23rd, 24th and 25th October, 1930. Programmes and Tickets for the above can be obtained from SCOTT & SON, Ticket Agents for the District, MUSIC WAREHOUSE 91 to 97 High-st., King's Lynn.'**

Scott & Son valued their commercial contracts, which also brought them a significant degree of prestige. One of their contracts was to provide and fit linoleum covering and edging to the staircase in Allen & Neale's new shop, at No. 55, High Street, on the corner of Norfolk Street. The photograph (right) appeared in the Lynn News & Advertiser on 14th November 1930, soon after the new building had been completed. It was set back from the original building line in accordance with the Town Council's street widening requirements. Allen & Neale's chemist's shop was on the ground floor, with its principal frontage to High Street and its entrance on the corner. There were two new shop units in Norfolk Street and two floors of offices above. The provision of the offices was of particular interest and the newspaper speculated that it was likely that future new shop developments would also include such accommodation on the upper floors. The architect for the new building was Mr Ernest E. Colman, who designed and supervised most of William Crawshay Scott's building projects.

At the start of 1931, the mayor launched an appeal for donations to purchase a painting of Lynn by Mr Walter Dexter, the well known local artist and Royal Academician, which was on display in the town. This appeal was successful and the painting was bought for 100 guineas and accepted by the mayor in July.

Scott & Son announced that they had stocked their store with new 1931 designs and they advertised three-piece and seven-piece drawing room suites 'in the newest coverings'. However, the recession was biting hard and by February 10th they were advertising reduced prices across the board – in furniture, bedding, prams, china, glass &

earthenware, gramophones, pianos, & musical instruments and hardware:- 'Markets are now at their Lowest - the Lowest for Years – and everyone should take this opportunity of Buying. PAY A VISIT TO OUR SHOWROOMS AND SEE THESE REMARKABLE VALUES'.

Other shops were also advertising reduced prices and Catleughs of Lynn published an explanation for the lower prices of the clothes in their store:- 'During the two years after the war we passed through a period of abnormal prices brought about by the war. 1920 – 21 saw the great slump; then for the next 9 years prices were more or less established but during the past 18 months great changes have been taking place in world conditions owing to over production or under-consumption, with the result that raw cotton and wool are today quoted at prices lower than pre-war days. It takes many months before a fall in raw materials can be passed on to the consumer owing to the necessity for forward contracts and the various manufacturing processes; but we have now reached the stage when the actual consumer can benefit'.

Scott & Son were well placed to take advantage of these lower prices for raw materials because they were still manufacturing much of the furniture that they sold in their store. In March 1931 they advertised 'New designs in 3-piece suites OUR OWN MAKES: Drop-end settees and 2 easy chairs, in Spanish Leather Cloth - £7/15/- (3 pieces)'. They were also offering seven-piece suites, comprising couch, two easy chairs and four small chairs. Their other main promotions that month included 'Bordered Rexoleum Squares'. Although they never had a specialist electrical department, Scott & Son had started to sell some electrical appliances, mainly just vacuum cleaners and washing machines. The 'Goblin Wizard' electric vacuum cleaner at £5/19/6 (illus. above) was another of their promotions that month.

The King's Lynn Chamber of Trade supported the 'Empire Marketing Board' in promoting an 'Empire Shopping Week' in the town between 1st and 9th May, 1931. This promotion was not welcomed by everyone in the town and there was a lively debate in the local press between supporters and opponents. The announcement of the event was issued by the Empire Marketing Board:- 'Buy Locally. The shop windows of King's Lynn are reflecting the great extent to which you can BUY BRITISH and the shopkeepers are vying with one another to show EMPIRE products to advantage. Buy Locally and make an Empire Purchase every day.

Under the auspices of the King's Lynn Chamber of Trade a great festival of Empire Shopping has been organised to emphasise the many natural advantages of purchasing Empire Products and to demonstrate the great trade resource of the British Empire.'

Scott & Son were clearly pleased with the performance of their Ford motor vans and in 1931 they placed a repeat order with J. F. Davy for another van on the same chassis. Davys placed an advertisement in the Lynn News on 2ⁿᵈ June that year with a picture of the van in Scott & Son's livery (illustrated on the previous page).

Mr E. Cockerill ran a china shop in Norfolk Street and, on his retirement in June 1931, Wm Crawshay Scott bought all of his stock, which was included in Scott & Son's summer sale:- 'SCOTT **& SON'S Great Summer SALE now on. GLASS, CHINA, & EARTHENWARE. The whole of Mr. E. Cockerill's stock has been removed from Norfolk Street and will be included in this Sale. Prices have reached the Lowest Level and with the Sale Reductions make this an opportunity not to be missed'.** Mr. Cockerill had commissioned the Potteries' company of Shelley to make some special china for him bearing the Lynn coat of arms. The company, which remained independent until 1966, continued to make batches of this pattern for some years.

Once again the question about the filling-in of the Purfleet was raised in the council chamber. For many years, the sanitary condition of the houses alongside the Purfleet had given cause for concern. As early as 1853, it was reported: '**Mr. George Andrews complains that the drainage from his own and two other houses passes under the kitchen floor, and he finds it very offensive. The stench from the privies is also very great. Examined Purfleet, - a most horrible place, when without water. Drains on all sides flowing in, and privies projecting upon timbers, and dropping the soil upon the uncovered banks of mud, fish, garbage, and other refuse. It goes through the centre of the town.'**

On Wednesday 8ᵗʰ July 1931 Mr. Raby moved: '**That in the opinion of this council it is desirable, if the necessary financial assistance can be obtained, that the work of filling in the Purfleet, together with the acquisition for demolition of the property on the south side of Purfleet-street, should be proceeded with, and that the health committee be empowered to take all necessary steps in the matter.'** Mr. Raby told the council that there were twelve lavatories in the street that discharged straight into the Fleet and that the buildings were overrun with rats. The Medical Officer of Health had scheduled two of the houses for demolition, two were unoccupied, one had already been purchased by the council and one was in use as a warehouse. It seems that Scott & Son had bought one of the properties, possibly a few years earlier, and that they were using it as a furniture store. During a lengthy debate, the main concerns expressed were that the cost could not be afforded and that permission and grant aid from the Ministry of Health would not be forthcoming. However, Mr. Raby's resolution was carried by 15 votes to four.

On 1ˢᵗ September 1931 Scott & Son advertised that they had purchased a quantity of blankets:- '**Special Delivery of real Witney Blankets: We were in the Market and bought 2,000 pairs direct from the Witney Mills when prices were at their very lowest. We are therefore able to pass this special advantage direct to the public and offer the whole of these at prices that have never been offered before.'**

Figured Walnut Bedroom Suite, as design, 37 Gns. Wardrobe 4ft. wide, fitted interior with full-length plate-glass mirror, rail and sliding hooks, shelf and door stop; 3ft. 9in. Dressing Chest, with large bevel-plate centre mirror and two bevel-plate reflex mirrors; 3ft. Dwarf Robe, fitted interior with shelves, sliding coat-hanger fittings and boot-rack. Full-size Figured Walnut Bedstead to match, £9/18/6 (Foreign).

Figured Walnut Bedroom Suite, £48/10/-. Wardrobe, 5ft. wide, three doors, two-thirds for hanging, one-third fitted drawers and shelves, mirror inside door; Dressing Table, 3ft. 6in. wide, best plate-glass mirrors; Chest, 3ft. wide, interior of cupboard fitted two drawers and shelf. Full-size Bedstead to match, £9/18/6 (Foreign).

OUR MOTOR VANS CONVEY ALL GOODS TO YOUR DOOR.   *Page Thirteen.*

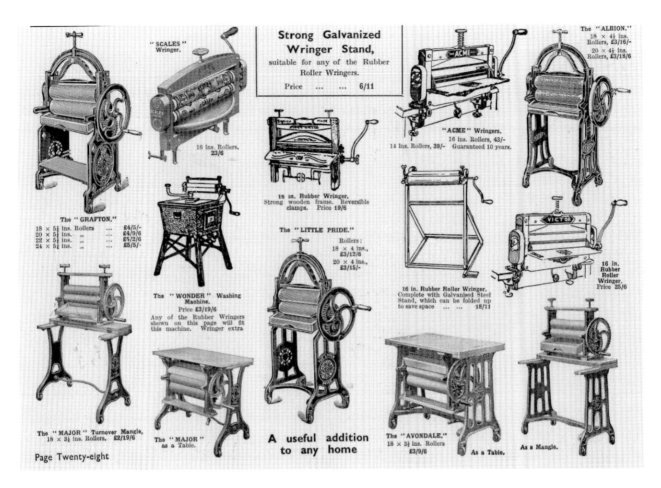

Although some labour-saving electrical appliances were being introduced, the main emphasis was still on relatively heavy manual devices, such as mangles and wringers. Scott & Son sold a range of these, including 'The Major' table mangle, costing 59/6 (illus. above), and 'The Avondale', which was 10/- dearer. 'The Acme' wringer was another line that was stocked by the firm and it sold well for many years. The design of the lettering for Scott & Son's name for use in advertisements was changed in September 1931 and the new one was a very distinctive and recognisable emblem of the firm that remained in use, with some changes, for many years.

In November 1931, advertising their next year's catalogue, Scott & Son listed the categories of goods that they stocked, including: dressing chests and washstands; bedroom suites; wooden bedsteads and cots; kitchen and wicker chairs;

metal bedsteads; bedding and spring mattresses; three-piece suites; seven-piece suites; dining chairs; adjustable chairs; mirrors; pedestals; occasional tables; china cabinets; oak sideboards; bentwood furniture; garden furniture; card tables; children's chairs; kitchen and scullery tables; whitewood furniture; 'Pedigree' prams; pianos; gramophones and music; floorcloth; linoleum; carpets and rugs; china, glass and earthenware; hearth furniture; trunks and suitcases; Witney blankets; lamps, stoves, wringers and hardware.

As the number of local jobless rose, there was increased concern about the plight of those who were out of work and their families. The debate about job creation continued in the council chamber and in the pages of the newspapers and the project to fill in the Purfleet was usually on the list of suggestions. On 5th January, 1932, the front page headline in the Lynn News and County Press read: '1,436: A BLACK "RECORD" Tragic Unemployment Total at Lynn Trade Prospects in 1932.'

The general feeling amongst traders in the town who were interviewed by the Lynn News, was that the depression had hit rock bottom and they were cautiously hopeful for the future. One in four of Lynn's population was out of work. A year earlier the total had been 1,047 and it had reached 1,411 a few weeks later. One month later, in February 1932, the jobless total was 1,575. 'HOW CAN LYNN HELP ITS 1,575 WORKLESS?' read the headline. A meeting was called in the town with spokesmen for the unemployed invited, at which schemes to create employment opportunities were to be considered. One welcome development was the Co-Op's proposal to build a model dairy. The meeting was held in the Corn Hall on the evening of Friday, 5th February and over 2,000 people attended. The mayor, Lord Fermoy, presided and several work-generating projects were proposed including, inevitably, the filling-in of the Purfleet.

On 18th October, some good news about employment opportunities was reported, with the announcement of a new canning factory. Messrs Beaulah Ltd., King's Lynn, were going to develop the factory, which would employ between 300/400 men and girls, at the old aeroplane sheds next to the works of Messrs. Savage Ltd. In addition to the jobs at the factory, there were seen to be opportunities for local growers to benefit by supplying vegetables for canning. The factory was formally opened on Wednesday 29th May the following year.

The continued depression triggered further price reductions at Scott & Son:- 'Great Slump in Prices Floorcloth down from 2/3 to 2/1 per yard.'

SCOTT & SON,
Complete House Furnishers,
91 - 97, HIGH STREET,
KING'S LYNN.
Tel. 495.   Est. 1874.

Perhaps reflecting the fact that they employed some disabled veterans from the war and had lost two of their staff during the conflict, each year Scott & Son carried Remembrance Day appeals within their regular advertisements (illus. left from the Lynn Advertiser on 6th November 1931).

There were regular, almost weekly, reports in the newspapers about the problems caused by parked vehicles in High Street. Motorists were being fined for causing obstruction, together with drivers of heavy goods vehicles and smaller commercial vans. The crack-down on offenders caused problems to many of the High Street traders because commercial salesmen and delivery van drivers complained to their employers, who became reluctant to supply their goods to the High Street shops.

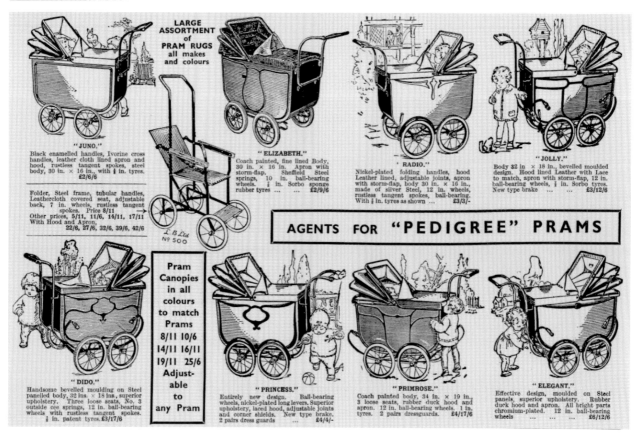

In spring of each year, Scott & Son would introduce the new ranges of prams and pushchairs that were being supplied by the major manufacturers. In 1932, they were advertising Pedigree Prams, the illustration on the previous page being from their catalogue that year.

The Lynn Gala on 1st August 1932 attracted some 8,000 people but this was less than in previous years. The band of the 5th Battalion Norfolk Regiment (TA) played in the afternoon. There were competitions for gardening, fur and feather (poultry, pigeons, cage birds and rabbits), athletics, and horse events. Apparently three men were charged with illegal gambling at the gala – being fined 40/- .

Mr. Oliver R. Jermyn, son of the late Sir Alfred Jermyn and head of the store founded by his father, was President of Lynn Chamber of Trade. In May 1933 he spoke to the members of Lynn Rotary Club on the work of the Chamber and, in a very perceptive address, described the spread of the chain stores all over the country as a "revolution which constitutes a serious menace to the private trader". He thought that within twenty years almost all private traders would have disappeared. Within ten years Jermyns was to be taken over by Debenhams.

Prices were still dropping and on 11th November of that year, Scott & Son advertised further reductions on their furniture. '**PRICES LOWER Than Ever at SCOTT & SON**', read the headline in their advertisements.

On 8th April 1933 the business was incorporated as a company limited by shares, with the title of Scott & Son (King's Lynn) Limited.

This advertisement for Congoleum, left, appeared in the Lynn News on 16th May 1933. Scott & Son were advertising Congoleum squares, sized from 3yds. x 2yds., costing 8/6, up to 4yds. x 3yds., at 19/11. It could also be supplied from the roll 2yds. wide at 1/9 per yard. A room 12ft. x 9ft. could be covered for 12/-. The alternative coverings were Linoette at 1/6 per yard and floorcloth at 1/9 per yard.

There was great anticipation of a Royal visit to Lynn in June 1933. The Lynn News on 20th June proclaimed:- '**Tomorrow (Wednesday) is a red-letter day in the history of King's Lynn, for we are to have the privilege of welcoming HRH the Prince of Wales, the world's most popular personality, who is coming to the town as President of the Royal Norfolk Show.**' To add to the excitement, the Prince arrived in a new aeroplane, a twin-engined de Havilland 'Dragon', which landed at the flying ground near to Exton's Place. The Prince, who was an hour late, was met by the mayor, Mr. H. L. Bradfer-Lawrence, and proceeded in a three-car convoy along Exton's Road, Goodwin's Road, Windsor Road and London Road to the Walks. After lunch, he took his place in the president's box and watched the parade of cattle before touring the trade stands. He fitted in a short visit to the West Norfolk and King's Lynn hospital before flying back to London. In spite of the presence of the Prince, visitors to the show were 4,000 fewer than the 20,000 who came on the two days in 1929. Many had been deterred from attending by the very heavy rain on the Thursday.

On 1st August 1933 Scott & Son advertised for a driver: '**Wanted capable motor driver; one used to large furniture vans – Apply: Scott & Son (King's Lynn) Ltd., High St.**'

The question of what to do about the Purfleet would not go away and a correspondent to the Lynn News, Mr. W. E. Taylor, wrote that the run-down properties on the south side of the street should be demolished, the river filled in and the street widened with car parking provided, suggesting that '**This could be made a source of income by making it into a parking-ground, with a man in attendance, to collect sixpence from car-owners as is now done in Doncaster and Hull**'. His letter was published on 1st August 1933.

Doubtless William Crawshay Scott would have been somewhat amused at this suggestion because, in addition to the shop on the south side of Purfleet Street that Scott & Son used as a furniture store, it is clear that he had already begun to buy up further properties alongside the fleet and that he had well-formulated plans for the site. These properties were nearly all, at least in part, in residential occupation. The dwellings were grossly substandard and subject to closing orders served by the council.

Although some improvements in water quality had occurred, as reported in the Lynn News, this stretch of the Purfleet was still most unsavoury looking and foul smelling in the 1930s. The buildings were also affected by a new building line that required any redevelopment to be set back to enable Purfleet Street to be widened. None of this mattered to William Scott, whose intention was to erect a furniture storage warehouse along the banks of the Purfleet. Indeed, the notices served by the council provided the opportunity he was looking for to negotiate with willing sellers. That the dwellings were occupied was no problem because the council had a liability to re-house those affected by the closing orders. No doubt the owners were only too eager to offload property that was a liability, in more senses than one.

Lynn people were kept informed through the pages of the local newspapers of national and international events, including the situation in Germany with the rise of Hitler and Nazism. The Lynn News carried regular articles concerning the re-armament of Germany and there was analysis by guest writers on the potential implications. In an article published on 15th August 1933 barrister John W. Benson, wrote of the inevitability of an arms race, concluding, **'Disarmament has been destroyed; for who will disarm in face of the policy of the National Socialists Workers' Party of Germany?'**

Queen Mary was a frequent visitor to Lynn and was in the habit of making shopping trips to the town when she was staying at Sandringham. On one occasion when she called in to Scott & Son's china department, she was not immediately recognised by one member of staff, who gently pushed past her!

Not everything that Scott & Son sold could be included in their catalogue and there were many special lines that were advertised from time to time in the local newspapers. One such item was the hand-painted fire screens offered in August 1933 (illus. above right). These were very stylish at the time, although it is not known whether Mary Cruickshank made a reputation for herself as an artist.

The Lynn News carried a special advertising feature in the weeks running up to Christmas during the 1930s. On 19th December 1933 Scott & Son offered a selection of items that they thought would make suitable presents:-

FOR LAST MINUTE SHOPPERS
Round up of the main shops advertising in the paper with 4 shopping days to go.
SCOTT & SON
It is practically impossible in a few words to produce an adequate impression of all that Messrs Scott & Son can offer as a solution to the gift problem. The glass and china department, renowned throughout East Anglia, has in stock something to delight everybody. Young folk are certain to find plenty in the toy department to delight their hearts, while those who want to give useful gifts can hardly fail to find satisfaction in the furniture, hardware, drapery or any other of the innumerable departments. Why not "say it with music" on the gramophone? Scott's have them. It is possible to do a lot of your gift buying under the same roof and to leave the premises unencumbered, for the firm's free delivery comprises a fleet of vans which can transport almost anything nearly everywhere.

Headline events in Lynn at the start of 1934 included the death of Mr. Charles W. Perry, who had been brought to the town as Alfred Jermyn's partner at the time that Thomas William Scott was running Jermyns' furniture department. Like his mentor, Charles Perry had been a towering figure in Lynn's commercial, religious and political life and had served as town mayor.

On the development side, it was the new post office on the Athenaeum site at Baxter's Plain that caused most interest. Built in two main stages, with the telephone exchange being completed first, the plans were published in January and a photograph of the steel framework being erected was printed in the newspaper on September 18th.

The mayor, Mr. T. A. Frost, had his eyes set on Lynn becoming a go-ahead regional centre and advocated the building of an airport for the town. An airport would be **'essential to the town's future prosperity'** he asserted.

Meanwhile, one of Lynn's oldest buildings was causing concern. **'Does Greyfriars' Tower Tilt?'** questioned the Lynn News on 30th January. The Town Clerk, Mr. J. W. Woolstencroft, thought that it was an optical illusion but, pressed by the newspaper, agreed to carry out tests, using a plumb-bob and tripod. By 22nd May, the results of these tests were revealed, with the Town Clerk confirming that the tower did not tilt and that it was just an optical illusion.

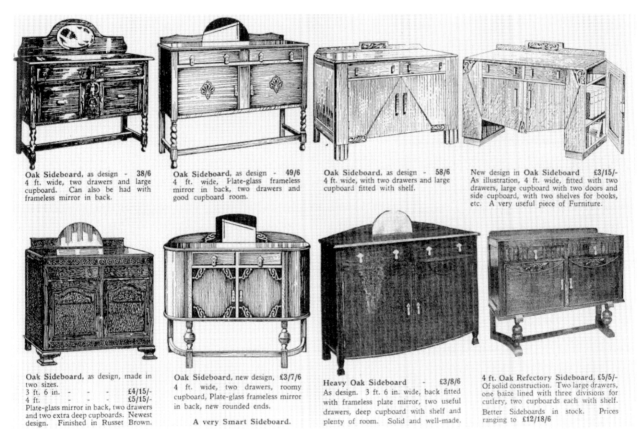

Oak Sideboard, as design - 38/6
4 ft. wide, two drawers and large cupboard. Can also be had with frameless mirror in back.

Oak Sideboard, as design - 49/6
4 ft. wide, Plate-glass frameless mirror in back, two drawers and good cupboard room.

Oak Sideboard, as design - 58/6
4 ft. wide, with two drawers and large cupboard fitted with shelf.

New design in Oak Sideboard £3/15/-
As illustration, 4 ft. wide, fitted with two drawers, large cupboard with two doors and side cupboard, with two shelves for books, etc. A very useful piece of Furniture.

Oak Sideboard, as design, made in two sizes.
3 ft. 6 in. - - - £4/15/-
4 ft. - - - £5/15/-
Plate-glass mirror in back, two drawers and two extra deep cupboards. Newest design. Finished in Russet Brown.

Oak Sideboard, new design, £3/7/6
4 ft. wide, two drawers, roomy cupboard, Plate-glass frameless mirror in back, new rounded ends.

A very Smart Sideboard.

Heavy Oak Sideboard - £3/8/6
As design. 3 ft. 6 in. wide, back fitted with frameless plate mirror, two useful drawers, deep cupboard with shelf and plenty of room. Solid and well-made.

4 ft. Oak Refectory Sideboard, £5/5/-
Of solid construction. Two large drawers, one baize lined with three divisions for cutlery, two cupboards each with shelf.
Better Sideboards in stock. Prices ranging to £12/18/6

Advertising their 1934/35 illustrated catalogue, Scott & Son confidently stated that **'We can Completely Furnish any Home at a Moment's Notice'**. This reflected the facts that they carried a large stock of goods in all departments and that they were able to deliver these in their own vans. In addition to warehouse facilities at their premises in High Street and Purfleet Street, they held stocks in their works on the South Quay and in a furniture store in Guannock Terrace, just off London Road, although this was mainly used for second-hand furniture.

There were now some distinctively 1930's designs on offer, including the range of sideboards shown in their catalogue (illus. above).

On 12th June 1934 they advertised a range of outdoor furniture (right). The type and design of garden and beach furniture hardly changed over many years. Folding garden chairs, deck chairs, with or without arms, deckchair canopies, garden or beach tents, bathing tents and folding tea tables were the principal items on offer.

The Lynn News again featured their annual Christmas shopping roundup in 1934, under the headline 'WHAT TO BUY AND WHERE TO BUY IT', and Scott & Son chose to promote their blankets and bedding as sensible gifts:-

SCOTT & SON

If you would fully enjoy your Christmas you must sleep well and warmly. There is nothing better than the genuine Witney blankets as stocked by Messrs. Scott & Son. They have eiderdowns, quilts, cushions and bed linen, for your bedroom, the spare bedroom or as gifts for your friends. As presents they are much cheaper than one would imagine and much more useful than some more expensive articles.

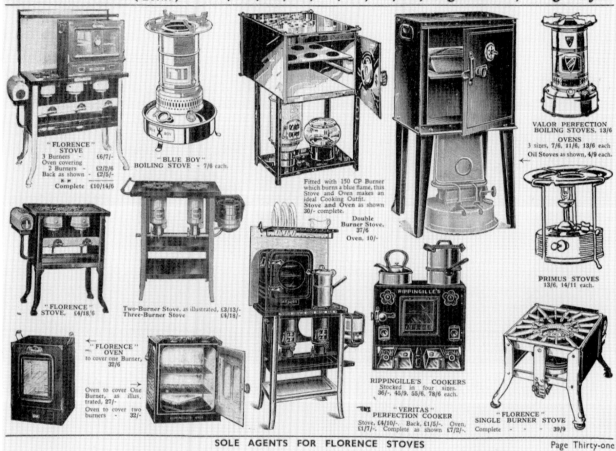

SOLE AGENTS FOR FLORENCE STOVES

Towards the end of 1934, negotiations between Scott & Son and the council concerning the development of the south side of Purfleet Street moved towards a conclusion. The council asked for a list of tenants in the properties owned by Scott & Son, which they supplied on 31st December: No.21. Hart. Wltr; No. 22. Weldrick G. T; No. 26. Simper. W. A; No. 27. Giddens. Jn. (Butcher); No. 28. Griffin. G. E. A; No. 28a. Thorn. Wm.

Some idea of the living conditions in these properties may be gleaned from the fact that Mr. and Mrs. Simper, who had been living in No. 26 for five or six years, had seven children, aged 15, 14, 13, 9, 5, 3 and 1. Mr. Simper was a labourer and paid 8/- rent to his mother-in-law, who owned the property and paid the rates. Walter Hart, who was to retire from Scott & Son in 1935, was living at No. 21. The photograph (right), taken by Goodchild of Lynn from the top of Burtons' new store, shows the new grain silos nearing completion opposite to the Purfleet Quay. The top of the Custom House can be seen above the roofs of the buildings on the right, which included some of those that were about to be demolished to make way for Scott & Son's new warehouse.

The council had already agreed to re-house the tenants and Scott & Son were now keen to proceed with their warehouse development. In addition to the properties listed above, Scotts also owned Nos. 23 and 24, Purfleet Street but the council owned No. 25, a shop and house. William Scott snr. had been negotiating directly with Mr. Reeve, the Town Clerk and, on his instruction, Ernest Colman wrote to the council in January 1935 seeking agreement to a land swap. The proposal was agreed by the council's Streets, Buildings and Markets Committee on the 16th January 1935 and confirmed by the Town Council on the 13th February. The Committee report read:-

A letter, dated the 7th January, from Mr. E. E. Colman, acting on behalf of Mr. W. C. Scott, was submitted, confirming the following negotiations with the Town Clerk for the widening and improvement of Purfleet Street: Mr. Scott to erect a new building on the south side of Purfleet Street; that as regards the premises Nos. 21 to 24, he is to set back the new building to a proposed line shown on the plan submitted, in exchange for the freehold premises No. 25, belonging to the Corporation, less the land in front of the new building line comprised in the last mentioned premises; further, that the Corporation agreeing to the above, Mr. Scott is to sell to the Corporation the land in front of the new building line to the existing premises Nos. 26, 27 and 28, at the rate of £1 per square yard, it being understood that as soon as the buildings to be erected by Mr. Scott are completed, the Corporation will carry out the necessary street paving works from Nos. 21 to 28 inclusive, with the necessary run-ins to the new premises, free of all cost to Mr. Scott. It was desired to learn as early as possible whether these proposals are acceptable to the Corporation.

Resolved: that the foregoing proposals be approved and adopted, that the Town Clerk be authorised to take all necessary steps to put the same into effect, including an application to the Ministry of Health to consents to the proposed exchange of properties, and that the Common Seal be affixed to the Deed of Exchange and any necessary documents.

The demolition commenced at the beginning of October and on 12th November, the Lynn News published a photograph (right) above the caption: **'The demolition of a large part of the south side of Purfleet-st. is almost complete, and work on the erection of a new warehouse for Messrs. Scott & Son Ltd., will begin shortly. The new building will be set back leaving a 30ft clearance between the buildings on either side of the street'.**

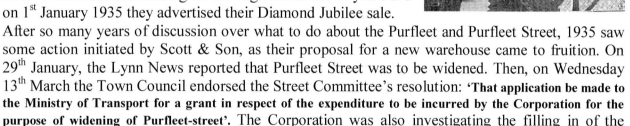

Scott & Son had been trading on the High Street for 60 years and on 1st January 1935 they advertised their Diamond Jubilee sale.

After so many years of discussion over what to do about the Purfleet and Purfleet Street, 1935 saw some action initiated by Scott & Son, as their proposal for a new warehouse came to fruition. On 29th January, the Lynn News reported that Purfleet Street was to be widened. Then, on Wednesday 13th March the Town Council endorsed the Street Committee's resolution: **'That application be made to the Ministry of Transport for a grant in respect of the expenditure to be incurred by the Corporation for the purpose of widening of Purfleet-street'.** The Corporation was also investigating the filling in of the Purfleet.

On 31st August 1935 Ernest E. Colman submitted the plans for the new three-storey warehouse. This was to be a huge single block, 138ft long and varying in depth from 39ft at the western end to 30ft at the eastern (High Street) end. It was 32ft tall, with a flat roof. The ground floor was 12ft from floor to ceiling, the first floor 8ft 6in and the top floor 8ft. The back wall ran alongside the northern bank of the Purfleet and followed the line of the river, hence the variation in the depth of the block. This wall was set on a reinforced concrete beam on fourteen concrete piles 38ft long. The ground floor was divided by two internal brick walls into three compartments. From west to east, these were:- a single bay containing a boiler house and a W.C; a three-bay vehicle storage garage, accessible by double sliding steel doors, in which there was set a personnel door; and a compartment consisting of five single bays for furniture storage, a double bay accessed by double sliding vehicle doors providing for the vans to be loaded and unloaded, and a double bay at the eastern end housing a wide staircase and a manually-operated furniture lift. The total area provided on the three floors was 13,890sq.ft, of which 10,160sq.ft was available for storing goods.

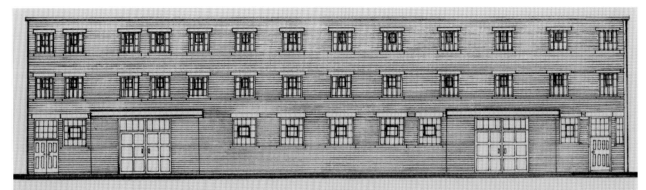

SCOTT & SON'S WAREHOUSE, PURFLEET STREET

The townspeople turned out to celebrate the King and Queen's Silver Jubilee in June 1935, the programme of events starting on the morning of Monday 6th with a civic procession and service on the Tuesday Market Place.

The great parade started out from the Gaywood direction, travelling in via Dodman's Bridge and Norfolk Street to the Tuesday Market Place. The first photograph, right, (courtesy of the East Anglian Film Archive - UEA) shows part of the Silver Jubilee parade in the Tuesday Market Place. One of Scott & Son's large furniture vans is following the huge 'New World Gas Cooker' man.

In the second photograph, below, (courtesy of Mrs. Muriel Browne), part of the parade is seen moving along Gaywood Road, near to the Highgate Infants' School. A.W. Green's Swan Dairy was close to where the photograph was taken and their van, car and milk floats, all dressed up for the occasion, can be seen in line, in front of the gas cooker man and Scott & Son's van.

That afternoon there was a cinema show for young people at the Majestic, sports for children over fourteen on the Walks and children's tea at the Corn Exchange and on the Tuesday Market Place. On Tuesday there was tea and entertainment for the unemployed at St. Nicholas' Drill Hall. On Wednesday the old folk were given a tea and entertained to a concert at the drill hall. On Thursday there was a band concert at the Walks bandstand. There was a British Legion tea and entertainment at the infant welfare centre on Friday and the week concluded with thanksgiving services at all the local churches and chapels.

The contents of Scott & Son's 1935 catalogue illustrate the contemporary designs that were popular before the Second World War and some pages are reproduced below.

Quality
FURNITURE
for the MODERN HOME

SCOTT & SON *of* KING'S LYNN
(KING'S LYNN) LTD.   91 to 97 HIGH STREET

OUR CATALOGUE	The Furniture illustrated in this Catalogue is of good design and construction, and although the prices are very moderate, the quality and workmanship employed in its production has been maintained. It is impossible to show designs of the whole of our stock, but if you are unable to visit us, we shall be pleased to send any further illustrations and details to suit your particular requirements.
OUR STORE	We cordially invite you to walk round our Showrooms and see the wonderful selection of fine Furniture. The very latest designs are always on show, as our stock is constantly being added to.
OUR FACTORY	By maintaining an experienced staff of Upholsterers and Cabinet Makers, we are able to produce a fine range of Upholstered Suites, which constitute excellent value for money. We specialise in Pure Bedding, which is widely known for its comfort and quality. "Excellent Value with Complete Reliability."
OUR POLICY	Every purchase made at these Stores carries our guarantee of satisfaction, which is backed by over 60 years' reputation founded on the basis of Sound Values and Fair Dealing. All goods sold we deliver Free in our own Motor Vans.
OUR TERMS	Our Terms are Strictly Cash. Our prices keen and competitive. This is without doubt to the benefit of our customers. Cheques and Postal Orders should be made payable to **Scott & Son (King's Lynn) Ltd.**, and all Correspondence addressed : Scott & Son (King's Lynn) Ltd., 91 to 97, High Street, King's Lynn.
OUR HOURS OF BUSINESS	Our Stores are open Daily, 9 a.m. to 6 p.m. ; Wednesdays, 9 a.m. to 1 p.m. ; Saturdays, 9 a.m. to 8.30 p.m. Telephone 495

SHOWN CLOSED—
Settee by Day

SHOWN OPEN—Bed by Night.
SETTEE-BEDS in a variety of designs, covered in strong Rexine, from £6/18/6
Covered in strong All-Wool Moquette - £10/18/6

FRAMELESS PLATE GLASS CHEVAL MIRRORS
Various designs.
29/6, 45/-

SHOWN CLOSED
3 ft. OAK-FITTED WARDROBE. as design - - - £3/12/3
Other makes—£2/8/6, £3/9/6, £3/18/6, £4/5/-, £5/5/-, £5/18/6
SHOWING INTERIOR
SEND FOR FULL RANGE OF DESIGNS AND PRICES.

THE POPULAR DIVAN SET
Complete Set - - - - 44/6
6 ft. 2 ins. long, 2 ft. 6 ins. wide. Comprising : 5 ins. deep, high-grade Boxspring, on 7 ins. polished Hardwood legs ; a 3½ ins. Bordered Mattress, filled with good quality Lindsey, and a 22 ins. square Pillow to match. Covered in Jaspe Cloth.

DIVAN SETS
In various styles and coverings. Prices : 37/6, 52/6, 59/6, 69/6, etc.
Headboards - - - From 7/6 extra.

SOILED LINEN BASKETS
Various designs and colours.
6/11, 9/11, 12/11, 14/11

OAK CHEST OF DRAWERS
3 ft. 6 ins. high, 2 ft. 6 ins. wide, with six large drawers - 39/6
3 ft. high, with five drawers 36/6
2 ft. 6 ins. high, with four drawers - - - 33/6

BEST POSSIBLE VALUE IN BEDROOM FURNITURE

Oak Pedestal, as design, 4/11
Other prices 5/11, 8/11, 10/11, 12/11, 14/11

Umbrella Stand, as design, 8/11. Other makes, 6/6, 7/11, 14/11, 16/11

DINING CHAIRS
In a variety of designs. Bulbous or twist legs.
7/11, 9/11, 14/11, 18/11

FRAMELESS MIRRORS. Assorted shapes, 4/6, 8/11, 9/11, 12/11, 14/11, 17/11, 21/-, 25/6, 29/6, etc.
All our Mirrors are Plate Glass.

Four-fold Draught Screens. in various colours and designs, 15/11, 18/11, 25/6, 29/6, 32/6

OAK HALL STAND
As design - - - 45/6
Other designs, 29/6, 39/6, 49/6, 58/6, etc.
Hall Seats, in Oak, 29/6, 37/6, 42/6

Oak Gate-Leg Tables
3 ft. x 2 ft. Oval Ends 25/6
3 ft. 6 in. x 2 ft. 6 in. " 35/-
4 ft. x 3 ft. " 45/-
3 ft. x 2 ft. Square En.Ins 28/6
3ft. 6 in. x 2 ft. 6 in. " 38/6
4 ft. x 3 ft. " 48/6

Polished Solid Oak Tables, with twist legs, size 24 ins. x 18 ins. As design. Also made oval, round and square.
9/11 each.

OAK NEST OF TABLES
As design - - 22/6
Other makes, 24/6, 32/6, 34/6, 37/6

Oak Tea Wagon, as design, 9/11
Fitted rubber castors.
With three trays - - 12/11
Other makes, 14/11, 18/11, 25/6

OAK COFFEE TABLES
Similar to design - 9/11
Also with three shelves, or concealed pull-out slides, etc.
25/6, 29/6, etc.

DRAW-LEAF TABLE
Size 5 ft. x 3 ft. when open, 3 ft. x 3 ft. when closed. Polished legs and frame, and strong White Plywood top - - Price 27/6

DRAW-LEAF DINING TABLE
3 ins. twist legs, polished top, size 5 ft. x 3 ft. when open, 3 ft. x 3 ft. when closed - 38/6
Size 4 ft. 9 ins. x 2 ft. 9 ins. when open, 2 ft. 9 ins. x 2 ft. 9 ins. when closed 37/6

POLISHED OAK DRAW-LEAF TABLE
Heavy bulbous legs. Top—size 5 ft. x 3 ft. when open, 3 ft. x 3 ft. when closed.
Price - - - - - 45/-

POLISHED OAK DRAW-LEAF TABLE
4 ins. heavy twist legs. Top with rounded corners, size 5 ft. x 3 ft. when open, 3 ft. x 3 ft. when closed - - - - Price 55/-

Settee and two Easy Chairs as design - - - - £9/18/6
A very smart Rexine Set, good quality Velour seats. Settee, 4 ft. 10 ins. ;
2 Easy Chairs, 32 ins. wide ; 24 ins. seat depth, well sprung.

Settee and two Easy Chairs as design - - - - £12/18/6
Covered in good quality Moquette. Seats and back well sprung. A variety
of Coverings to select from. A very attractive Suite.

Settee and two Easy Chairs as design - - - - £19/19/-
Covered in Moquette and Velvet. Stuffed pure Black hair. Double sprung
and contains 415 springs. Wonderful Value.

Three-Piece Suite - - - - - £12/18/6 the Three Pieces
Comprising Settee and two Easy Chairs, covered in modern Moquette and
Velvet. Sturdily constructed. Well sprung backs and seats.

SMALL
CHAIRS

Settee and two Easy Chairs - - - £13/18/6 the Three Pieces
Covered in the new Jaspé Moquette Velvet. Also in Patterned Moquette.
Well sprung and strongly made.

IN
VARIOUS
DESIGNS
Covered
to match
any Suite
From
£1 Each.

Settee and two Easy Chairs as design - - - - £19/19/-
Covered in good quality All-Wool Fancy Jaspé Moquette and Brown
Velvet. Double sprung seats. A luxurious Suite. Very comfortable.

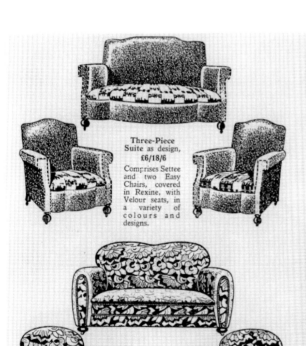

Three-Piece
Suite as design,
£6/18/6
Comprises Settee
and two Easy
Chairs, covered
in Rexine, with
Velour seats, in
a variety of
colours and
designs.

Skittle Pattern Settee and two Easy Chairs - £7/18/6 the Three Pieces
as design. This Suite is well made and sprung, and covered in a very good
quality Velour, or in Art. Tapestry and Velvet. Same price.

Settee and two Easy Chairs - - - - £8/18/6 the Three Pieces
Covered in good quality Rexine, with four feather-filled Cushions, well-sprung seats
and backs.
Superior quality - - - - - £10/18/6 the Three Pieces
On larger frames, covered in Brown, Green, or Red Rexine, piped in Black, with four
feather-filled Cushions in Velveteen to match.

Settee and two
Easy Chairs as
design - £9/18/6
Comprises large
Settee and two
large Easy
Chairs covered in
Rexine with
Moquette seats,
4 feather-filled
Cushions in
Moquette and
Velvet.

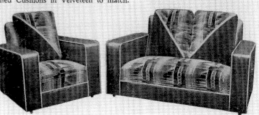

ORIENTAL CARPETS | SCOTT & SON (KING'S LYNN LTD.)

IN THE LATEST COLOURINGS

INDIAN and TURKEY CARPETS and RUGS

Hundreds in stock, many qualities and designs. All of the best value. Periodical consignments bring us the newest colourings. It is impossible to give all sizes, colours and prices in stock, so have selected a few at random.

Size	Ground Colour	Pattern Colour	Price
9' 5" x 6' 4"	Cream	Blue	£1/19/6
10' 3" x 6' 4"	Cream	Green	£2/2/6
9' 1" x 9' 1"	Camel	Red	£2/17/6
10' 6" x 9' 2"	Camel	Tan	£3/2/0
12' 4" x 9' 3"	Camel	Brown	£4/9/6

Above are low priced Indian Carpets. We have all sizes and colours in better grades. Call and select from our huge stock.

INDIAN RUGS

5 feet x 2 feet 6 inches	From	12/11
6 feet x 3 feet	"	14/11
7 feet x 4 feet	"	29/6

GENUINE TURKEY CARPETS AND RUGS

Heavy Luxurious Pile, Rich Red Grounds with Blue and Green design, fast colours. A lifetime's wear in every piece. Stocked in all sizes.

Rugs	6 ft. 6 in. x 2 ft. 6 in.	£3/18/6
	6 ft. x 3 ft.	£4/9/6
Carpets	6 ft. x 6 ft.	£9/18/6
	7 ft. 3 in. x 5 ft. 2 in.	£10/18/6
	9 ft. 3 in. x 9 ft. 1 in.	£16/10/0
	11 ft. 2 in. x 9 ft. 3 in.	£14/17/6
	10 ft. 2 in. x 9 ft. 8 in.	£18/10/0
	11 ft. 8 in. x 9 ft. 6 in.	£19/5/0
	13 ft. 4 in. x 9 ft. 11 in.	£28/0/0
Runners	11 ft. 2 in. x 2 ft. 4 in.	£6/18/6

Also several fancy Turkey Carpets in stock.

THIS PHOTOGRAPH OF OUR CARPET SHOWROOM GIVES AN IDEA OF OUR WONDERFUL STOCK

INDO-TURKEY CARPETS AND RUGS

Real Turkey colours, Red Ground with Blue and Green design. heavy all-wool Pile, made in British India.

Size		Price
5' x 2' 6"		29/6
6' x 3'		45/0
9' 10" x 7' 2"		£7/17/6
10' 6" x 9' 2"		£10/15/0
12' 3" x 9' 1"		£12/10/0

Page Twenty

PERSIAN REPRODUCTION CARPETS, RUGS, RUNNERS AND MATS

Excellent quality, Persian and Chinese designs have been faithfully copied. Beautifully blended colourings. (Foreign).

Carpets			Rugs		
9' x 7' 6"	£2/15/0		2' 10" x 1' 10"	3/6
9' x 9'	£3/5/0		4' x 2'	4/6
10' 6" x 9'	£3/18/6		4' 4" x 2' 2"	5/11
12' x 9'	£4/10/0		4' 10" x 2' 3"	6/11
Runners 9' 2" x 2'	15/11		5' 2" x 2' 10"	12/11
			6' x 4'	16/11
Stair Carpet, 18" wide	Yard 3/6		Slip Mats 28" x 12'	1/11

REVERSIBLE WOOL RUGS

Suitable for bedrooms, etc. Plain or Patterned

7/11	9/11	11/6	14/11	18/11	21/6	23/6	27/6

Axminster Rugs

48" x 24"		3/11
54" x 27"		4/11

Good quality, many designs.
Better Quality.

6/11	7/11	9/11	11/6	12/11	14/11

New designs, all colours.

Spool Axminster Rugs

Choice designs, full range.

8/11	10/6	14/11	17/11	21/-

Corridor Rugs

Axminster with Turkey and fancy designs.

7' 6" x 2' 3"	19/11
9' x 2' 3"	25/6
10' 6" x 2' 3"	28/6
12' x 2' 3"	34/6
7' 6" x 3'	27/6
9' x 3'	34/6
10' 6" x 3'	38/6
12' x 3'	42/6

116

The hardware department stocked a standard range of oil lamps - hand, table, hanging and wall-mounted. They also supplied all the necessary spare parts, including wicks, burners, chimneys, globes and shades. Their range of lamps from their 1935 catalogue is illustrated above. From time to time, special lines that had not been included in their catalogue were bought in. The table lamp, illustrated left, was advertised in the Lynn Advertiser on 15th October 1935.

For their toy advertisements for Christmas 1935, Scott & Son chose this image of Father Christmas from the range on offer at the Lynn Advertiser. On sale that year were the traditional boys' toys, including:- tool sets priced from 6d up to 7/11; a 'Frog' aeroplane with 11½ in. wingspan that could fly 330ft., at 5/-; boxes of soldiers, from 6d to 2/6; building bricks, from 6d to 2/11; and model forts, from 2/11 to 6/11. Girls were expected to help in the kitchen with their pastry board and rolling pin sets, from 9d to 2/6. They could also help with dressmaking and mending with their fitted workboxes priced from 1/- to 2/6. Toys from the 1935 catalogue are shown on the following page.

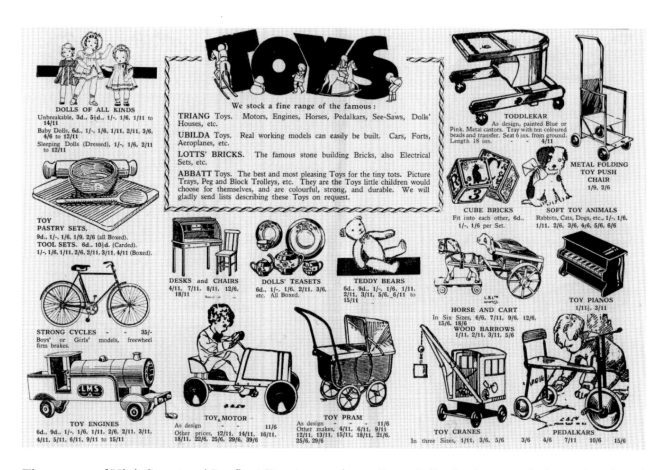

The corner of High Street and Purfleet Street opposite to Scott & Son's shop was being redeveloped and there was a grand opening of Montague Burton's new store at 98 & 99, High Street on Friday 13th December 1935. The building was designed by Ernest E. Colman, who was responsible for Scott & Son's new warehouse, just round the corner in Purfleet Street.

The unemployment figures released in January 1936 gave some small cause for optimism that prosperity was improving in the town. There were 87 fewer men out of work in December 1935 compared with the same month a year earlier, 29 fewer women and 26 fewer unemployed juveniles. The published employment figures revealed that, out of a total of 7,080 jobs, the main categories included: 1,089 labourers; 679 shop assistants; 788 servants; 493 railway workers; 365 road transport workers; and 88 charwomen.

The Lynn News carried tributes to King George V in their issue of 21st January 1936 and an account of the accession proclamation for King Edward VIII on Wednesday 22nd. The ceremony at Lynn Guildhall was heralded by the sounding of a fanfare at 12.30pm, following which the mayor, Mr. J. W. Raby, attended by members of the Lynn Corporation and officials, read the proclamation. At the conclusion of the proclamation, a second fanfare was sounded, the mayor led three cheers for the King and the watching crowd sang the National Anthem. The Mayor and Corporation then proceeded in procession to the Tuesday Market Place where the accession of the King was again proclaimed in front of a large crowd, from the steps of the Corn Exchange. Mr. Raby was, of course, unaware that he was to create an unusual mayoral record by reading the proclamation for two Kings in one year!

Household essentials were always promoted at the beginning of the year, with the emphasis on spring cleaning. In their advertisements in February 1936 Scott & Son offered such practical items as household steps, five-legged dolly pegs, polishes and stains (illus. right), draining boards, copper lids, clothes-horses and pastry boards. The illustration below is from Scott & Son's 1935 catalogue.

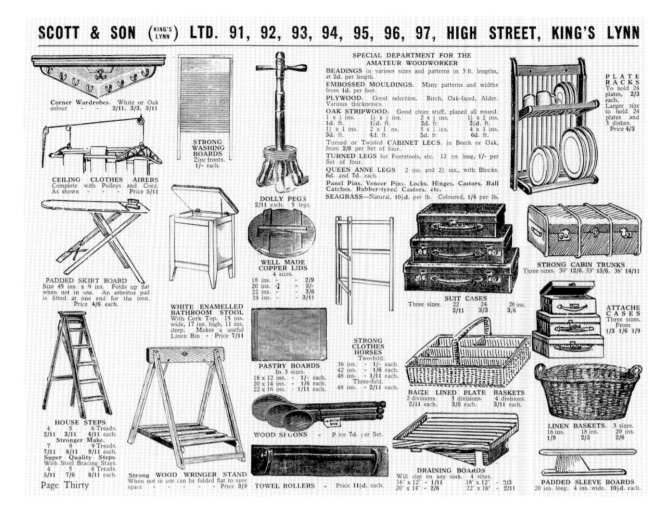

Corner Wardrobes. White or Oak colour - - 2/11. 3/3, 3/11

CEILING CLOTHES AIRERS Complete with Pulleys and Cord. As shown - - - Price 5/11

STRONG WASHING BOARDS Zinc fronts. 1/- each.

PADDED SKIRT BOARD Size 45 ins. x 9 ins. Folds up flat when not in use. An asbestos pad is fitted at one end for the iron. Price 4/6 each.

WHITE ENAMELLED BATHROOM STOOL With Cork Top. 15 ins. wide, 17 ins. high, 11 ins. deep. Makes a useful Linen Bin - Price 7/11

HOUSE STEPS
4   5   6 Treads.
2/11 3/11 4/11 each.
Stronger Make.
7   8   9 Treads.
7/11 8/11 9/11 each.
Super Quality Steps.
With Steel Bracing Stays.
4   5   6 Treads.
5/11 7/6   8/11 each.
Page Thirty

Strong WOOD WRINGER STAND When not in use can be folded flat to save space - - - - Price 3/9

DOLLY PEGS 2/11 each. 5 legs.

SPECIAL DEPARTMENT FOR THE AMATEUR WOODWORKER
BEADINGS in various sizes and patterns in 3 ft. lengths, at 2d. per length.
EMBOSSED MOULDINGS. Many patterns and widths from 1d. per foot.
PLYWOOD. Good selection. Birch, Oak-faced, Alder. Various thicknesses.
OAK STRIPWOOD. Good clean stuff, planed all round.
1 x ½ ins.   1½ x ½ ins.   2 x ½ ins.   1½ x ½ ins.
1d. ft.   1½d. ft.   2d. ft.   2½d. ft.
1½ x 1 ins.   2 x 1 ins.   3 x 1 ins.   4 x 1 ins.
3d. ft.   4d. ft.   5d. ft.   6d. ft.
Turned or Twisted CABINET LEGS, in Beech or Oak, from 2/6 per Set of four.
TURNED LEGS for Footstools, etc. 12 ins. long, 1/- per Set of four.
QUEEN ANNE LEGS 2 ins. and 2½ ins., with Blocks. 6d. and 7d. each.
Panel Pins. Veneer Pins. Locks. Hinges. Castors. Ball Catches. Rubber-tyred Castors. etc.
SEAGRASS—Natural, 10½d. per lb. Coloured, 1/4 per lb.

WELL MADE COPPER LIDS 4 sizes.
18 ins. - - 2/9
20 ins. - - 3/-
22 ins. - - 3/6
24 ins. - - 3/11

PASTRY BOARDS In 3 sizes.
18 x 12 ins. - 1/- each.
20 x 14 ins. - 1/6 each.
22 x 16 ins. - 1/11 each.

WOOD SPOONS - Price 7d. per Set.

STRONG CLOTHES HORSES Two-fold.
36 ins. - 1/- each.
42 ins. - 1/6 each.
48 ins. - 1/11 each.
Three-fold.
48 ins. - 2/11 each.

SUIT CASES
Three sizes. 22   24   26 ins.
             2/11 3/3   3/6

BAIZE LINED PLATE BASKETS
2 divisions.   3 divisions.   4 divisions.
2/11 each.   3/6 each.   3/11 each.

DRAINING BOARDS Will clip on any sink. 4 sizes.
16" x 12" - 1/11   18" x 12" - 2/3
20" x 14" - 2/6   22" x 16" - 2/11

TOWEL ROLLERS - Price 11½d. each.

PLATE RACKS To hold 24 plates, 2/3 each. Larger size to hold 24 plates and 3 dishes. Price 4/3

STRONG CABIN TRUNKS Three sizes. 30" 12/6. 33" 13/6. 36" 14/11

ATTACHE CASES Three sizes. From 1/3 1/6 1/9

LINEN BASKETS. 3 sizes.
16 ins.   18 ins.   20 ins.
1/9   2/3   2/6

PADDED SLEEVE BOARDS 20 ins. long. 4 ins. wide. 10½d. each.

A tragic event occurred in High Street on 9th March 1936 when the well-known and much respected local butcher, Tom Andrews, was killed when moving a large sausage machine from one shop to another. Tom Andrews was the nephew of William Crawshay Scott and the whole family was terribly shocked by his death. Thomas William Andrews was only 43 years old and was married with three children. A member of the Lynn Rotary Club, he had attended their lunch before walking back to his wife's shop at 108 High Street. The sausage machine, weighing about half-a-ton was to be moved to his larger shop at 120/121, High Street. In lifting the machine from the counter to a small hand trolley, the boards that had been placed over the mat well gave way. Tom Andrews lost his footing and was crushed and killed instantly. The loss of another independent High Street trader, albeit in extraordinary circumstances, continued the trend that Oliver Jermyn had forecast.

Fire destroyed the Theatre Royal during the night of 9th/10th May and there followed considerable discussion and speculation about what would replace the building. The press and local people would have liked the Corporation, who owned the site and leased it to the Union Cinema Co., to build a 'much-needed public hall'.

As the construction of Scott & Son's new warehouse in Purfleet Street progressed, on 25th May 1936, the Lynn News reported a narrow escape for two of the building workers:-

FELL INTO PURFLEET
While working near the top of Messrs. Scott & Son's new premises in Purfleet-st., Lynn, and engaged in shifting a plank yesterday morning, William Collinson, bricklayer, 15, Lansdowne-st., Lynn, fell about 40 feet into the water of the Fleet. A fellow workman, Mr. H. Batterham, was also knocked off the plank into the mud. Collinson, though suffering from a sprained ankle in consequence of the fall, managed to swim to the bank, while Batterham shouted for help. It was with difficulty that he was able to make himself heard above the hammering on the new building, but help was eventually forthcoming, and the men were taken to their respective homes. Besides a sprained ankle, Collinson received bruises about the arms and legs. Batterham escaped with bruises only.

Building work was also progressing at Baxter's Plain on the new post office. Staff had to move out of the old building, into temporary accommodation in Paradise Road, while the post office was demolished. The new one was due to open in 1938. The old Athenaeum building had been in use as a post office since September 1883.

The Lynn News gave over their front page on 8th December to the dilemma facing the King, who **'MUST CHOOSE THRONE OR MARRIAGE.'** A week later, the Mayor was once again reading the proclamation for a new King from the steps of the Town Hall and the Corn Exchange.

Within nine months of the Theatre Royal burning down, another of Lynn's entertainment venues had been destroyed by fire. On Thursday 11th February 1937 the St James's Kinema and dance hall was burned to the ground. The previous St James's Kinema had been destroyed in November 1904. There was a real public hunger for a big new development on the site, because the rebuilding of the Theatre Royal had been limited in scale by the Corporation setting an expenditure ceiling of £13,600. The new Theatre Royal was being designed to seat just 1,050 and there were to be no other public facilities. The architects for the Theatre Royal project were Messrs. Allflatt & Courtney of Tuesday Market Place, King's Lynn.

In its continuing series of articles informing their readers about the situation in Europe, the Lynn News published a report of an address by Gen. Sir E. Peter Strickland, former Colonel of the Royal Norfolk Regiment, given to the annual dinner of the Lynn Branch of the Regiment's Association. The General concluded by giving this warning: **'There is a lot of loose talk just now about war. As far as I know there isn't going to be one, and at the present moment there is not the slightest sign of it. A lot of good would be done by stopping all this loose talk. It is creating such a state of nerves that people are beginning to act as if we are already at war. We don't want that!'** Some of the actions that he may have been referring to were the information and training programmes being made available to the public about precautions that could be taken in the event of aerial attacks. This included instruction on defence against gas attacks, with gas mask drills.

Linos and Congoleum were advertised by Scott & Son on 19th May 1936 (illus. left). Floor coverings remained amongst the store's strongest selling items. Cork lino squares were very popular at this date. Supplied in sizes from 3yds x 2yds at 8/6, up to 5yds x 4yds at 45/-, these were strongly patterned and coloured. The principal manufacturers were Barrys, Armstrongs and Williamsons.

A year later, the town was preparing to celebrate the Coronation of King George VI. The Walks were **'transformed into a fairyland of lights'** in red white and blue. The Corn Exchange, Red Mount and several private buildings were floodlit. The shopping streets were festooned with bunting and flags, the shops being stocked with flags, decorations and souvenirs. Scott & Son had special offers of souvenirs of coronation ware bearing pictures of the King and Queen, including:- beakers (6d and 9d); mugs (9d); jugs (1/-, 1/6, 1/11, 2/11); tankards (1/11); ash-trays (6d); biscuit barrels (4/11); three-piece sets of plate, cup and saucer (1/6); half pint mugs, and sets of four serviette rings (5/6). Their advertisement was in the Lynn News on 4th May 1937. The celebrations began on Sunday 9th May with a service at St Margaret's Church and a Sunday school demonstration on the Walks. On Wednesday 12th there was a crowded programme, starting with a civic procession and open-air service on the Tuesday Market Place. This included a display by aircraft based at Bircham. There was six-a-side football on the Walks recreation ground, children's tea parties in the Corn Exchange and in a marquee on the Tuesday Market Place, and a bowls drive at the Grammar School field. The main event was the Coronation Parade around the town, which included 'mock Councillors in mock robes'. A parade of decorated boats performed the 'storming of the Boal Quay' and there were river races for rowing boats and other craft. In the evening there was a bonfire and fireworks display on the West Lynn bank of the river and the day concluded with a dance and a cabaret. There were many street tea parties and Bertram Mills Circus was in town for the week. The coronation illuminations were to be left up until the end of the month but on the afternoon of Wednesday 26th May the town was hit by one of the worst storms since the gales of 1908. The lights in the Walks were wrecked, several trees were uprooted and many branches were broken off.

The factory on the South Quay was working flat out to satisfy the demand for reasonably-priced, sturdy three-piece upholstered suites and Scott & Son offered a range of these in different materials, at prices from £4/5/0 up to £11/18/6. In their annual stocktaking sale in January 1938 the special offers included:- 'Dining-room sets comprising Draw-leaf table, Sideboard and 4 Chairs at; £5/15/-, £6/9/6, £6/18/6, £7/18/6, £9/18/6, and £12/18/6. Bedroom Suites at Special Sale Prices; £3/15/-, £4/17/6, £5/15/-, £6/15/-, £7/15/-, £9/10/-, £11/9/6, £12/10/-, etc'. The illustrations below and on the following pages, from their spring catalogues for 1937 and 1938, show some of these sets.

Spring

SCOTT & SON
(KING'S LYNN) LTD.

SPRING

THE Poet may see Spring as a reason of Romance— The housewife sees it as a reason of hard work, carpets to come up, curtains to come down and maybe the painters in as well. No wonder she feels the need of some new things for the home to act as a tonic when the annual upheaval is over. A visit to Scott's should precede the Spring Clean so that the new furniture, floorcoverings, curtains, etc., can be delivered at the most appropriate moment.

91-97 HIGH STREET, KING'S LYNN
ESTABLISHED 1874   PHONE 2495

THIS Booklet is published with the object of helping you to make your home cosy and beautiful, but does not by any means give a list of our whole stock. If you will drop us a Post Card, we shall be pleased to forward to your address, FREE AND POST FREE, one of our LARGE 40 page illustrated catalogues which is a complete guide to House Furnishing, better still, accept this invitation, and pay us a personal visit, we shall be only too pleased to conduct you round our showrooms which are filled with the very latest designs at the lowest prices. Every article sold carries our Guarantee. All goods are delivered in our own motor vans.

Owing to the continued advance in the prices of all commodities, prices will have to be advanced when our present stock is cleared. It is therefore to the advantage of the Public to buy as early as possible.

THE *Lounge* and it's Furnishings

SCOTT & SON can satisfy customers who want quiet comfort in the lounge with furniture that won't "date," just as easily as those who aim at an ultra-modern room with an atmosphere of stream-lined smartness.

If you are on the look out for an upholstered suite, fireside chair or occasional piece which will make your lounge complete, Scott & Son's is the place to find it.

Three-piece Suites in Rexine from **£4/5/0**

In Velour from **£7/18/6**   In Cowhide from **£11/18/6**

Scheme for the Dining Room

MODERN education has achieved great things, but it hasn't so far succeeded in teaching small boys (and girls) not to scrape their feet on the table legs at meal times. So a Dining Room Suite cannot afford to be a "show piece." It must be sturdy enough to withstand the daily wear and tear of the family breakfast, dinner and tea, and yet smart enough to give the hostess a thrill of pride on state occasions.

Scott's Dining Room Furniture combines these two features happily and inexpensively.

Complete Dining Sets from **£5/15/0** to **£19/19/0**

Walnut FOR THE BEDROOM

HAVE you admired the glossy elegance of figured Walnut in shop windows and other people's homes and wished your bedroom could be furnished like that.

If so, you can give yourself a pleasant surprise to-day by looking in at Scott's and examining the very latest Walnut Bedroom Suites. They were selected by our buyers at the British Industries Fair and cost from as little as £11/15/0.

Sleep

"Tired Nature's Sweet Restorer"

MANY a time the complaint "I can't sleep well" should really be "I can't sleep well on a mattress like this." Don't worry about your health and your diet until you've had a look at the thing you are lying on night after night. Then come to Scott's and compare it with the deep-sprung, luxurious, rest compelling mattresses which modern science has devised to give you sound, refreshing sleep.

A comfortable mattress is a good investment.

Full size Spring Filled Mattresses **55/-** to **£10/10/0**

page seventeen

White Hemstitched Sheets.
A strong bleached cotton sheet that will give lasting satisfaction.
Size 108″ × 70″ **7/11** pair

Superior Quality White Hemstitched Sheets.
Size 99″ × 80″ **8/11** pair

Fine White Sheets.
Made from super quality cotton. Each sheet hemstitched, each pair wrapped in cellophane, will give lasting wear.
Size 108″ × 70″ **15/11** pair

White Pillow Cases.
Strong, buttoned, remarkable value.
6d. each

White Pillow Cases.
Coloured scalloped edge with coloured flower, green gold, blue, pink white. Housewife shape.
6d. each

Housewife Pillow Cases.
Embroidered ends, in fast colours. A strong and durable cloth.
10½d. each

On 11th January 1938 their advertisement proclaimed: '**ANOTHER BIG PYREX OFFER**'. Scott & Son were promoting Pyrex by combining the manufacturer's special three-for-two offer, with a discount on the items from 12/- to 6/6. The free third item was a mug.

Meanwhile, in the council chamber the debate turned once again to the vexed question of the proposed widening of Purfleet Street. Scott & Son had set back their new warehouse to allow for the widening of the street but the old properties at both the High Street and King Street ends of Purfleet Street were still standing. At the King Street end, Nos. 18, 19 and 20 had been bought by the council for £500 but they had not taken possession of them. At the High Street end were:- No. 29 – Mr. C. Regester, Baker and Confectioner **(Home-made cakes. 'Dough Boys a speciality'.)**; No. 30 – a small house bought by William Scott from Mr. Winkfield who had let it to Mr. J. C. Hornigold; No. 31 – Mr. F. A. Dale, Pork-butcher; No. 32 - B. Hornigold's tobacconist's and sweet shop, also owned by Mr. Dale.

The council were debating the motion: **'That it be an instruction to the Streets Committee to take the necessary steps to acquire the remaining property on the south side of Purfleet-st., at the High-st. end'.** The debate was quite heated because this was a topic that kept cropping up for debate but without much action being taken. It was left to Mr. Catleugh to explain to his fellow councillors that agreement had been reached with Scotts to set back their property but that acquisition of the other shops was subject to private negotiation. The headline in The Lynn News and County Press on 18th January 1938 was very prophetic: **'Purfleet-st May be Widened – This Year, Next Year, Sometime!'** The leader in the newspaper that day complained about the lack of action to widen the street, which stretched back some thirty years. The Editor's view was that widening would bring several benefits, including the removal of a traffic bottleneck and the opening-up of unobstructed views of the Custom House. He considered that it would also bring to a head the question over whether the Purfleet should be culverted. This old town fleet was still an open drain which ran along the back of Scott's new warehouse. As far back as 18th July 1863 the newspaper had carried an article arguing that the Purfleet should be tunnelled over. Seventy-five years later, the editor of the Lynn News, whose office was in Purfleet Street, opined: **'The widening of Purfleet-st will raise another matter: the culverting of the Purfleet, an open sewer about which we have written a good deal. As visitors go round the town admiring its cobbled streets and quaint buildings they little imagine that, bounded by a mass of brick and mortar close to High-st, is a scene strikingly like a Gustave Dore illustration to Dante's "Inferno." Indeed, not only visitors, but most residents are unaware of the appalling sight – and smell – which meets the explorer of this Purfleet. At low tide banks of mud and slime are exposed on either side of a trickling stream of water. Down this open channel is borne about a quarter of Lynn's sewage, releasing noisome fumes full of danger to health. Long exposure has brought comparative immunity to the inhabitants of the neighbourhood, but newcomers to nearby establishments have been affected. Who knows what ailments have had their origin in the germ-ridden sewer of the Purfleet?'**

Later that year, the three Purfleet Street properties owned by the Town Council were demolished and a photograph was printed in the Lynn News on 13th September showing the newly opened-up view of the Custom House. Other developments of note that year included the opening of two cinemas in the town. In February, Lynn's new Theatre Royal was completed, replacing the building that had been destroyed by fire. The theatre, close to Greyfriars' Tower in St James Street, was opened on April 4th. In Pilot Street, the site was cleared in August for the second new cinema and this one, named the 'Pilot Cinema', was opened in November.

Scott & Son started advertising the new **"Pedigree"** **Baby-Carriages** on 1st February 1938 at prices ranging from £4/15/- up to £10/15/-, and **"Pedigree"** **Folders** from 37/6 up to 75/-. The following month they invited readers to **'Send for our New 40-page Illustrated Catalogue and Furnishing Guide, Free and Post Free to any address'.**

Their catalogue that year included the **'ROL-A-DOR'** revolutionary space-saving wardrobe, priced at 16/9. This embodied the principle of the roll-top desk to protect the two compartments of the

ROL-A-DOR The Space Saving Wardrobe

DUSTPROOF and MOTHPROOF. Specially constructed to keep out dust—raised floor to prevent dampness. Fitted with a Humidor containing an effective Moth Preventative.

STANDARD MODEL Size 5 ft. high, 21 ins. wide, 21 ins. deep With Magic Spring Door

18/6

GIANT MAGIC ROL-A-DOR - **25/.**

IMPORTANT FEATURES
● MAGIC DOOR — automatically springs open.
● MOTHPROOF.
● DAMP PROOF.
● DUSTPROOF.
● Holds 20-30 Garments—lengthy gowns too.
● SPACE SAVING— no swinging doors.
● Selected wood frame.
● HUMIDOR — an effective protection against moths.
● SHOE RACK— keeps shoes tidy and in place.
● SIZE—66″ x 24″ x 21″—4 cubic feet larger than the Standard Rol-a-dor

Price 25/.

ROL-A-DOR PRODUCTS
"SHOE CABINET" with Rol-a-dor, holds 12 pairs shoes, sturdy wood frame, size 48 ins. high, 15¾ ins. wide, 12¾ ins. deep .. .. Price 21/-
"SLIDE AWAY"—The family Unda-bed Chest Size 48 ins. x 22 ins. x 8 ins. On ball-bearing castors. Polished wood frame .. .. Price 8/11
'DE-LUXE' CHESTS. Ideal for Linens, Blankets, Clothes, etc Size 30 ins. x 16 ins. x 20 ins. In Mahogany fibre board .. .. Price 5/9
"PACKAWAY" CHESTS in Mahogany fibre board. Handy and compact size. 20 ins. x 14 ins. x 12 ins. .. .. .. In Sets, 5/9 the set of 3

wardrobe. Benefits advertised were that this kept out the dust and moths. The wardrobe was set on a plinth to avoid the problem of damp – an indication of the conditions to be found in the majority of houses in an age prior to the installation of damp proof courses and central heating.

It was on 5th July 1938 that the Lynn News announced the death of William Crawshay Scott snr. He had died on 2nd July and his funeral was held at Gaywood church on Wednesday 6th July at 2.30pm. Many of the staff of Scott & Son attended the funeral, including the following:- Messrs. E B. Smith (manager, furniture department); A. E. Smith (works manager); Miss F. Finbow (manageress, china department); Messrs. C. A. Cook, W. T. Green, E. Mott, H. Gazley, S. Rainbow, E. Eke, D. Whitby, D. Pegg, A. R. Booty, H. Dowdy, and the Misses M. Green, M. Benefer, E. Johnson, W. Withers, S. French, R. Brock, B. Simpson, M. Brookbank, J. Lakey, I. Withers, M. Greaves, E. Webber, A. Sampson, M. Williamson, A. Lawson, D. Richardson, V. Bray, F. Jarvis, H. Cowen, J. Castleton, J. Croucher, and I. Gordon.

The works manager, Albert Edward Smith, had worked his way up from being an apprentice to take charge of Scott & Son's furniture factory on the South Quay. He was married to Maria Osborne Watts ('Ossie'), who was the granddaughter of Thomas William Scott, the founder of the firm. Miss Joan Croucher was later to become the wife of Maurice Scott.

Business continued under the joint management of the two brothers, William Crawshay and Maurice Septimus Crawshay, known as Mr. Will and Mr. Maurice to the staff.

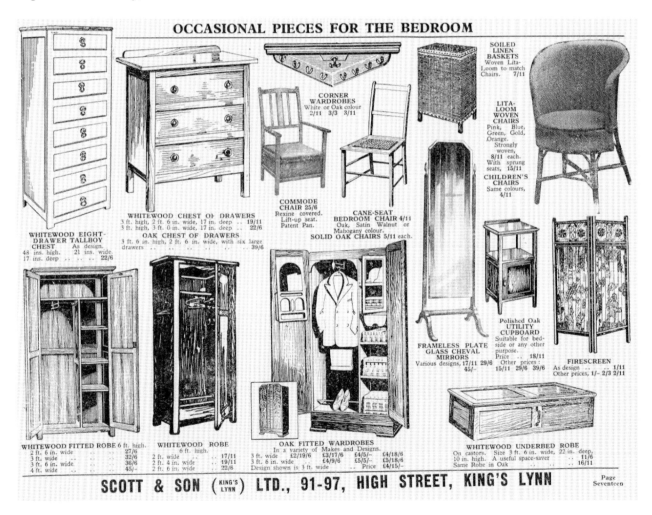

Through the months of September and October 1938 a series of advertisements illustrated the different makes and designs of bedroom furniture available from the shop, including the oak fitted wardrobes as shown in their catalogue (illus. above). Although most of the furniture that they sold was being bought in from other manufacturers, there was no let-up in the output from their own works for their three-piece suites.

Also in September of that year, Scott & Son were advertising table and hand lamps in their hardware department again. There was a strong demand for oil lamps in Lynn and the surrounding area right up until the Second World War. In their 1938 catalogue they offered a range, although it was somewhat smaller than in earlier catalogues. Spare chimneys and wicks were still stocked, too.

Other items for the home included clocks, which were illustrated in their catalogue and advertised in the newspapers in November 1938 (illus. right).

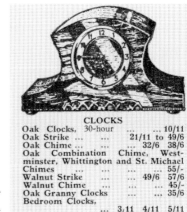

There was no getting away from discussions about Purfleet Street in the council chamber – this time on the question of the standard of design of new buildings in the town. Alderman R. Taylor led off against the modern buildings but was mainly sniping at the new council houses. Cllr. Raby, who had opened the street widening debate earlier in the year, then launched a thinly-veiled attack on the appearance of Scott's new warehouse. On 20th September, 1938, the Lynn News reported what had been said by Cllr. Raby in the debate:- **'There was a certain street in the town in which he had been interested for a number of years and a building there did 'command the street,' as Ald. Taylor said, a building which was in close proximity to one of the most beautiful buildings in the town. When this was put to them he did not remember such criticism from Ald. Taylor as they now heard. Some of them did try to secure some modification by suggesting a certain type of brick, but the main point was that the criticism of this barrack-like building was before the Council'.**

It has to be admitted that Alderman Taylor and Councillor Raby had a valid point. Over the next thirty years or so, there must have been thousands of amateur photographers who cursed the fact that they could not get a good shot of the Custom House from Purfleet Street without Scotts' warehouse creeping into the viewfinder. However, it is clear that Cllr. Raby and others had not been sufficiently persuasive in arguing their case when the application for the warehouse had been submitted. In approving the plans on 11th September 1935 the Council imposed the following conditions: **'Subject to front of building being built in Rustic Fletton bricks and pointed up with white Cement and windows in reveal'.**

The headlines in the newspapers were preparing their readers for war. On 17th January 1939 the Lynn News read:- **'CALL TO NATIONAL SERVICE. The trumpet call to National Service has been sounded this week. And for the first time millions of people will see shortly in facsimile the handwriting of the Prime Minister. The desire of all of us is to live at peace with our neighbours. But to ensure peace we must be strong'.**

New National Service committees were being set up across the country, with local offices of the Ministry of Labour being kept open on certain evenings for people to obtain information and guidance. A guide was issued giving information about recruitment to the Navy, Army and Air Force and the whole range of civilian services for which volunteers were needed. A schedule of reserved occupations was issued from which persons were not to be moved to other services at time of war. There was an age limit for most classes. Doctors and nurses were needed and women were sought for ARP services, including driving ambulances and attendance at First Aid Posts.

In February, Scott & Son's sale (illus. right 3rd Feb.) coincided again with the Lynn Mart, which went ahead as usual and featured a number of animals: **'AT KING'S LYNN MART YOU MUST SEE THE 1939 SENSATION THE RACING CHEETAHS Who have caused a SENSATION at the LEADING LONDON DOG-TRACKS by beating the WORLD'S FASTEST GREYHOUNDS'.** Evidently there were eleven of these racing cheetahs, the most famous of which was called 'Pongo'. It seems that when he wasn't racing, Pongo was relatively docile. The newspaper printed a photograph of Pongo standing on a dining table at a smart London hotel, with guests still sitting down and the table laid for luncheon! Also at the Mart was 'Nero' the largest St Bernard in the world.

King's Lynn's new £40,000 post office was officially opened by the Assistant Postmaster General on Wednesday, 29th April, 1939 and there was a big gathering to watch the event. The mayor, Alderman Catleugh, bought the first stamps and many of the town's traders attended, being entertained to lunch at the Town Hall afterwards. Also opening, after an extensive refurbishment, was the Café Imperial in High Street. The timing of this, two months before the outbreak of war, could not have been more unfortunate and it seems very unlikely that the investment made to provide a new Café Lounge and Restaurant with seating for 150, was recouped for several years. The former owner was Mr. Charles Winlove Smith but it was now under the management of Mr. Victor Beesley, who was seeking to attract custom for morning coffee, luncheons, afternoon teas and dinners.

On 1st September, the headline in the Lynn News was:- **'HITLER'S REPLY AWAITED. Full Mobilisation of British Fleet. Evacuation of Children Begins Today. THE CRISIS IN WEST NORFOLK – All Ready to Receive Evacuees'.**

It was reported that local demand for blackout material had generally been satisfied. Lighting restrictions were in place but, in spite of this, there did not seem to have been any marked increase in road accidents. To help motorists see the way ahead, intermittent dividing white lines had been painted on the main roads, some pavements had been painted a light colour and shielded red lights had been erected at certain corners. Steps were being taken to protect the civic treasures, including the King John Cup.

Prime Minister Neville Chamberlain announced that war had been declared at 11.15 am on Sunday 3rd September and within a few days the impact on the town of the situation faced by the country was to become apparent. Householders in the town had offered to take 3,000 evacuees but places were needed for 5,500 and some compulsion seemed inevitable if Lynn was to meet its quota. By 8th September 1939 there were already 2,700 evacuees in the town. The first train had arrived on the Friday afternoon bringing children evacuated from London's East End. The town's air raid sirens were tested and those private residents who were able to completed the construction of air raid shelters in their gardens. Schoolchildren in Lynn were photographed digging 'shelter trenches' in the school grounds, reinforced with sand bags. On 6th October it was reported in the Lynn News that forty street air raid shelters, each capable of holding sixty people, were to be built immediately in Lynn. The cost of each shelter was £250. Fuel rationing at 75% of household use was introduced. The evacuation impacted on the local schools, with the Grammar School arranging part-time tuition for 300 boys from Hackney Downs secondary modern school.

On 20th October 1939 the newspaper gave details about the following day's enlistment arrangements. Men had to report to the local offices of the Ministry of Labour at prescribed times, arranged alphabetically by surname.

SCOTT & SON
(KING'S LYNN) LTD.
91-97 HIGH STREET, KING'S LYNN
ESTABLISHED 1874   PHONE 2495

Unfortunately this Catalogue had gone to Press some time before War was declared, and we find that in some instances prices have since been increased and some of the supplies may be difficult to obtain, but we hope that our customers will co-operate with us and treat this list as a general guide. We wish to assure them that these disparities are not through lack of sincerity on our part, but due to circumstances beyond our control.

Scott & Son's catalogue for 1939 was prepared prior to the outbreak of the war and contained an introduction explaining that some prices had already been increased (illus. left).

The impact of war upon the population became more and more severe as the Government introduced further measures to save on consumption of fuel, raw materials and food. In June 1940 the Ministry of Food published the arrangements for issuing new ration books. Traders in the town were having to respond to the new conditions. Lighting restrictions were difficult for them to comply with, however, and there were several instances of shopkeepers being prosecuted for breach of the regulations. At dusk Scott & Son closed their shop entrances, apart from their main door, so that they could limit the areas that were prone to let out light.

They reacted quickly to the needs of residents to black out their windows and to furnish their 'refuge rooms' with suitable materials and adaptable furniture. If the shelter rooms were to be used, they would need to accommodate the whole family. It was necessary, therefore, to have smaller items and ones that could have a dual use – for both day and night time occupation. Scott & Son responded to these requirements by offering folding chairs, adjustable bed-chairs, divan sets, couches, folding beds, and soft mattresses that could be rolled or folded up. Protection against blast damage included rolls of adhesive tape, adhesive curtain net, and a solution that could be painted onto glass, all designed to prevent the glass from shattering across the room (illus. below right 9th August, 1940).

Life in the town continued as normally as possible and in February 1940 the Lynn Advertiser celebrated its 100th anniversary with a special edition, in which the history of the newspaper was recalled. Their loyal advertisers were invited to place congratulatory messages in the newspaper and Scott & Son submitted the following:- **'Scott and Son, the Lynn House Furnishers, write: We should like to congratulate the Lynn Advertiser, our near neighbour in Purfleet-st., on the occasion of its Centenary. Lynn owes much of its position as a busy shopping centre to the power of your paper as a medium of advertising. The Lynn Advertiser has rendered us good service in this respect during the past 67 years. In wishing you 'Many happy Returns of the day' we hope for a continuance of the pleasant business relations which have for so long existed between us'.**

As the days became shorter and the nights became colder, there was a need to draught proof rooms at home and to make them as comfortable as possible, with fuel now being restricted in supply. Scott & Son continued advertising furniture, blankets and black-out materials that were suitable for these circumstances. On 6th September 1940 they placed an advertisement in the Lynn News that listed materials suitable for creating **'a perfect black-out'** (below left).

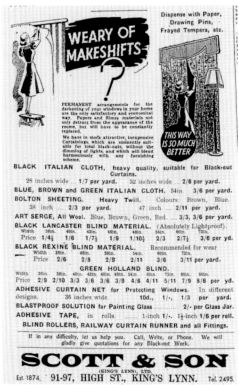

These materials had to be really thick and they came in black, brown, blue and green Italian cloth. Blind materials that were completely light proof were available, too. In addition to these and to the anti-blast protection materials previously supplied, they were now advertising **'Resistaflame'** fire retardant paint. This could be brushed or sprayed on and was claimed to minimise fire danger and to resist damp and decay. Also on offer were **'Perma-led'** strips that could be glued to the glass and which would reinforce it to give some blast protection. The idea was to create the patterning of authentic leaded lights.

There was nothing normal about trading during the war years and Christmas time was the most difficult period. By October of 1940, Scott & Son had received all the toys, games, books and dolls that they expected to come in for their Christmas sales. They urged their customers to come and buy their presents early, to avoid disappointment,

128

because they did not expect to receive any later orders. They were also keen to point out that they were not selling any imported toys, advertising:- 'TOYS OF ALL KINDS – ALL BRITISH'.

As they had done during and after the Great War, Scott & Son included an appeal in their advertisements at the beginning of November for people to give generously for their poppies. Also in November, they placed a series of Christmas toy advertisements in the Lynn News and the Lynn Advertiser. The traditional toys were still the mainstay of their stock but boys had a slightly wider variety to choose from. 'Minic' wind-up cars, lorries and a steam roller were the star attractions, with prices ranging from 1/3 to 6/-. Some came with battery-powered electric lights.

Towards the end of 1940, Scott & Son took the decision to reduce the size of their advertisements in the local newspapers. It may be that the publishers were having to cut down on the amount of newsprint they used as it became scarcer. In their smaller advertisement placed in the Lynn News on 27th November, Scott & Son thanked their customers for their co-operation and understanding throughout the past year, saying, 'we have maintained our stocks, moderate prices and deliveries as well as restrictions have allowed'.

Maurice Scott had been called up and was stationed with the Army Pay Corps at Chester. Other staff of Scott & Son were also serving in the armed forces. Fortunately, there was a core of experienced staff who were not eligible for call up, including veterans of the Great War, and they were able to recruit extra female assistants, so the shop was able to function as near to normally as was possible. William Scott was left to keep the business going and had joined the Special Constabulary. On 14th January 1941 the Lynn News ran the headline 'SPECIALS ON PARADE'. The members of the Lynn Special Constabulary had paraded at the Tuesday Market Place on the previous Sunday. They were inspected and complimented by the mayor, Ald. J. H. Catleugh, and then marched to St. Margaret's Church where they attended the morning service.

In the wartime photograph (above) of the Special Constables, taken on the Saturday Market Place in front of the Town Hall, William Scott is standing on the far right in the back row.

In the same edition of the newspaper, there was further news about the possible widening of Purfleet Street: 'PURFLEET– st. The purchase of 29, Purfleet-st (formerly occupied by Regester's bakers shop) by the Corporation for £700, has brought the widening scheme another step nearer completion'.

The Lynn News of 28th January 1941 asked whether a Savings Group could be established in every street in town. An appeal was launched for residents and traders to take the initiative in setting up these war savings groups. The arrangements involved having a group secretary who would call on the members of his or her group each week to sell them the Savings Stamps to put into their own books. The secretary then took the money round to the Post Office or the Trustee Savings Bank and bought some more stamps.

February 2nd to the 8th 1941 was designated 'WAR WEAPONS WEEK' and Field Marshal Sir William Edmund Ironside came to Lynn to inaugurate the Borough's campaign. Scott & Son placed a War Weapons Week appeal in their advertisements that week (illus. right).

The townspeople responded admirably to this appeal and the target of £100,000 was reached within the first two days of the launch. By the Saturday evening, the total raised by the people of Lynn and district during War Weapons Week had risen to £240,000.

On 19th August 1941 the Lynn News reported that the Greenland Fishery Museum had been damaged by a bomb. On the whole, however, reports of air raids were short of detail, presumably to ensure that the enemy did not benefit from information that might indicate to them how successful a raid had been. Also, there was a public morale issue and the press concealed information that could cause people to fear that the enemy were gaining the upper hand or that could lead to some degree of panic. This led to some rather bizarre reports of air raids on 'a village in East Anglia' or 'a street in town'. Doubtless the townspeople knew exactly where these raids had occurred and what damage had resulted.

In the same edition of the Lynn News, there was a report of King's Lynn's streets being used for the location shots for a new film. Nelson Street was one of the locations used for scenes in the film 'One of Our Aircraft is Missing'. The street had been chosen to represent the Dutch setting of the film. The stars were Googie Withers, Ralph Richardson, Eric Portman, Bernard Miles, Hugh Williams, Hugh Burdon and John Justin. During the filming, a swastika flag flew over the house of the Borough's Medical Officer of Health, Dr. J. W. McIntosh.

All the local traders urged their customers to shop early, taking advantage of the daylight hours. Scott & Son carried an appeal in several of their advertisements (illus. left from the Lynn News, 30th September 1941).

The third week in November 1941, was designated 'DIG FOR VICTORY WEEK' and Scott & Son advertised garden implements for sale suitable for the task: 'DIG FOR VICTORY WEEK FORKS from 6/11, SPADES from 5/11, WHEEL BARROWS, with wood wheel – 19/11, WHEEL BARROWS, with rubber tyre – 27/11'.

At the end of a difficult year for everybody, the uncertainty of what lay ahead was reflected in Scott & Son's Christmas message: 'SCOTT & SON SEND GREETINGS TO ALL AND WISH THEIR MANY CUSTOMERS AS HAPPY A CHRISTMAS AS POSSIBLE WITH THE HOPE OF BETTER TIMES IN 1942'.

The second week of February 1942 was designated for another savings appeal, this time it was 'WARSHIP WEEK' (illus. right).

One of the problems of running the shop with a depleted complement of staff was the provision of cover over the lunchtime period. On 3rd March 1942 Scott & Son announced in the Lynn News that they would be closing the shop for lunch between 12.45pm and 2.00pm every day, except for Tuesday. Their advertisements continued to concentrate on materials and furniture that would be useful for black-out and shelter purposes and for protection against bomb blasts. On 17th March, 1942, they advertised 'light-proof' materials for the black-out. 'Sizalkraft reinforced paper' was said to have several uses, being water and tear-proof it made a 'perfect black-out material'. Other practical

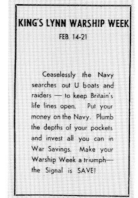

materials and equipment being offered were strong stirrup pumps, roofing felt. **'Sankeys famous flower pots'**, watering cans, spades, forks and wheelbarrows.

In March 1942, coal, gas and electricity rationing was introduced. Like every other trader, Scott & Son had to curtail their use of vehicles, save electricity and comply with the blackout requirements. They took some of their vehicles off the road and closed some of their workshops as twilight approached. Twelve-volt accumulators were taken up into the attic at the shop and wired up to provide dim lighting. What work that could be done under such restricted lighting was transferred to this floor, where the small windows made it much easier to create an effective blackout. Scotts were well placed, of course, to make up their own heavy curtains, which they did by using thick, blue cloth doubled up to prevent any light from penetrating through.

The Government issued orders to restrict the movement of delivery vehicles to reduce the continued use of petrol, and vehicle pools were arranged by the local Chambers of Trade. Jermyn & Sons and Scott & Son combined to provide pooled transport for furniture and larger goods, including those of other traders in the town. Announcements of the arrangements were made by the two companies in notices placed in the Lynn News on 14th April 1942 (illus. right).

Other restrictions over deliveries were announced in a notice from the Lynn Chamber of Trade in the Lynn News on 28th April 1942. At the request of Government Departments, they introduced a scheme to cut down on deliveries of goods, divided into three categories: groceries and greengroceries were not to be delivered by motor vehicles at all – traders could use bicycles or other means of making deliveries; drapery, furnishings and allied trades, for which the pooled deliveries of Jermyns and Scotts was to operate; and butcher's meat and fish, which could be delivered by motor if their customers lived more than a mile from their normal shop. The restrictions did not apply to the delivery of bread, milk and newspapers. Customers were urged to collect their food from their usual shops, on the days that they would previously have been delivered.

The very circumspect reporting of air raid details was much evident in the Lynn News of 16th June 1942. The report was of a raid on an unspecified hotel the previous Friday evening, the 12th June. This was the Eagle Hotel in Norfolk Street which suffered a direct hit, resulting in 42 deaths. In August, there was another savings initiative; **'TEN TANKS WEEK'**, and Scott & Son included an appeal in their advertisement in the Lynn News on 4th August (illus. left).

Ralph Richardson and Googie Withers were back in Lynn for the shooting of another film, again set in Holland, 'The Silver Fleet' and this was reported in the Lynn News on 8th September 1942. A photograph showed a scene from the film being shot in the Saturday Market Place, with the Lynn Guildhall being used to portray the German naval H.Q. in a Dutch town.

'The Silver Fleet' came to town in the second week of April 1943 and was shown at the Theatre Royal. Doubtless many residents of Lynn came to see whether they could spot themselves or their friends in any of the scenes. There were several Lynn locations for people to identify, too.

Railings and ironwork throughout the town, as elsewhere in the country, were cut down for scrap to aid the war effort. Not much was spared, including the redundant bridge which stood alongside the arched concrete Cut Bridge. The concrete piers stood alongside the road bridge for many years afterwards, as a stark reminder of the old bridge.

By April 1943 Scott & Son's advertisements had become much reduced in size and did not contain any illustrations. However, they were still prepared to include wartime appeals and on 6th April, they included an appeal in support of 'WINGS for VICTORY WEEK' in the town (illus. right).

In June 1943 there was an event to help lift the spirits of the staff at Scott & Son, when one of their colleagues was married. On 9th June Florence Finbow married Theodore Dawes at East Winch church. Their reception was held at the home of Mr. and Mrs. H. Burfield and they honeymooned at Bury St. Edmund's. Miss Finbow had commenced working at Scott & Son in about 1915 and was the manageress of the china department. She and her husband received gifts from all the departments at the shop. She came back to work at Scott & Son after her marriage and became one of their longest serving members of staff.

In September 1944 the Lynn News and the Lynn Advertiser combined to form the Lynn News & Advertiser. The newspapers had already reduced their size, to cut down on the use of paper, and Scott & Son's advertisements were one quarter the size of their previous ones. They were now advertising 'Utility Furniture' made largely from laminated timber and using much smaller-sized materials to save on wood.

At long last the war came to an end and the people of Lynn were ready to celebrate. The Lynn News & Advertiser published a VE Day special on 8th May 1945. Shops were mainly closed through two days of holiday. Flags, bunting, banners and streamers decked houses and shops throughout the town. Outside Dr. J. H. Humphris' house in King Street, a celebration bonfire was lit in the middle of the street and people kept it burning with a wide variety of articles which had association with the deprivations and anxieties of wartime, including blackout materials.

As a climax to the celebrations, a service of thanksgiving was held in the Tuesday Market Place on Sunday and there was a big parade. The mayor took the salute as the Army, WAAF, and USAAF contingents marched past, together with Land Army girls, Home Guards, Civil Defence workers, West Norfolk & Lynn Nursing Corps, the St. John's Ambulance Brigade and associated organisations. St. Margaret's Church and St. Nicholas' Chapel were filled for the services and there was a joint service of all the local churches conducted from the steps of the Corn Exchange.

Although the war had ended, there were still severe restrictions on the supply of food and other goods, and Scott & Son continued to place small advertisements for items that would be useful in times of austerity. These included cold frames, fruit netting, potato baskets, tomato stakes, wheelbarrows and cloches. Utility Furniture was all that was available and customers were advised that **'if you bring your dockets we can supply blankets, sheets, mattresses, floor covering and curtain material'**.

On Friday 6th July 1945 the Lynn News & Advertiser reported that polling had taken place in the General Election on the day before. Standing in the Lynn Division were Donald McCullough (Nat. Cons.), Maj. Fred Wise (Lab.), Mr. A. P. D. Penrose (Lib.), and Comdr. G. T. Bowles (Liberty). The voters of Lynn reflected the mood elsewhere in the country and Fred Wise won the seat for Labour for the first time. Two other Norfolk constituencies, previously held by Conservatives, also went to Labour candidates.

There was a farewell gathering of the Hackney Downs school staff who were leaving after six years at Lynn, attended by the mayor, Mr. O. R. Jermyn.

In August the townspeople celebrated VJ Day even more enthusiastically than they had VE Day the previous month, because the war really was over. The Lynn News & Advertiser carried reports from Lynn, Downham and elsewhere in west Norfolk. There were two days of holiday and free dances were held at the Lynn Corn Hall on both days. There was such a rush to use the telephone for trunk calls that priority had to be given to business calls. The main cause for the over-demand was the number of U.S. servicemen in the town celebrating and wanting to ring home. Queues formed for the Hunstanton bus as people flocked to the seaside to celebrate. The crowds were very good natured and there was no drunkenness – beer and spirits were still in acutely short supply. There were long queues for the cinema, with the greatest draw being Deanna Durbin in 'Can't Help Singing'. Further queues formed for restaurants. The mayor lit a huge bonfire on the recreation ground by the Walks. However, a party of revellers decided that he should have stayed up for the all night celebrations and tried to wake him by shouting and singing outside his house at 4.00am in the morning, to the accompaniment of clashing dustbin lids. They failed to wake him!

With the war over, everybody could relax. Those who had served in the forces were de-mobbed and the volunteer services were disbanded. Amongst those celebrating locally were the Special Constables who were invited to join the Borough Police and the War Reserves to a special dinner at the Grosvenor Hotel, Norfolk Street on Friday 26th October, where they were served sausage and mash at 3/6 per head.

CHAPTER FIVE
Post War Revival and the Swinging Sixties
Scott & Son: 1946 – 1971

5. POST WAR REVIVAL and the SWINGING SIXTIES:
SCOTT & SON 1946 - 1971

One of the signs that west Norfolk life was getting back to normal after the upheaval of the war years was the return of the Royal Family to Sandringham. Queen Mary was the first to arrive, in December 1945 and she soon resumed her occasional shopping visits to King's Lynn. Scott & Son was one of the shops that she sometimes visited and customers and other shoppers would quickly become aware of her presence in the High Street. On 1st January 1946 the Lynn News & Advertiser reported that crowds had flocked to see the King and Queen, the two Princesses, Elizabeth and Margaret, Queen Mary and the Duke of Kent, when they attended church at Sandringham the previous Sunday.

Keen to inject an element of competition into the sale of Utility Furniture, which was controlled at both the manufacturing and purchasing ends of the chain, Scott & Son placed advertisements emphasising that there was a difference between the quality of items supplied by the major manufacturers. They also stressed the personal service that they offered:- '**UTILITY FURNITURE is Standard in design wherever you go. But even in standard designs there are varying degrees of quality. SCOTT'S can assure you that there is a difference and that we only stock Utility Furniture which has been made by the BEST makers. Into every piece goes good quality woods, upholstery and careful finish. SCOTT'S offer quick delivery, helpful service and best attention'.**

The availability of some Utility Furniture from stock was Scotts' strongest selling point. They invited customers to bring their buying units and priority dockets to their shop for immediate delivery (illus. right from the Lynn News & Advertiser 28th June 1946).

The unavailability of materials to manufacture everyday items had caused huge problems to traders throughout the town, who struggled to keep their businesses going. 'Make do and mend' was the byword for survival in the home and this applied just as much to the High Street traders. Many of the larger factories in the country had closed down completely, whilst others had turned solely to supplying War Ministry contracts. Retailers such as Scott & Son had to turn to other, very much smaller, manufacturers and suppliers. They sold whatever they could get their hands on. After the war was over, it was several months before some of the larger furniture manufacturers were able to offer new contracts to Scott & Son. Once again, they felt obliged to explain the situation to their customers and included the following statement in their advertisement placed in the Lynn News & Advertiser on 2nd July 1946: '**Buying furniture to-day is a lot different than it used to be. Now buyers, after obtaining permits, are demanding above all else, definite assurance that their Utility Furniture is of the highest enduring quality, made of good woods, and is honest value for money. These are the features that SCOTT'S have been best known – and best liked for – in the years gone by. And this range of Utility Furniture is the very best in material, workmanship and advanced 1946 designs. Prompt delivery made of many items in Bedroom Suites, Bedsteads, Wardrobes, Dressing-chests, Dining Room Suites, Kitchen Cabinets, Tables and Chairs. Also, a fine range of Glassware, Hardware, China and Earthenware'.**

The recovery from the traumas of the war years was hardly helped by the severest winter weather in living memory. Two short spells of cold weather, in December 1946 and early January 1947, were followed by the big freeze that lasted from 21st January to 16th March. It was the coldest February on record. To make matters worse, the thaw brought disastrous flooding to Fenland, leading to food shortages.

The Custom House had suffered some damage from a wartime accident and this was to be repaired. During the war, the wire cable of a barrage balloon, attached to a ship that was moored in Lynn Harbour, apparently got tangled around the golden ball and weather vane on the top of the building and carried them away. These were replaced in April 1947.

Although the war was over, the country still faced severe deprivations, occasioned mostly by the National Debt. The Government took measures that were to impact directly on everyone in the country.

One such measure was to cut imports of paper, coming mostly from Canada and Newfoundland, to save on the dollar deficit. This affected the Lynn News & Advertiser, which had to reduce its size and circulation once again. Scott & Son's advertisements, like those of other traders, were cut down in size. The tea ration was also being reduced. These measures were announced in the Lynn News & Advertiser on 25th July 1947.

In August 1947 Scott & Son advertised some 'New and Better Occasional Furniture – NO UNITS REQUIRED'. They were keen to attract customers to exchange their Utility Furniture units as soon as there was a new issue. The advertisement, right, was in the Lynn News & Advertiser on 29th August, 1947, and the one below on 29th April that year.

National energy consumption was running at a level that was creating a supply crisis that reached a head in September 1947. It was announced that Lynn Town's Electricity Committee was meeting with the representatives of nineteen local firms. These firms employed over 1,700 workers between them and the aim of the meetings was to reduce energy consumption by one third compared, with December 1946. There was talk of reducing and staggering working hours. After two meetings of the Electricity Committee with the local firms, a plan was formulated to reduce consumption to comply with the Central Electricity Board's general electricity economies which were about to be introduced. Some firms were even bringing back into use vintage steam engines which had long been idle. Others were shutting down one day each week. The firms involved included the Lynn Docks Company, Messrs. Patrick & Thompson, Lincolnshire Canners Ltd., and Messrs. Savages Ltd. Domestic users in Lynn were warned that they faced a one day per week cut if they did not save. The town was divided into five zones for potential rotation of cuts on specified days of the week. Salvage became a controversial topic once again and local councils were criticised in the press for doing nothing to encourage recycling. To

make matters worse, there was a serious drought that had badly affected farmers. Only one inch of rain had fallen between July and the end of October and unemployment in agricultural-related industries was escalating.

At the end of November 1947 the basic petrol ration was withdrawn, causing considerable problems to most people apart, it seems, from farmers. The Lynn News & Advertiser reported on 5th December that there were as many cars as ever in the town on market day, because every farmer had received a priority allowance. Other essential services were less well served, including some teachers who reported that they could not get to school. Local councillors were outraged that they had not received their allowance and were prevented from attending meetings. More bizarrely, perhaps, the Hunstanton Golf Club complained that their members could not obtain petrol coupons and that the club's takings had been affected.

The local newspaper reported that many old folk were receiving barely enough food to survive and that the situation in rural communities in west Norfolk was a disgrace. An example of the meagre rations that some old people were receiving was given in the Lynn News & Advertiser on 13th January 1948:-

'BREAKFAST: dry toast and tea. DINNER: toast with a little margarine. EVENING MEAL: parsnips and Brussels sprouts sprinkled with a little gravy saved from last week's joint'.

In spite of all the deprivations and restrictions, including the energy crisis, the consumer market was beginning to see the introduction of labour-saving domestic appliances, such as electric washing machines. Scott & Son began putting on demonstrations in their shop of the new 'SERVIS' electric washer and wringer:- 'A DEMONSTRATION OF THE "SERVIS" Electric Washer and Wringer Will be held in our showroom each day from Monday, January 26th to Friday, January 30th at 10.45am and 2.45pm (WEDNESDAY AFTERNOON EXCEPTED) WE WELCOME ALL WHO ARE INTERESTED'.

There was a growing desire by the people of Lynn to have something positive to latch onto – anything that would help them to break out of the austerity straitjacket that still constrained them in their everyday life. This was to be provided by an initiative of the Lynn Civic Society and the Chamber of Trade working with others to promote the first ever Lynn Civic Week in June 1948. Opened on Sunday 20th June, the aim was to revive interest and pride in the many treasures of the town and the accomplishments of its inhabitants in the spheres of industry, commerce, art, handicrafts, drama, music and sport. The events and activities contained something to interest almost everyone.

The week started with special civic services, with the mayor and civic dignitaries attending morning service at St. Margaret's Church. There were art and photographic exhibitions and a programme of 'Open Premises', allowing people to look round places that were not usually open to the public. These latter included industrial and commercial business premises, such as C. G. Barrett & Co.'s laundry at Gaywood.

At an open-air theatre near the Red Mount Chapel, local amateur groups joined together to present a special production of 'Songs from the Shows', which proved to be a very popular entertainment. Town centre shops took part in a shop window display competition. To help with sponsorship and to overcome the continuing newspaper advertising restrictions, Scott & Son and other traders provided promotional space (illus. above).

The power crisis continued throughout 1948 and on 15th October the Lynn News & Advertiser published a district-wide plan of potential weekday power cuts on a day-by-day basis, issued by the Eastern Electricity Board.

Scott & Son continued to restrict their advertising and their only promotions through the latter half of 1948 were for Utility Furniture and ideas for Christmas presents for children. These included **TRIANG** Pedal Tricycles, **TRIANG** 'MINIC' wind-up toys and the **TRIANG 'MINIC'** Pedal Car.

In February 1949 a start was made on relaxing the rationing system on groceries and tinned peas and beans were taken off points.

Scott & Son started demonstrating pressure cookers at their shop, commencing on 14th February with hourly demonstrations of the 'Tempo' cooker (illustrated on the next page). The savings in cooking time that pressure cookers promised, with potatoes in 6–8 minutes and a stew in 15 minutes, were especially relevant at this time of power shortages, and sales were strong right from the launch.

In spite of parking restrictions, there were regular traffic jams in King's Lynn's narrow shopping streets. There had been discussion from time to time about the potential relief that might ensue from the introduction of a one-way scheme. On 22nd April 1949 the Lynn News & Advertiser published information about an experimental one-way system that was to be introduced for one week only. Police Superintendent Fred Calvert emphasised the fact that this was to be an experiment only and would be withdrawn at the end of the week. Starting in Norfolk Street, at its junction with Broad Street, traffic would proceed west towards High Street where it would turn left. On reaching the Purfleet Street junction it would be one way from there towards the Custom House on King Street. Although this inconvenienced the movement of Scott & Son's delivery vans on their journeys between the South Quay and Purfleet Street, there was no arguing against the need for some measures to ease the traffic flow through these narrow streets.

On 7th June 1949 Scott & Son's advertisement appeared to indicate that the restricted design limitations of utility furniture had been lifted. They were offering 'Freedom of Design' through a range of walnut and oak bedroom suites, dining-room suites and three-piece suites. Scott & Son's advertisements had been gradually increasing in size and were soon to take up more than double the space that they occupied during the latter years of the war.

The Tempo Company was not the only one to promote pressure cooking and another of the well-known brands that Scott & Son stocked was Prestige. Their new cooker was being demonstrated at Scott's shop in July 1950 (illus. right).

In November 1949 a Lynn Festival Council was formed to plan a music and arts festival for June the following year. The originator of the idea was Lady Fermoy, who was well known in Lynn for her own accomplishments as a pianist and accompanist, having performed many times in the town. At the previous year's Civic Week, she had accompanied the world renowned viola player, Lionel Tertis. Lady Fermoy announced

that the Queen had agreed to be patron of the Festival, which was also planned to include the formal opening of the newly restored St. George's Hall in King Street. She said that it was her hope that the festival would not merely be something around which the opening of the refurbished hall could be celebrated but that it would become the first of an annual arts and music festival in the town. "This will be our try-out", she said.

Five years after the war and with an end to the 1940s, there was a mood amongst the young people of the town to really let their hair down, to celebrate the New Year and to welcome in the new era of the '50s. So determined were they to celebrate in style that 200 people gate-crashed the New Year dance at the Corn Exchange, swelling the numbers to around one thousand – well over the limit for the hall of 850. The added attraction was Vic Lewis and his dance orchestra, who were mobbed by the throng of enthusiastic fans. Every venue and pub in town was packed out. According to the report on the New Year's celebrations in the Lynn News & Advertiser on

Tuesday 3rd January, '...by midnight, orderly merriment was the rule when everyone joined hands to sing Auld Lang Syne. Round at the Town Hall, smiling, pretty little Miss 1950 – twelve-year-old Christine Walton – joined the two hundred dancers at the Dr. Barnado's Homes Ball as they sang the same song as 1949 went out'. The New Year sales were also popular and drew greater crowds than ever before. The queue outside the Belfast Linen Warehouse at 88, High Street started at 6.30am and extended past the front of Scott & Son's shop and right around the corner into Purfleet Street.

Further signs that things were getting back to normal, so far as trading in the town centre was concerned, included the return of Burton's full page advertisements, which had ceased during the war, of course, and the first new large-scale building redevelopment in Lynn. This latter was a new shop and works for the printing and stationery firm of Watts & Rowe, on a site between the Rummer Hotel and the Methodist Schoolroom in Tower Street. The redevelopment was necessitated by the compulsory purchase of their premises at the junction of St. James Street and St. James Road for the new £75,000 police station.

The first King's Lynn Festival was now being planned as the town's part of the Festival of Britain celebrations in 1951 and the draft programme was agreed by the Lynn Festival Committee at the beginning of May 1950.

The end of the points rationing system for groceries on Saturday 20th May 1950 caused the Lynn News & Advertiser's reporter to reflect upon the irony of the situation that, instead of customers queuing at the retailers, it was the shopkeepers who had to queue at the

3.00pm – Arrives via Wootton Road, Lynn Road, Gaywood Road, Littleport Street, Norfolk Street, High Street, Tuesday Market Place to Guildhall of St. George.
3.25pm – Arrives at Guildhall. Inspection of Naval Guard of Honour.
3.30pm – Enters Guildhall for opening ceremony.
4.35pm – Her Majesty leaves Guildhall of St. George for the Town hall for tea.
5.05pm – her Majesty received at St. Margaret's Church, west door.
6.15pm – The Queen leaves St. Margaret's Church and returns to Sandringham via St. James Road, Railway Road, Norfolk Street, Littleport Street, Gaywood Road and Wootton Road.

suppliers. In order to secure sufficient stocks to serve the demands of their customers, the shopkeepers were obliged to queue early at the wholesale depots. At the end of that month, petrol rationing ended, too.

Tuesday 24th July 1951 was a landmark date in the cultural life of King's Lynn. 'Lynn is Ready for Great Festival. Popular Interest in Queen's Visit to Open Ancient Hall', ran the headline in the Lynn News & Advertiser on Friday 20th July. Buildings had been spruced up and freshly painted and flags had been put out on shops and houses in the town, especially along the route that the Queen was going to take when she arrived. The first King's Lynn Festival, under the auspices of St. George's Guildhall Ltd., in association with the Arts Council, was held at various venues throughout the town, but centred on the Guildhall itself. The refurbished building was to be opened by the Queen to mark the start of the Festival. The newspaper printed her planned programme, from arrival on the outskirts of the town to her departure (above right).

Scott & Son marked the start of the festival in their advertisement in the Lynn News & Advertiser on 24th July (illus. left).

There was a veritable galaxy of stars appearing throughout the festival week, including:- Peter Ustinov; Kathleen Ferrier; Sir Osbert Sitwell; the London Symphony Orchestra, conducted by Josef Krips; the Boyd Neel Orchestra; Peter Pears; and Benjamin Britten. There were throngs of people lining the streets to see the Queen's arrival and departure and the whole week was a great success.

The build-up to the General Election in October 1951 involved some lively political rallies in Lynn. Amongst the main party meetings was that of the Labour party, attended by the Prime Minister, Clement Attlee. Although every meeting had its fair share of hecklers, by far the liveliest was that of the Tories at the Corn Exchange on Friday 19th October, when 700 people attended. Many were standing to barrack former MP, Mr. Richard Low, who was supporting the local Lynn Division candidate, Comdr. R. Scott-Miller. In spite of the apparent hostility towards the Tories, both Scott-Miller and Mr. D. G. Bullard, for South-west Norfolk Division, regained seats for the Conservatives.

'King George Dies at His Sandringham Home: Peacefully in His Sleep. Deep Sense of Loss in West Norfolk', read the headline in the Lynn News & Advertiser on Friday 8th February 1952. The Royal Proclamation of the accession to the throne of Queen Elizabeth II was to be read from the steps of the Town Hall at 11.00am that day by the mayor, Mr. F. Basil Humphrey. The King had died on Wednesday 6th February and his coffin was borne on a gun carriage from Sandringham Church to the station at Wolferton on Monday 11th. Thousands of local people lined the route to pay their respects to the Norfolk-born King. A memorial service at St. Margaret's Church was conducted by the vicar, Canon R. L. Whytehead. In his address, he referred to the late King's love of Norfolk "... where he always felt at home. The county was one of the few places where he could utterly relax from the inescapable bindings of kingship", he said.

Many hundreds of people gathered outside the Town Hall to hear the proclamation read by the mayor. The big bell of St. Margaret's tower sounded out the hour of eleven and bugles rang out to herald the proclamation. A flag, until then at half-mast, was hoisted by a Sea Cadet to fly from the top of the mast, high above the heads of the crowd outside in the Saturday Market Place. "Long Live the Queen!" shouted the crowd. On Friday 15th February a last, silent tribute was paid to the late King. At 2.00pm a two-minute silence was held and people in their homes, places of work, schools and in the towns and villages joined in.

After a number of experimental schemes had been tried with varying degrees of success, Supt. Fred Calvert unveiled his master plan for controlling traffic in the centre of the town, which was published in the Lynn News & Advertiser on 19th February 1952. His proposed one-way system turned out to be the opposite of that which was ultimately adopted. His plan was for traffic to turn right towards the Tuesday Market Place from Norfolk Street into High Street junction. Purfleet Street was to be one way, with traffic travelling eastwards away from the Custom House towards New Conduit Street. Traffic at that junction was to be controlled by a policeman between the hours of 8.30am and 6.00pm every weekday, who was to be stationed in a 'Police Point' - a raised box in the centre of the road. The scheme was met with a large degree of scepticism but was put in place for an experimental period. By 28th March the local newspaper was already reporting that the Council had resolved not to prolong the traffic experiment that had started at the beginning of the month. Supt. Calvert considered that the experiment should be continued but appears to have been very much in the minority in holding this view. The traders of Lynn issued a very restrained comment in which they concluded the traffic experiment was '...not a success'. They went on to say that the general view was that the previous scheme had been working well and should have been continued and extended, rather than to introduce a new one with the reversal of the flow in some streets.

The second King's Lynn Festival opened on Saturday 19th July 1952 and the town was again honoured by the presence of the Festival's patron, HM Queen Elizabeth, the Queen Mother.

On the 23rd of the month, a new building was opened – The Woolpack on the Tuesday Market Place, designed by Lynn architect, Harold Marsh.

In November, the fourth traffic plan in three years was proposed. This one concentrated on extending the parking restrictions in and around High Street and Norfolk Street.

On Tuesday 16th December the western end of Purfleet Street was flooded, but it did not extend as far as Scott & Son's premises. The firm was not so fortunate when, two months later, the east coast floods hit the town. Fifteen people were drowned in Lynn during the floods and there was extensive damage. Scott & Son's works on the South Quay were seriously flooded, as were their warehouse and premises in Purfleet Street. Some goods were not recoverable, including a large consignment of toilet paper that had just been received. However, some flood-damaged goods were salvaged and offered for sale (illus. below right).

There was much sadness throughout the town when Queen Mary died on 10th March, 1953. On one of her Christmas shopping trips to Lynn she visited Scott & Son and asked where the toy department was. Upon being told that it was on the first floor, she expressed surprise and said that it should be downstairs at the front, where everybody could see it. Whether it was due to her comments or not, the toy department was later moved to the ground floor, at the front of the shop.

A special Coronation souvenir was enclosed with the Lynn News & Advertiser on Friday 22nd May 1953, which included an advertisement for Scott & Son linking the Coronation with the founding of the firm (illus. below left).

Established during the reign of
Queen Victoria
in the year
1874

Almost 80 years ago, Thomas William Scott opened a little shop in King's Lynn, and later, in partnership with his son, the business was moved to its present site. With hard work, together with a high standard of service to the public, it prospered.

This year, 1953, sees the Coronation of our Queen Elizabeth II, and the seventy-ninth anniversary of this family business, the thriving, vital result of enterprise and industry.

The old tradition of personal service will be maintained; young people of today may be assured of the satisfaction their forefathers enjoyed.

SCOTT & SON
COMPLETE HOUSE FURNISHERS
91-97, High Street, KING'S LYNN   Telephone 2495

'Brilliant Lynn Coronation Carnival Defies Weather, Rewards all Concerned', was the headline in The Lynn News & Advertiser on Friday, 5th June. The paper reported that thousands had crowded the route to see the spectacular half-mile procession in spite of the atrocious weather – it was cold, wet and blustery. A dozen floats had to be withdrawn because the heavy downpour during the day had ruined their displays. Nevertheless, people put up with it, determined to celebrate and to enjoy the event. The streets were deserted until the crowds began gathering just an hour before the parade was due to start at 6.30pm. Most fortunately, the heavy rain held off for the two hours that it took for the parade to pass all the way along the route – Tuesday Market Place / High Street / St. James Street / London Road / Windsor Road / Guanock Terrace / London Road / St. James Road / Railway Road / Norfolk Street and back to the Tuesday Market Place. The procession took fifteen minutes to pass any one point. At its head was the kilted Clan-na-Gael Drum and Pipe band from Peterborough. Behind them were brilliantly-costumed horse riders, the tableaux, decorated vehicles, trade floats, comic entries and men, women and children in fancy dress. At regular intervals behind the pipe band came marching the Lynn Town Band, the Band of the Lynn Sea Cadet Corps and the RAF Band from Marham. Evidently the weather was so cold that 'Lady Godiva' wore a cardigan! The scantily-clad 'Hawaiians' caused much merriment by singing 'Stormy Weather' as their float travelled through the streets. Part of the parade is seen in the photograph on the following page passing Scott Son's shop, which was decked with flags and red, white and blue swags looped below the fascia.

September 26th to October 10th 1953 was 'Carpet Fortnight, promoted by the carpet manufacturers'. This was a time when fitted carpets were the exception, rather than the rule, and they were being heavily promoted by all the carpet retailers in Lynn, including Scott & Son.

Competition for the furniture trade in the town increased with the opening of Charles Hall Ltd., in Norfolk Street on 2nd October 1953. They had branches in Cambridge and elsewhere in the country and offered 'No Deposit Terms' and '24 Months to Pay'. Their motto was 'The National Furnishers with a Personal Touch'. Also advertising in the Lynn News & Advertiser at this time was

H. W. Peak Ltd., House Furnishers, of Saturday Market Place and St. James Street, and Brown's Furniture shop of 119, High Street, who had branches at Yarmouth and Lowestoft.

There were further reports in the Lynn News & Advertiser on 16th October 1953 of Lynn Chamber of Trade's response to the latest traffic control measures that had been proposed for the town centre. These involved the extension of no waiting restrictions along New Conduit Street. The traders' response was summed up by a 'Traders Lamentation', reflecting their view that the council's preoccupation was the free flow of traffic, never mind the consequences upon the trade of the town.

The three houses in Purfleet Street bought by the council for street widening were demolished in February 1954. Photographs appeared in the Lynn News & Advertiser on 16th February and 12th March, the first showing the demolition under way and the second the unobstructed view of the Custom House after the houses had been cleared away.

Her Majesty Queen Elizabeth the Queen Mother was granted the Freedom of the Borough at a ceremony in the town on Monday 26th March 1954. She arrived by car via St. James Street, Church Street, and Priory Lane, and was greeted at the west door of St. Margaret's Church by the Duke of Gloucester. The Saturday Market Place was closed to traffic from 9.30am to 2.30pm, along with Queen Street and Purfleet Street. Essential traffic, which included Scott & Son's delivery vans, was allowed to pass to and from the South Quay.

By the beginning of the 1950s, major investment was being committed towards construction and repairs to Lynn's infrastructure. The Lynn Conservancy Board began a £100,000 reconstruction of the South Quay in 1953 and this was completed by the spring of the following year. This was amongst the first and largest post-war civil engineering project to have been completed in the town and the formal opening on Monday, 26th April, 1954 was a significant event, with over 300 people gathering on the quay. The opening ceremony was conducted by the Mayor of Lynn, Lord Wise. He had boarded a motor launch at Purfleet Quay and had then been taken for a cruise up and down the river before coming alongside the South Quay. The ceremony took place a few yards from Scott & Son's works, which form the backdrop to the photograph of the mayor making his speech (illus. above right), which appeared in the Lynn News & Advertiser on 30th April.

During 1954, Scott & Son were giving demonstrations of the new 'Goblin' washing machine. These single-tub washers had hand wringers and were priced at £33/15/9, inclusive of purchase tax. They also began to take greater advertising space in the Lynn News & Advertiser and would devote half a page to their sales promotions (illustrated on the following page from 3rd June 1954).

In the run-up to Christmas 1954 the Lynn News & Advertiser ran a special advertising feature, which included detailed descriptions of the goods and services offered by some of the main traders in the town. Scott & Son took a column in this feature on 3rd December. This promotional text, which is transcribed in full below, is interesting from two viewpoints. Firstly, it is descriptive of the goods and services provided by the firm and, secondly, it conveys some of the expectations and prejudices of that post-war period. Of particular interest is the assumption that 'the wife' would be delighted to receive as a Christmas gift some device that may, or may not, have saved time or effort in the course of everyday cooking or housework.

SCOTT & SON. Some giant chain stores boast that they can provide anything from a battleship to a hen egg. Not so Scott & Son, of High Street, Lynn, but the House of Scott does guarantee an unrivalled Christmas service as far as household commodities are concerned.

If there is anything you want for the house for Christmas, a tea set for the wife, an easy chair for father, or a toy cycle for the baby, Scotts can provide it. "We have everything for the home… no matter what it is", says manager Mr. E. B. Smith.

Scott & Son's huge premises are a housewife's paradise. Not only can she wander around the departments at her leisure – examining furniture, drapery, china and glassware, toys and hardware – but when she has made her purchases the firm offers a free delivery service to her home.

The firm of Scott & Son is prepared for a "boom" Christmas trade and all departments are fully stocked for the big shopping rush which has already started.

Ideal Christmas gifts? The range and scope of the gifts is only limited by the imagination of the purchaser. If it is household furniture that is required kitchen cabinets, stools, tea wagons, hearth furniture, coffee tables, fire-side chairs, rugs and the inevitable television table come into the medium price category.

A three-piece suite may be called for, and an attractive suite in moquette is available for £23 19s 6d and another covered in rexine with velveteen spring interior cushions, for £33 5s. Many models of upholstered suites are made in their own factory.

Sheets and quilts, bedspreads and blankets, table cloths and pillow cases, travelling rugs, cushions, towels and floor pouffes can all be obtained in the drapery department, while many a housewife's eye will glint at the sight of the latest kitchen aids, electric cleaners and washing machines on view in the hardware department. Invaluable in any home nowadays are the range of "Pyrex" and "Phoenix" oven to table glassware; a 21-piece china tea set can be obtained for £3 11s 6d (top price being £21 19s 6d) and for the enthusiastic collector Doulton and Dresden china figures are available in large quantities.

For the youngsters there are Mobo toys and Tri-ang pedalkars, pedal motors, dolls' prams, Minic toys and the fascinating little Bubble Express for 19s 6d.

In January 1955 Scott & Son promoted their New Year sale with another half page advertisement.

In the last week of August 1955 the King's Lynn Chamber of Trade held a Trades Exhibition

on the Red Mount Field, near to the hospital. It was billed as the biggest and best trades show ever held in the town. The last one had been held in the Corn Exchange 22 years earlier.

The eight huge, linked marquees, covering some 36,500 square feet in area, housed 38 trade stands, with a further nine in a free-standing tent next to the entrance. The tents had been supplied and erected by Messrs. Trenowath & Son of Lynn. Free car parking was provided, with access off London Road, and an entrance charge of 6d was made. Richard Murdoch performed the opening ceremony at 2.30pm on Wednesday 24th August in front of the mayor, civic and trades' leaders and a large crowd. He had appeared in several films and was the star of 'Band Wagon' at the London Palladium, but he is perhaps best remembered for the radio comedy 'Much-Binding-in-the-Marsh' with Kenneth Horne and Sam Costa. Throughout the week there were fashion shows, as well as various displays and demonstrations. Scott & Son were on Stand No. 37 in one of the six side tents, and the programme contained a note about the firm (illus. above right).

It is particularly interesting to note that Scott & Son are indicating, even at this fairly late date, that some of their products are made at their own 'factory' in King's Lynn. Earlier that month they had been advertising 'Scott & Son are manufacturers of three-piece suites'. It is also apparent that they were holding a large stock of goods.

The manufacturers were only too pleased to take an active part in the exhibitions put on by the traders and Scott & Son had assistance in both the provision of display material and in demonstrating the various products. The principal items promoted on this occasion were the new 'Goblin' cylinder vacuum cleaner and their washing machine, on sale for 27 guineas. Also on display were 'Prestige' pressure cookers and kitchen knives and their 'Minit Mop'. This latter was one of those multi-purpose housework aids that were supposed to let you dispense with all your other mops, polishers and brushes. A system of detachable heads enabled you to change from a sponge mop, squeezed dry by a lever on the handle, to a polishing mop or to a brush.

On the first day of the show, 2,863 people attended but the numbers gradually increased, with over 6,000 on the Saturday. With another 5,310 coming on the last day, the total reached 30,341, which was judged to be a wonderful success. The Lynn News & Advertiser of 26th August contained this report of Scott & Son's stand: **'At the stand of Scott & Son Ltd., a family firm founded in 1874, housewives found much of interest. These complete house furnishers are concentrating especially on pressure cookers and washing machines, and representatives from Prestige pressure cookers and Goblin washing machines were present. Items for the kitchen were well to the fore'.**

The stand was constructed by Scott & Son's own cabinet makers, including John Mitchell. They built the stand at the Purfleet Street warehouse before dismantling and transporting it to the show ground. The first of the two publicity photographs that are reproduced below shows Scott & Son's stand at the 1955 Trades Exhibition, with the display of Goblin vacuum cleaners and their 27 guineas washing machine. On the right is a display of **'Colclough'** bone china tea ware. Each item of china could be bought separately. To the far right, in the next section of Scott & Son's stand, can just be seen a table with a gas cooking ring ready for the demonstrations of the Prestige pressure cookers.

Another part of Scott & Son's stand at the 1955 Trades Exhibition is shown in the second photograph. The Goblin washing machine is on the far left and in the centre is the **'Minit'** mop display. The demonstrations of pressure cooking were conducted by representatives of the manufacturers, the Prestige Company. Prestige also manufactured the Minit mop and Scott & Son stocked their range of kitchen knives and cutlery. On display at the rear of the stand is a set of **'Skyline'** kitchen cutlery. The kitchen cupboards on display were from the **'Hygena'** range, which had been introduced to create a fully fitted kitchen with matching units, as opposed to the individual, freestanding dressers and odd cupboards and tables that were in most kitchens at this date. Hygena offered fourteen interchangeable units comprising cabinets, low cabinets, wall cupboards, tables and stools.

The range of three-piece suites displayed by Scott & Son was available in different finishes:- moquette, from £23/19/6 to £59/19/6; moquette with loose spring interior cushions, £38/19/6 to £57/19/6; leathercloth with moquette seats, £25/19/6 to £31/18/6; rexine with velveteen spring interior cushions, £32/15/- to £42/10/-; and in cowhide, from £52/10/-. Bungalow suites in moquette were priced between £21/15/- and £34/19/6. Bed-settees, complete with mattress, cost from £46/5/- to £59/12/6. Many of these suites were made up by Scott & Son at their South Quay works.

The advertisements for Scott & Son show how the ranges and styles of furniture changed during the 1950s. In June 1956 they were advertising **'Astral'** bow-fronted, interchangeable bedroom furniture. These were finished in oak veneer with mahogany linings inside. In September that year they promoted the **'Link'** range of lounge and dining room furniture, offering flexibility at budget prices.

The High Street shops were beginning to increase their Christmas displays and illuminations. Scott & Son were well placed to have the maximum impact from their display, commanding the corner site at the Purfleet Street junction. In 1955 they decided to illuminate their first floor windows and the effect, although very simple, was quite striking.

One of the biggest boosts to the town's commercial expansion, economy and employment opportunities came in 1957, with the announcement that the American company of Campbell's Soups Ltd., were to build a factory on Hardwick Road. The news broke on 26th January and was confirmed on 8th March.

Three years after the success of their first trades exhibition, the King's Lynn Chamber of Trade decided to repeat the event, making it even bigger and better this time around. The erection of the main tents commenced on Monday 18th August 1958, the contractors this time being Messrs. J. Rands and Jeckell Ltd., of Ipswich, who had provided the tents for the Royal Norfolk Show that year. The area provided for trade stands amounted to 44,000 square feet. The opening ceremony was performed by Lady Barnet, star of the television panel games 'What's My Line?' and the 'Brains Trust' and of the radio programmes 'Any Questions?' and 'A Matter of Opinion'. The exhibition ran from 27th August to 3rd September and was sited on the same field as before. The Lynn News & Advertiser ran a Trades Exhibition Review with a 'Round the Stands' advertising feature. Scott & Son's summary for their stand was:

'SCOTT & SON (KING'S LYNN) LTD. (Complete House Furnishers). Stand No. 41. There will be daily demonstrations of cooking and the preparation of food using the largest range of pressure cookers and kitchen utensils – the Prestige range.

There will also be demonstrations of all models of Goblin washing machines. For the first time the new Pyrex Gaiety ware will be shown and also samples of china and glass by all the leading British and continental manufacturers.

Samples of the large and comprehensive stock of furniture serve as a reminder that the firm, established in 1874, has devoted all this time to complete house furnishing'.

By the late 1950s, the range of furniture, china, glass, floor coverings, bedding, drapery, hardware and kitchen appliances stocked by the firm had increased considerably. There was much more money in people's pockets and this was reflected in the high quality china and glass that was on display in the shop. This included Royal Doulton, Royal Worcester, Royal Cauldon, Poole Pottery, Susie Cooper, Minton, Spode, Wedgwood, Aynsley, Coalport, Shelley, Tuscan, Beswick, Edinburgh Crystal and Whitefriars Crystal.

In the upper photograph of Scott & Son's stand at the King's Lynn Trades Exhibition in August 1958 (left), Mr. Bill Holland is on the far left. Standing behind the display is the Prestige Company's demonstrator and on the far right of the picture is Mrs. Ellen Bambridge. In the lower photograph, Mrs. Hazel Loasby is on the left and Miss Pauline Mott is on the right of the china department's display.

By far the largest furniture manufacturing company at this time was Harris Lebus of Tottenham. They supplied a range of furniture sold by Scott & Son.

Although Scott & Son had been advertising that they made three-piece suites as late as 1955, their manufacture of furniture had tailed off and they were only upholstering chair and settee frames that they had in store. Their workshop was almost solely devoted to the repair and renovation of customers' own furniture. This included re-polishing, cabinet repairs, re-upholstering, and the re-making of mattresses. They also undertook carpet-laying, including the lifting and re-laying of customers' own carpets. Good quality wool carpets were exceptionally hard wearing and people would often take their carpets with them when they moved house. This would necessitate the cutting and sewing of carpets to fit the rooms in the new house. Pelmets, blinds, curtains and loose covers were made to measure and fitted, if the customer required. Scott & Son had a team of experts to undertake this work, several of whom served the firm faithfully for many years, although the rates of pay were not the best in the business.

When John Mitchell was recruited as a cabinet maker and French polisher in 1950, his starting wage was set according to the scale of the National Labour Agreement for the Furniture Trade. John (known as Jack to his colleagues) had learned his trade in the workshops at Cranwell, whilst doing his National Service in the Air Force. His work had included making and mending furniture and the wooden frames of gliders.

Hours of work for the cabinet makers at Scott & Son were from 8.30am to 5.30pm, except for Wednesdays (8.30am to 5.00pm) and Saturdays (8.30am to 1.00pm). By this date, the cabinet-making shop had moved from the South Quay, where it had been on the top floor of the works, to Gibson's Yard at the back of the main shop. Apart from an electric drill, the work was all done with hand tools. There were three benches available for the cabinet makers but these were rarely all in use at any one time. Wood-turning for chair or table legs and the cutting-out of unusual shapes was contracted out to Savages. The main stream of work came from customers who brought in their broken or damaged furniture. The cabinet makers also undertook polishing of their own work. However, the expert French polisher was Jim Gathercole, another of the older members of staff who had worked at Scott & Son for several years. Sometimes customers came in with an order for an item to be made to their suit their specific requirements. Other purpose-made furniture included seats and tables for the pub trade, and Scott & Son completed several of these contracts, including some for Steward & Patterson's chain of pubs. Free-standing sets of seats were made for the New Inn at South Wootton and for Wenn's Hotel in High Street. They also constructed their own display stands for the shop. John Gazley, one of the cabinet makers, was engaged for some time on this work.

Chair frames were still being purchased for making up in the upholstery shop at the works. This gave Scott & Son the flexibility to offer customers the choice of finish from a wide range of material samples. Many customers were loath to part with their three piece suites and preferred to have them recovered or completely re-upholstered. There was also a steady demand for loose covers, which were made to the customer's own requirements and choice of material. For many years, the work of meticulously cutting-out the material for loose covers and for re-upholstering chairs was undertaken by the works manager, Albert Smith. The upholsterers would also make hoods and covers for prams and pushchairs.

At the South Quay works, there was a carding machine to tease out the horse hair used for stuffing the chairs and cushions. The team of upholsterers included Harry Bushell, Tom Reeve, Albert Booty and Percy Hall, who was the one-legged veteran of the Great War. Percy also undertook the seaming-up of carpets. For this work, space was cleared on the second floor of the Purfleet Street warehouse, enabling large pieces of carpet to be laid out and cut to the required size, before being stitched. Any man visiting the upholstery workshop was ill-advised to wear a tie. Along one of the beams at the works was tacked a colourful display of tie-ends, all cut from the decorative neckwear of visitors who were not conversant with the upholsterers' tradition of taking a souvenir with a quick snip of their huge upholstery shears!

By the middle of 1959 the new factory for Campbell's Soups was nearing completion and trial runs through the plant were started in June. On Tuesday 14th July the company advertised for staff: 'Campbell's Soups Limited, Hardwick Road Factory, King's Lynn offer regular Employment to women interested in food processing work in ideal factory conditions – wages during training £6/6/0 per week'.

The 1960s brought a surge of changes to Lynn, including a new look to the distinctive Ladymans' store in High Street. Out went the overhead cash railway, the wooden arches and heavy timber ceiling beams, the old-fashioned lighting and antiquated heating system. In came the bold new world of gleaming vitreous enamelled fixtures, in white and pale blue, and bright fluorescent lighting.

Campbell's Soups were running at full production by the beginning of 1960 and had to recruit more staff to satisfy the demand. They opened an additional town centre employment office as part of their recruitment drive.

Dow Agrochemicals' new factory was three months ahead of schedule and would be producing 'Dowpon', a weed killer to control couch grass and other perennial weeds. The Duke of Edinburgh performed the formal opening ceremony of the new £1m factory on 18th November.

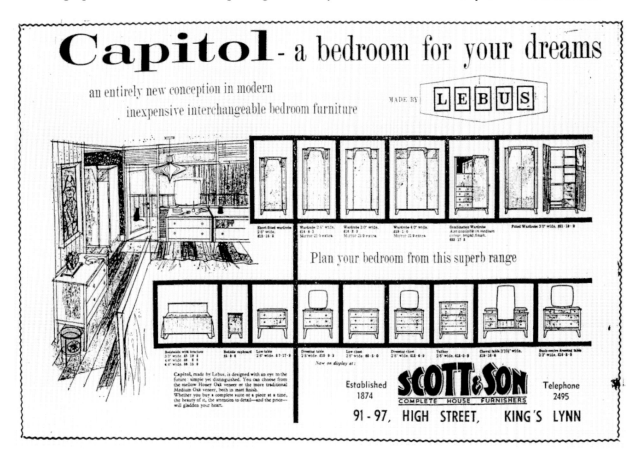

The Lebus Capitol bedroom furniture range advertisement (above) appeared in the Lynn News & Advertiser on 1st May 1959 and the one for Dunlopillo (below right) was in the issue for 4th August that year.

Scott & Son's sale advertisement for January 1960 indicates the range of goods that they stocked. A noticeable trend at the start of the new era was the popularity of studio couches. These became strong- selling items for several years, offering flexibility where space was at a premium and they were particularly useful in bed-sitting rooms. This reflected the fact that more young people, in particular, were moving out of the family home, either permanently or, as students, during the academic year. Many householders in the town furnished one, or more, of their rooms for letting out to students. Cheap and useful furniture for the home, flat or bed-sit was provided by the range of whitewood furniture offered by Scott & Son. Ready-assembled, it just needed painting. The range was advertised alongside studio couches in Scott & Son's January sales' advertisement in the Lynn News & Advertiser on 1st January 1960 (illustrated on the following page).

Heavenly Dunlopillo
brings you
a new kind of sleep

In September 1960 Lynn's first supermarket opened. The Elmo Supermarket was at 112, Norfolk Street and advertised:- **'One-stop shopping comes to Lynn. Developing Friday night shopping – open until 7.30pm.'**

During November, International Stores at their shops at 37 & 42, High Street, on the opposite side of the street to Scott & Son, responded to the Elmo initiative with one of their own. At No. 42, High Street, they offered **'Self Service with Free Delivery'** and at No. 37, High Street, they offered **'Personal Service with Free Delivery'.**

Lynn suffered flooding again in the spring tides of March 1961 and Scott & Son's South Quay premises were affected once more, as was St. Margaret's Church, where the water reached a depth of 2ft.

Later in that year, competition for Lynn's drapery business increased with the arrival of the B & W Linen

Shop at 103, High Street in September. This was a branch of their Haymarket, Norwich shop. They sold sheets, blankets, bedspreads, towels, curtains, loose-cover fabrics, and fancy linens.

The King's Lynn Chamber of Trade promoted another trades exhibition in the town in 1961, as advertised by Scott & Son on 6th June 1961 (illus. above right). Scott & Son's exhibition on this occasion was themed, with kitchen, living room and bedroom displays, together with china and carpets. **'Prestige'** pressure cookers and **'Minit'** mops were again demonstrated, but this time they had competition from **'Skyline'**, whose pressure cookers, kitchen cutlery and **'fabulous, miracle CHOPPER'** were demonstrated during the three days of the exhibition. The carpets on show were very strongly patterned and not at all to today's taste. Alongside the **'Goblin'** cylinder vacuum cleaner was their latest upright model. The room displays are of particular interest because they reflect the designs that were fashionable in the early 1960s. They continued to advertise three-piece suites made in their own workshops, alongside furniture made by the principal factories in the country. Amongst the range of floor coverings on offer was 'Hardura', the trade name for a coarse-fibre felt, faced with extremely tough bituminised paint. Hardura was used in cars for mats and boot lining.

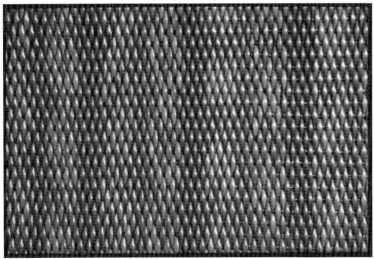

The whole exhibition was under canvas, occupying ten large marquees. To the left of the entrance was the Fashion Theatre, where there were two displays each day, and to the right was the catering tent. At the other end was the open-air arena for outdoor exhibits and displays. There were two approaches: one via the Broad Walk from London Road, with free car parking off County Court Road; the second from Tennyson Road, with a free car park at the football ground. Music was from the Regimental Band of the Royal Fusiliers, the King's Lynn Town Band and the St. John's Ambulance Brigade Cadet Band. Scott & Son's display took up six stands in the central tent space, close to the open-air arena. The top photograph shows Scott & Son's central china display with Wedgwood, Spode and Royal Doulton on display. In the centre is a stand of Pyrex ware, with more laid out on the ground and on the stand over to the left. Edinburgh Crystal is shown on the circular table and a large Tudor Crystal vase is on the tall pedestal towards the right.

The middle photograph shows Scott & Son's carpet display. In addition to the traditional ranges by manufacturers such as Crossley, they were promoting 'Dandycord' mats. These mats, designed for kitchen and bathroom, were made from rows of plastic tubing woven together (illus. bottom left). Available in a range of bright colours, they were advertised as being 'non-soiling, non-slip, non-fade and non-curl'. It was also claimed that they were 'warm to the feet and a dream to clean'.

The top photograph, left, shows the bedroom display on Scott's stand at the show. The layout includes items from the 'Carnival Unit Furniture' range and a 'Somnus' divan bed.

The middle photograph (below left) shows the living room display on the stand with furniture that is typical of early 1960s design.

In the bottom photograph, kitchen units and utensils are displayed. 'Minit Mops' and 'Prestige' pressure cookers were on show alongside an extensive range of 'Sky-line' products, including their pressure cookers. The influence of television is apparent: 'See the fabulous Sky-line miracle chopper … from potatoes to ice chopped in a trice - as seen on TV', is the slogan on the advertising card in the centre of the picture. The first 'TV chef' was Philip Harben, who appeared on the BBC in 1946, and he was promoting 'Prestige Imperial Ware' with a book on frying.

Another new factory was opened in Lynn in September 1962 when Dornay Foods, a division of Mars Ltd., confectionary manufacturers of Slough, started production. They launched a recruiting drive for staff that month.

The Lynn News & Advertiser ran a Christmas advertising feature on 27th November 1962, headlined 'SHOPPING IN LYNN HIGH STREET AND NORFOLK STREET'. Scott & Son included the following write- up in the feature: 'SCOTT & SON. Messrs. Scott & Son, of High Street, offer a large selection of pleasing gifts in their chinaware department. Particularly attractive are the Royal Doulton Toby and character jugs, quite reasonably priced from 12s. to 39s. according to size. Christmas, of course, is the major event of the year for small children, and their needs are certainly well catered for in the toy department.

Something new in the department this year are the "talking" dolls and teddy bears. These cuddly, life-like toys really do have quite an extensive "vocabulary" and "speak" up to about eight to ten sentences. The smaller talking dolls are £5 9s 6d and the teddy bears are £7 19s 6d. For the home, Pyrosil oven dishes are an ideal buy from the hardware department'.

Part of their advertisement in the Lynn News and Advertiser 27th November 1962 is shown right.

The advertisement above is from the Lynn News & Advertiser 19th February 1963.

Venetian blinds became a fashionable alternative to curtains in the 1960s and the advertisement for 'Quill' blinds by Scott & Son (below, right) appeared in the Lynn News & Advertiser on 12th March 1963.

On Monday 25th March 1963 Lady Fermoy was conferred with the Freedom of the Borough of King's Lynn, in recognition of her services to the town. She was only the third woman to receive the award. The ceremony was held at the Trinity Guildhall.

Two High Street stores celebrating anniversaries were Le Grice Bros (75 years), and Jermyns (91). Arguably, only Le Grice's claim was genuine because Jermyns advertised as 'Your Debenham Store', having been taken over by the national chain in 1943. Debenhams continued to use the Jermyns' name and to celebrate the anniversaries of the founding of the store by Alfred Jermyn in 1872.

In their hardware department, Scott & Son stocked gardening tools and seeds and they always had a spring promotion. In April 1964 they advertised 'Atco', 'Qualcast', 'Folbate', 'Suffolk' and 'Falcon' petrol mowing machines (illus. left). 'Sankeys' flower pots, which had been stocked by the firm for many years, were still selling well.

Further competition to the old-established King's Lynn furniture stores, such as Scott & Son, came in early July 1964 with the opening of a branch of the Norwich firm of Wallace King. Theirs was the first to open in a new development of shops in St. James Street, on the site of the old St. James' Club. Advertised as 'Lynn's New Furnishing Centre' they offered parking at the rear of the store for the convenience of customers.

It was often said of Scott & Son that they would deliver a single cup and saucer to a customer. Their Bedford delivery vans were garaged at the works on the South Quay and were loaded up at the Purfleet Street warehouse before going out on their daily round. On Mondays they set off towards Littleport and Ely, on Wednesdays it was Hunstanton and the coast, and on Thursdays it was Terrington. Large rolls of carpet, lino or other floor covering were delivered on the big vans, but the carpet layers would travel out in their

little Bradford vans. These latter were replaced by small Bedford vans in later years. In those days, long before the advent of satellite navigation systems, the drivers knew most of the routes, without even referring to a map. Even many of the single-track roads, some of them un-maintained, were familiar to the more experienced drivers, which at this date included Reggie Mace, David Lomax, Derek Brown and Eric Peacock. Head driver Joe Dixon was reputed to navigate by the numerous pubs in the district, which provided distinctive landmarks. However well they knew the route, there was often the unexpected to cause difficulty. The most frequently encountered problem was that of the tiny 'cupboard' stairs that were to be found in many of the rural cottages. It was a struggle to get even the smallest of bedroom furniture up these narrow winding stairs. It was essential, therefore, to know what furniture items could be taken apart, and to be prepared to carry them upstairs in pieces before re-assembling them. Sometimes one of the cabinet makers had to accompany the delivery drivers in order to take the furniture apart and reassemble it. If all else failed, the furniture had to be lifted onto the roof of the van and pushed through the upstairs window, sometimes after the window had been taken out. On one occasion, Joe Dixon was carrying a roll of lino around the back of a cottage in the fens near Terrington, when there was a strange rattling of chains, rather reminiscent of an anchor being let down. As he rounded the corner of the cottage, he was confronted by a large, black Alsatian dog, flying towards him at head height. Before Joe could stop, the clanking noise ceased and the dog dropped like a stone as it reached the end of its tether and the chain tightened around its neck. On such occasions, a recuperative cup of tea from the big flask in the cab of the van was required before setting off for the next delivery. The photograph above shows Joe Dixon with his van on the South Quay.

In October 1964 Purfleet Street was transformed into a scene set in a Dutch/German border town in 1943. The film was 'Operation Crossbow', with an all-star cast that included Sophia Loren, George Peppard, Trevor Howard, Anthony Quayle, Tom Courtenay and Jeremy Kemp. The story was only very loosely based on the real wartime operation of the same name, in which the German missile development site at Peenemunde was heavily bombed. The filming had to stop whenever Scott & Son's assistants went to collect a customer's pram from the warehouse. One Wednesday afternoon when filming was underway in Purfleet Street, the director and crew were much put out when the big sliding doors to Scott & Son's warehouse suddenly opened and two cars drove out! This was Messrs. William and Maurice Scott preparing to drive home after work. This incident was not caught on film. The former Central Hotel in Purfleet Street, owned by Scott & Son, was transformed into a café for the film but the Purfleet Street scenes included the film are too brief for any of Scott & Son's premises to be recognised.

Part of Scott & Son's Christmas advertisement from the Lynn News & Advertiser 1st December 1964 is reproduced on the following page.

On Tuesday 4th May 1965 a new supermarket opened at Nos. 5, 6 & 7, High Street. Victor Value offered '**The lowest possible prices anywhere, Plus S&H PINK STAMPS**'. This was the 25th Victor Value to be opened in the country and, according to the Lynn News & Advertiser, they attracted 'floods of housewives' on opening day.

An experimental traffic ban in High Street and Norfolk Street went ahead on three Saturdays in September 1965. First announced by the Town Council the year before, the whole length of High Street and the top end of Norfolk Street were to be closed to traffic from 1.30pm to 6pm. After this initial trial, the council decided to test the scheme over an extended period of three months the following year.

On Tuesday 4th September the Lynn News & Advertiser carried an advertisement from Scott & Son, which listed some of the products that they stocked (illus. left). Beds and bedding had been one of Scott & Son's principal lines from

the outset. Their original reputation was made on the basis of the quality of their own lines, manufactured in their factory. They had ceased making any new bedding by this date, although they continued to undertake some re-upholstering of traditional sprung mattresses, which many people still preferred to the modern alternatives.

Their bedding department stocked mattresses, divans and pillows from the best-known manufacturers, including 'Eventide', (illus.), 'Vono', 'Reynard', 'Dunlopillo', 'Sure-o-Sleep', and 'Somnus'. In their baby carriage department, they were selling prams and pushchairs by 'Pedigree', 'Silver Cross', 'Tan-Sad', 'Leeway', and 'Swan'.

Toys were by now becoming much more sophisticated and more expensive. The most popular ones were influenced by current films and television characters. In April 1966, 'Thunderball' was the theme of an advertisement from Scott & Son, who were offering: 'Thunderballs at 3/11 each; 007 Gun with Silencer for 5/11; 007 Rifle for 14/11; Badges 1/- each; and James Bond hats at 5/6'.

Scott & Son had 'Tich & Quackers' ventriloquist dolls for sale. These were a spin-off from Ray Allen's TV show. Tich was a very scruffy, and rather naughty, schoolboy and Quackers was a most vociferous and even naughtier duck. Ray Allen was also responsible for introducing the nation to 'Lord Charles', another TV dummy. These dolls were 16in. tall and cost 92/6 each. Even more expensive were the talking, walking Victorian dolls at 159/11. More modestly priced were the dressing-up clothes for Sindy, her boyfriend Paul and her little sister Patch. The illustration, left, of Sindy, Paul and Patch on their bicycle made for three was part of Scott & Son's advertisement in the Lynn News & Advertiser dated 21st November 1967.

There were only two High Street shops that managed to provide car parking for their customers: Scott & Son and Le Grice Brothers. The culmination of a five year programme of improvements was completed towards the end of 1965 at Le Grice's shop, at Nos. 21 & 22, High Street. The shop was given a new front and a 30-space car park was provided at the rear, following the demolition of some cottages, a garden and a pub.

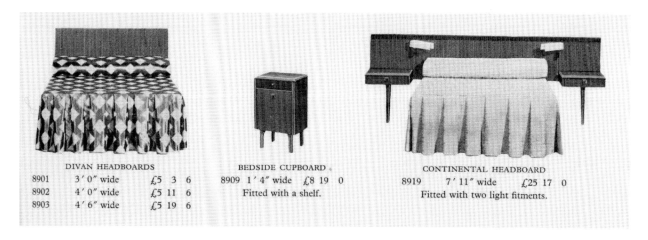

DIVAN HEADBOARDS				BEDSIDE CUPBOARD			CONTINENTAL HEADBOARD		
8901	3' 0" wide	£5 3 6		8909 1' 4" wide £8 19 0			8919 7' 11" wide £25 17 0		
8902	4' 0" wide	£5 11 6		Fitted with a shelf.			Fitted with two light fitments.		
8903	4' 6" wide	£5 19 6							

Although Scott & Son had long since ceased issuing their own catalogue, they provided customers with illustrated furniture catalogues that were produced by the main manufacturers and overstamped with the shop's address. The Lebus range of bedroom furniture, above, is taken from their Autumn 1965 catalogue.

Floor polish was still an everyday requirement in many homes and the hardware department sold 'Mansion', 'Goddards' and 'Johnsons'. New materials were being introduced regularly towards the end of the 1960s, including Marley 'Consort' vinyl flooring (illus.) and 'Fablon'. This latter was a self-adhesive plastic material used, amongst other things, for transforming the appearance of old furniture. In later years there was just cause for people to curse this use of the fabric, which was extremely difficult to remove when it had been in place for a long time. Fablon was sold in rolls 18in. wide, for 4/- per yard, and 36in. wide, for 9/- per yard.

The Lynn Chamber of Trade held a **What's New? In '66** promotion in March of that year, aimed at demonstrating that service was second to none in the town **'and more than 500 shop assistants are aiming to prove this beyond doubt'** they proclaimed. The advertisement below was included with the Chamber of Trade's promotion in the Lynn News & Advertiser on 18th March 1966.

Meanwhile, the marketing of carpets in King's Lynn was given a new look by Reg Skipper's **'Modern Carpets Selection Centre'** at 122, Norfolk Street. He introduced an innovation in the form of a mobile showroom in September, 1967. **'All you have to do is call or phone us and arrange for the van to call at a time which is convenient to you. The van has a very large range of carpets to choose from',** he announced. There is no record of how successful his venture proved to be.

The Elmo supermarket, at 112, Norfolk Street, became a branch of Fine Fare in October 1967.

Tragically, at the comparatively young age of 45, the proprietor of Le Grice's clothing store, Franklin E. Le Grice, died in 1967 and the decision to close the business was announced towards the end of the year. Their closing down sale ended on Saturday 13th January 1968 and another of the old-established independent traders vanished from Lynn's High Street.

Devaluation of the Pound was causing concern that month and the manager of Jermyns, Mr. J. C. Stokes, stated that people appeared to be buying larger household items in anticipation of escalating prices later in the year. He was reported as saying that on the first day of his firm's January sale people had concentrated on buying furniture, bedding and carpets, taking advantage of the current prices before the devaluation kicked-in.

The big new, 75-bedroom extension to the Dukes Head Hotel, costing £400,000, was completed for Trust Houses Ltd., in January 1968. Later that year, on 29th June, the King's Lynn High School Old Girls Association held a retirement dinner for the long-standing headmistress, Miss F. Winifred Dore, at the Town Hall.

One of Scott & Son's most prominent front windows was given over to a rather unusual display in the last week of June 1968. It was transformed into a hospital ward to show the public modern methods of nursing. Designed both to recruit nurses and to instruct the public in the most up-to-date techniques and equipment, the week-long exhibition attracted a great deal of interest and many enquiries. The photograph, above right, is from the Lynn News & Advertiser, Friday 21st June 1968. The grey-haired lady with her hand on the bed is Mrs. F. M. Dawes (née Finbow), manageress of the china department.

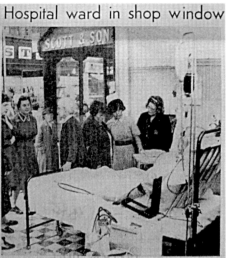

Hospital ward in shop window

The King's Lynn Festival was in its eighteenth year and Scott & Son had become regular advertisers in its programme. In the Lynn News & Advertiser's special festival supplement on 12th July 1968, Scott & Son placed an advertisement that summarised the departments in their shop. They advertised the availability of a free car park for customers, but this was under threat from the council's proposals for rear access to the High Street. A Compulsory Purchase Order (CPO) had been served by the council on various owners to facilitate the assembly of the land needed to create rear access to the land between the backs of the properties in High Street and King Street. Access was to be via Purfleet Street, where Scott & Son had the entrance to their customers car park. This was one of four CPO's served by the council. Scott & Son were one of the objectors to this but their objections were dismissed and the order was confirmed in July 1968.

In the latter years, Scott & Son sometimes used a shortened version of the company's name and a more modern typeface for their advertisements in the newspapers. Usually this was 'Scotts' but frequently a stray apostrophe appeared, as in the Christmas toys advertisement, left, from the Lynn News & Advertiser on 22nd November 1968. The Lynn News & Advertiser reported on 21st February 1969 that the Town Council were planning to introduce the Saturday town centre pedestrianisation scheme on a permanent basis later that year: **'Saturday Ban on Vehicles in High Street. Lynn town centre pedestrian scheme to start in May? The town centre's pedestrian scheme for Saturday shoppers should be in operation within three months'**.

In addition to the robust, value-for-money furniture that was the mainstay of the company's business throughout its life, some more expensive furniture was offered, too. In the late 1960's this included high quality reproduction oak furniture with a stain and heat resistant finish. This range comprised: Tudor Sideboard - £46-12-0; Midland Table - £26-7-0; Ladder Back Chairs - £6-19-0; Bureau - £40-18-0; Cabinet - £37-19-6; Rug Box - £13-18-6; Nest of Tables - £16-9-0; Long John Table - £12-17-0; Hall Table - £12-17-0; and Swivel Top Table - £9-9-0.

The first public indication that Scott & Son may be about to close came with an article in the Lynn News & Advertiser on Tuesday 25th November 1969. The newspaper had noticed that a planning application had been submitted by an Essex investment company to redevelop the site of Nos. 91

to 97, High Street and Nos.1 to 8, Purfleet Street. They reported that Frincon Investments of Frinton-on-Sea had agreed to buy the premises and that their spokesman had said "We have applied for total demolition of the premises and now the big question mark is the planning consent. If we get that we could have new shops up in about 15 months." Alan Scott was quoted in the same report as saying "At present we have not sold any premises and have no further comment to make".

Agents appointed by William and Maurice Scott had been negotiating for some time with Frincon but agreement depended upon the grant of permission to demolish the present buildings and to erect two new shop units; one three storeys high and one of two storeys, on the site, however, on Friday 28th November the newspaper reported that planning permission had been refused. The headline on this occasion read **"Scotts of High Street, Not Closing Down".** The Town Council's Planning & Development Committee had refused planning permission for the proposal from Frincon Investments. The Committee decided that the plans did not leave enough room for parking away from the road and that the congestion caused would be a danger to other traffic. Frincon appealed against the decision.

> ## Scott's High St. store to be sold?

Faced with questions from the press, William Scott responded by stating that whatever happened the firm would keep trading. He was quoted as saying "We have no intention of ceasing to trade and if we do move we hope we will continue to trade continuously. We will stay where we are if the deal falls through."

William was now 68 years old and was seeking to retire and he was already working part time at the shop. His brother Maurice, 56, was proposing to stay in the business and they had planned to convert the three-storey Purfleet Street warehouse into a shop. Their sons, cousins Robin and Alan Scott, both wanted to continue in business, the former specialising in china and glass, the latter in furniture. However, their plans for the warehouse were not to go smoothly, and Robin was to decide that the proposed adaptations and arrangement of departments would not provide a sufficiently prominent showcase for fine china and glass.

SCOTT'S
OF KING'S LYNN
81 97 HIGH ST.
Telephone 2495

SCOTT & SON (K.L.) LTD.   Est. 1874

We are
NOT closing down
and are trading as
normal.
We expect to move to
more suitable premises
in due course.

The denial by William Scott that the business was to cease trading seems to have done little to quell the rumours of imminent closure and the company felt compelled to publish a notice on 2nd December 1969 that they were continuing to trade (illus. left).

In the light of the problems encountered over the planning applications, by Frincon for the redevelopment of the shop site and by Scott & Son for the conversion of the warehouse, the business continued as usual, although there was now a cloud hanging over its future, causing uncertainty and worry to the staff.

In September 1969 the King's Lynn Chamber of Trade promoted a Trade & Industry Week, with a window dressing and 'Spot It' competition (below).

KING'S LYNN TRADE & INDUSTRY WEEK, SEPTEMBER 20 - 27
WINDOW DRESSING AND "SPOT IT" COMPETITION.   SEE IF YOU CAN SPOT THE ARTICLE IN OUR WINDOW DISPLAYING A NUMBERED DISC AND WINDOW BADGE

Advertisements for Scott & Son appeared in the Lynn News & Advertiser as before, with promotions for Christmas gifts appearing in the edition on 25th November, 1969 (illus. below).

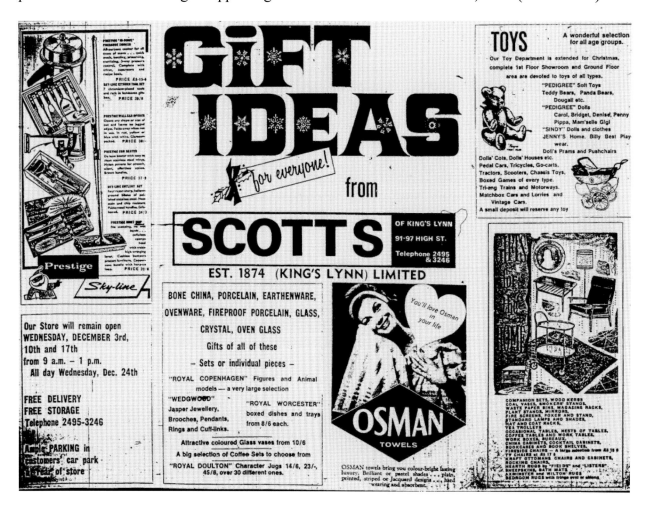

In the early hours of Saturday 31st January 1970 a thief who was, perhaps, rather too eager to take what he could from the shop before it closed, escaped with very little, as reported in the Lynn News & Advertiser the following Tuesday: '**PORCELAIN GOES IN SMASH AND GRAB. Lynn Police rushed to the High Street shop of Scott & Sons Ltd., early on Saturday after a smash-and-grab raid. A £159 porcelain ornament, depicting three leaping Grant's gazelles, was stolen. However, it was discovered that the leg of one of the gazelles had been broken off and was lying among the broken glass. Mr. Robin Scott said later that this would depreciate the value of the ornament to a certain extent, but not completely. Mr. G. H. Brown, manager of a nearby shoe shop, raised the alarm about 2.00am after he had heard glass breaking. He jumped out of bed in his flat over the shoe shop and looked out of the window but saw nobody. As he went to make a 999 call he saw that Scott's china cabinet window had been broken, and a brick was lying on the pavement. GLASS CUTTER. A glass cutter had been used on the window, which was then smashed in with a brick. The German-made Lorenz Hutschenreuther ornament was the only article taken from the window although others were broken. The gazelles are coloured fawn, with a white underside and black spiral horns. They stand about 1ft high and about 1ft 5ins long. Although valued at £159, Mr. Scott thought that the ornament could be sold in London for about £225. It was the only one of its kind in stock at Scott's shop'.**

More High Street closures and moves were being announced, the most significant being the loss of the iconic Ladymans' store at Nos. 39 & 40, when they moved into smaller premises in New Conduit Street. Although the magnificent heavy beamed interior had suffered an insensitive 1960 makeover, and the wonderful overhead cash railway had long since gone, the black and white frontage, with the red teapot hanging over the pavement, was very much a local landmark. The old building was to be demolished to make way for a new Littlewoods store.

Palmer and Harvey Ltd., tobacconists of 112, High Street was another casualty. Their manager, Mr. G. W. Rice, who had only been there for twelve months, announced that sixteen employees would be made redundant. With thirty branches, Palmer and Harvey were the largest wholesale tobacconists in the country.

Another of Lynn's iconic structures was also about to be demolished – the concrete arches to the Cut Bridge, so long the landmark gateway to Lynn from the midlands and the north, were to be taken down and the bridge altered to give it a flat look. The £190,000 contract for the work was awarded to the Dredging and Construction Company Ltd., of Lynn, in May 1970.

'Miss Anglia goes on a shopping spree with the Lynn News & Advertiser' was the headline to a special advertising feature in their paper on Tuesday 2nd June 1970. For **'vivacious, sparkling-eyed Miss Anglia, 22-year-old Jennifer Cresswell'**, west Norfolk was just one of 80 visits since her 'election' in October 1969. Jennifer lived in Hull with her mother and had travelled to Lynn to do the rounds of the shops for the feature. Jennifer was photographed in Scott & Son's shop promoting Slumberland beds (illus. left). The caption read: **'EVERY GIRL likes her comforts, and Jennifer is no exception. A soft, comfortable bed is one of the most important things in her life. At Scott & Son Ltd., she had an opportunity to try out a Slumberland bed, reputed to be the most comfortable yet – and an opportunity to fall in love with one of the biggest, cuddliest teddy bears she had ever seen, Jennifer likes furniture in general, and she also had a quick look at Scott's large range of dining room, sitting room and bedroom furniture'.**

The 20th King's Lynn Festival was held in July 1970. Later that month the arches to the Cut Bridge were demolished. In September, another new supermarket, Downsway, which was to open in a new development at Nos. 128–132, High Street, was granted an off licence. At the hearing of their application, the presiding justice, Mr. Daniel F. Burlingham, spoke of his concern over the development of the town centre. He said that it was not going according to plan and that there were perhaps 20 to 25 shops in the centre waiting to be let. He was not optimistic about the future and warned that "…the number of empty shops in a year or two may well be 50 or so." At the beginning of November, the new Littlewoods' store opened where Ladymans had formerly stood and, on the 17th of the month, TV and radio personality Vince Hill opened Lynn's new Tesco store at Nos. 21 & 22, High Street, Le Grice Brothers' former premises.

One week later, on 24th November 1970 the Lynn News & Advertiser carried the story that Frincon Investments Ltd. had won their appeal against the refusal of permission to redevelop Scott & Son's site, under the headline: **'SCOTT'S SITE PLAN GETS THE GO-AHEAD'.**

Planning permission to redevelop Scott & Son's prestige site on the corner of Lynn's High Street and Purfleet Street with two shop units has been granted by the Secretary of State for the Environment to Frincon Investments. The public inquiry had been heard at Lynn before inspector Mr. K. G. Robbins. The proposal was in accordance with the shop zone in the approved comprehensive development area, and there was no problem over the design and servicing arrangements for the proposed three-storey and two-storey shop units. The issues at stake concerned the lack of provision on site for customers' car parking. The local authority's standards would have required 75 car parking spaces to be provided. However, it was intended that within a year or two both High Street and Purfleet Street would be pedestrianised. Under these proposals, the capacity provided for public car parking was to be dramatically increased from 700 to 5,000. In the light of these circumstances both sides at the inquiry agreed that on-site parking would be inappropriate. The newspaper noted that Scott & Son's shop had been a well-known High Street landmark for many years and that the inspector had concluded that the design of the new development would be acceptable in scale and design for its important location. At this stage, there was no indication as to what types of shops would be provided on the site.

Decimalisation was introduced on 15th February 1971 and the shops had to train their staff to handle the new currency. Like other stores, Scott & Son's advertisements included the decimal equivalents alongside the old prices. The new coins came into use just before the introduction of pay and display long and short term car parking for Lynn's shoppers on 26th April 1971.

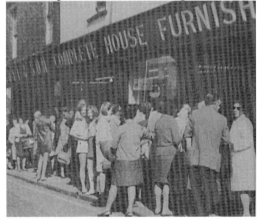

Another new store opening at this time was Maples Quality Furniture Store at Nos. 5–7, High Street. This almost coincided with the announcement by William and Maurice Scott that their shop was going to close, which was reported in the Lynn News & Advertiser on 21st May 1971. Although Scott & Son (King's Lynn) Ltd. was to cease trading, it was also announced that Robin Scott was to continue running the china department, as an independent business, with the name 'Scotts China Shop'.

During the first two weeks of May 1971 Scott & Son had placed normal advertisements in the local newspapers. As soon as the news broke of their impending closure, however, they started advertising their clearance sale. The first advertisement appeared on 21st May (illus above).

This was now a very difficult time for all concerned, but especially for the staff, many of whom had only ever worked for Scott & Son. There were 39 staff affected by the closure, although some were to be employed by Robin Scott at Scotts China Shop. About 30 were made redundant, some of whom were amongst Scott & Son's most faithful and longest-serving employees who had already reached retirement age.

In spite of the personal concern that the directors felt over the redundancies and the closure of a business founded by their grandfather in 1874, there is no room for sentiment in business and difficult decisions had to be made.

The nature of trading on High Street was changing more rapidly in the early late 1960s and early 1970s than at any other time. It was unrecognisable from the High Street on which Thomas Scott and his son William Crawshay had opened the first Scott & Son at No. 89 in 1892. Although the numbering in High Street goes from 1 to 123, several shops occupy more than one unit. In 1892, there were 99 separate trading units, including shops, banks, public houses, plumbers, painters, saddlers, and a sail and tent maker. The majority of these, 53, were manufacturers of at least some of the products that they sold. This included, of course, Scott & Son who made much of their furniture and bedding. The others included those already mentioned, together with three milliners, seventeen drapers, two glove and gaiter makers, a sugar boiler, an umbrella maker, a gun maker and a tinner and brazier. It could be argued that the list of manufacturers should also include the five chemists, who made their own patent medicines, and the beer, wine and spirits merchants who were attached to local breweries and blending houses. Only five of these 99 traders were branches of businesses with their headquarters outside Lynn.

By 1972, this trading pattern had changed completely. Out of 94 trading units, only 11 were 'manufacturers', four of them being bakers. The chain stores now dominated, there being only 26 independents.

Just as dramatic was the reduction in the number of people living on High Street. In the early 1890's there were almost 500 people living there. Over 320 of these were the family members of the traders, all of whom lived on the premises. The remainder included assistants or servants, who boarded with the families and many families who lived in the small yards off High Street. By 1970, there were fewer than 25 people living at addresses in High Street.

The end for Scott & Son came with their closure on 29th May 1971 but there was still some work to be done. A temporary shop and office was opened at 23, New Conduit Street, where Maurice Scott supervised the finalising of the accounts, honouring of all the orders that had been placed but not yet delivered, and the winding-up of the business, including selling off the remaining furniture stock. He was assisted by one or two of the staff and by his son Alan, who found himself having to undertake a wide variety of jobs, including that of van driver. Alan Scott continued to work in the furniture trade for many years, at Reed's of Downham Market.

Meanwhile, Robin Scott opened Scotts China Shop in Norfolk Street and traded there for another 37 years. There was, therefore, continuous trading by Thomas Scott and his descendants in King's Lynn from 1874 until 2008 - a period of 134 years.

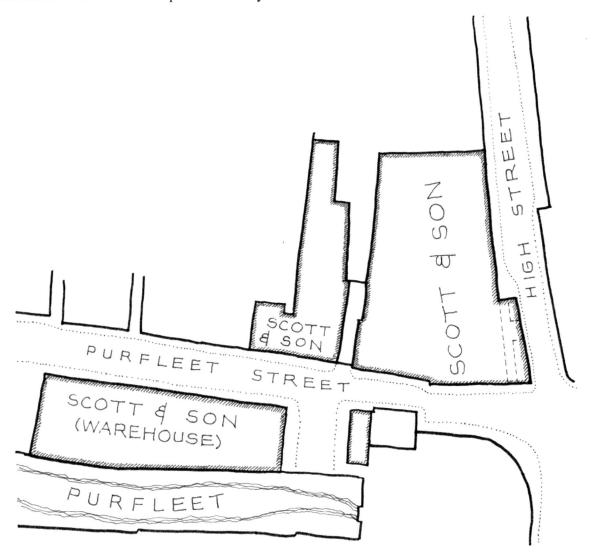

The plan above shows Scott & Son's premises c1935, soon after the warehouse in Purfleet Street had been built. The High Street bottleneck can clearly be seen at the point where the china shop (Nos. 95, 96 & 97) jutted forward.

In 1899, when Nos. 93 & 94 were redeveloped, Scott & Son were required to set the new shop back to comply with a new building line imposed by the council. Nos. 95 to 97 came into the ownership of Scott & Son at various dates between 1904 and 1910, and the council asked them to redevelop these properties to the new line. For the next 35 years or so, the council continued desperately to try to persuade the company to demolish these old properties and thereby remove the biggest traffic bottleneck in the centre of Lynn. In 1927 Scott & Son redeveloped Nos. 91 & 92 and set these back to the approved line. This prompted the council to renew their efforts to persuade them to treat Nos. 95 to 97 in a similar fashion. However, their requests continued to be rejected.

Scott & Son had found it most frustrating when dealing with the council over the rebuilding of Nos. 93 & 94, the negotiations taking fifteen months between April 1898 and June 1899. It is evident that they had no desire to go through that process again. Indeed, it would seem that they resolved to devise a scheme that would give them the maximum benefit of the available floorspace within the old buildings and to resist the council's requests to demolish them. The photograph above left shows the distinctive corner shop looking north.

The view in the opposite direction is shown right and shows the blank, brick, wing wall that was built in 1899 when Nos. 93 & 94 were set back to the improvement line prescribed by the council. At ground level below this wall can be seen the gated entrance to the china department arcade. When the shop was open, shoppers could walk through this arcade instead of having to use the narrow pavement (the street had been pedestrianised by the time that this photograph was taken).

The last approaches by the council to Scott & Son requesting them to set back the corner buildings appear to have been made towards the end of WWII. Eventually, however, new ideas for the treatment of town centre shopping streets began to take hold and the council decided to drop the idea of widening the street for the benefit of traffic and to introduce pedestrianisation instead.

There is a final twist to the story of Scotts' projecting corner shop. After the demolition of their old shop, the council decided that they preferred the appearance of the street scene with a building that stepped forward at the junction.

The new building that houses Boots the Chemists reflects the front building line of the old shop, stepping forward at first floor level with a walkway below. In the photograph below left, the old shop is being demolished in 1971, and the new buildings are shown in the one on the right.

ANNUAL TAKINGS at SCOTT & SON 1893 - 1970

Year £

Year	£		Year	£	
1892		Scott & Son opens @ 89 High St	1930	33,095	
1893	2,223		1931	33,165	
1894	2,869		1932	30,863	
1895	3,024		1933	36,860	Royal Norfolk Show
1896	3,372		1934	41,060	
1897	4,001	Trades Exhibition	1935	42,320	Purfleet St. warehouse built
1898	5,445	St. James St. factory fire.			Silver Jubilee
		Nos. 93 & 94 High St. open	1936	42,925	Death of George V
1899	4,430	Barnum & Bailey's 'Greatest			Edward VIII abdicates
		Show on Earth'	1937	42,035	Coronation of George VI
1900	4,660		1938	42,715	Death of Wm Crawshay Scott I
1901	3,893	Death of Queen Victoria			
1902	4,685	South Quay factory built	1939	44,715	) Great Depression ends
		Coronation of Edward VII	1940	50,645	)
1903	4,815	Music shop @ 42 High St. opens	1941	56,425	)
1904	5,315	No. 96 High St. opens	1942	39,775	) World War II
		No. 89 High St. vacated	1943	37,906	)
1905	5,405		1944	42,485	)
1906	5,781		1945	53,750	)
1907	6,040		1946	97,337	
1908	6,445	No. 97 High St. opens	1947	97,460	
1909	6,365		1948	99,150	
1910	6,680	No. 95 High St. opens	1949	114,740	
		Death of Edward VII	1950	114,220	Food rationing ends
1911	7,195	No. 91 High St. opens	1951	120,010	First King's Lynn Festival
		Coronation of George V			
1912	7,835	Music shop @ 42 High St. closes	1952	114,557	Death of George VI
		Thomas William Scott retires	1953	127,165	Coronation of Elizabeth II
1913	7,545		1954	122,662	
1914	8,399	)	1955	127,005	Trades Exhibition
1915	7,665	)	1956	129,364	
1916	5,710	) World War I	1957	127,315	
1917	6,465	)	1958	130,355	Trades Exhibition
1918	7,955	)	1959	130,370	
1919	20,536		1960	133,002	
1920	22,032	Royal Norfolk Show	1961	142,485	Trades Exhibition
1921	24,400		1962	143,305	
1922	27,763		1963	145,086	
1923	26,408		1964	158,880	
1924	27,274		1965	161,033	
1925	30,545	Royal Norfolk Show	1966	158,510	
		Trades Exhibition	1967	159,630	
1926	29,808	General Strike	1968	181,740	
1927	33,079	New shop 91 & 92 High St. open	1969	181,495	
1928	32,220	Trades Exhibition	1970	183.985	
1929	32,295	Royal Norfolk Show	1971		Scott & Son closes
		Great Depression starts			

Staff of Scott & Son
1892 – 1971

Thomas William Scott.
Founding partner (1892 – 1912).

William Crawshay Scott.
Founding partner (1892 – 1938).

William Crawshay Scott jnr.
Partner (1928 – 1971).

Maurice Septimus Crawshay Scott.
Partner (1938 – 1971).

SCOTT & SON – Staff (1892 – 1971)

This list of over180 staff at Scott & Son includes many of those who worked there between the 1920's and the closure of the shop in 1971. It has been compiled with the help of former employees or their descendants but is incomplete and dates are uncertain. In a few cases it has not been possible to indicate the department in which the member of staff worked. This applies to a number of those who attended the funeral of William Crawshay Scott snr. in 1938, which are marked (c1938). Prior to 1920, information about staff is very scant.

Dates refer to the time spent working at the shop.

PRE 1920
Mr. Thomas William Scott (Founding partner 1892-1912)
Mr. William Crawshay Scott ('The Governor')
 (Founding partner 1892-1938)
Mr. William Edward Carter (Upholsterer c1892-1916)
Mr. Walter Carrison Hart ('Old Hart') (Furniture packer and delivery driver 1895-1935)
Mr. Herbert H. Styles (Shop manager from c1897)
Mr. Albert Edward Smith (c1897-c1950) (Works Manager)
Mr. Arthur Breeton Meggitt (Cabinet maker 1899-c1963)
Mr. Albert Victor W. Little (Cabinet maker c1905-1910)
Mr. Sydney John Rainbow (French polisher c1907-c1940)
Miss Florence Elizabeth Scott (c1911-c1924)
Miss Caroline Peake (Chief cashier c1911-c1960)
Miss Marjorie Emma Scott (Office accounts c1914-c1920)
Miss Dorothy Edith Scott (Office accounts c1914-c1920)
Mr. William Crawshay Scott jnr. ('Mr. Will')
 (Works apprentice c1914. Partner 1928-1971)
Mr. David Dey (Music department manager c1915).
Miss Nora Ethel Scott (Music department c1915-c1924)
Miss Florence May Finbow (Later, 1943, Mrs. Dawes)
 (China dept manageress c1906-c1960) (Part time to c1967)
Miss Frances Mary Finbow (China dept. c1911)
Miss Maggie Brookbank (Drapery manageress c1919-1971)
Mr. Frederick William West (Van driver c1914-1918)
Mr. Joseph Dixon ('Joe') (Head delivery driver c1919-c1960)
Mr. Percy William Hall (Upholsterer c1919-c1964)

Above, from top: Florence, Marjorie, Dorothy, Nora, William, Lillian and Maurice Scott. 1925.

OFFICE 1920-1971

Miss Lillian Edna Scott (c1921-1933) (Manager)
Miss Gwendoline Green (1928-1936) (Manager)
Mr. Maurice Septimus Crawshay Scott ('Mr.Maurice')
 (Started c1929, partner 1938-1971)
Miss Muriel Green (aka Miss Brown) (1931-1938. Married, returned part time during WWII, as Mrs. Browne) (Manager) (Gwendoline's sister) (Part time 1950s/60s)
Miss Edna M. Hull (Later, 1941, Mrs. Spinks) (c1932-1960s)
Miss Irene E. Withers (c1938)
Mr. Charles Parson (c1930s/40s) (Part time bookkeeper)
Miss Marjorie Greaves (c1938)

OFFICE 1920-1971 cont.

Miss Jean Bell ('Ginny') (1940s) (Later, 1950, Mrs. Pidgeon)
Miss Mary Stoakley (1942-1946)
Miss Vera Batterbee (c1940s/50s)
Mr. H.V. Barnard (1940s/50s)
Miss Brenda M. Wilkin (Later, 1952, Mrs. Skoyles) (1951-1953)
Miss Beryl A. Spinks (Later, 1961, Mrs. Softley) (Mrs. Spinks' niece) (1960s-1971).
Mrs. Pat Pearson. (c1960-1964)
Miss Bridget Green (Later Mrs. Richardson) (c1960s)
Miss Doreen E. Mendham (c1960s)
Miss Valerie J. Bunn (1960s – 1971)
Miss Margaret Woods (1960s)

FURNITURE: 1920-1971

Mr. Ernest Bullen Smith ('Bill') (Manager c1937)
Mr. Ernest W. Eke ('Ernie') (c1929-1971)
Mr. Horace Gazley (c1919-c1960)
Mrs. Doris A. Eastwood (née Richardson) (c1950s-1960s)
Mrs. Ellen Bambridge (Nell) (c1960s-1971) (See Miss Andrews – Toys & Prams)
Mr. Nudds (c1950s-1960s)
Mr. Tony Pitt (1960s)
Mr. Michael J. Piper (1960s)
Mr. Robin Back (c1950s-1960s)
Mr. Alan Crawshay Scott (1959-1971) (Manager)
Miss June C.E.Roberts (1961-1967)
Miss Dorothy Simmons (1960s. Later, 1962, Mrs. Holland – married Bill Holland from hardware dept)
Mr. Bernard Tuttle (c1960s)
Mr. Barry Purple (1960s)
Mr. Paul Griffiths (1962-1966) (Left, retrained and returned as cabinet maker – see workshop staff)
Mr. Les Spinks (Part time late 1960s)
Miss Anne Ripley (1969-1971)

TOYS and PRAMS: 1920-1971

Miss Joan Croucher (c1935-1940) (Married Mr. Maurice Scott in 1941)
Miss Doris A. Richardson (c1930s Later, 1938, Mrs. Eastwood – see Furniture)
Mrs. Ethel Gill ('Gilly') (c1950s - 1960s)
Miss Ely (c1950s – 1960s)
Miss Cathryn I. Lown ('Cathy') (c1950s-1960s)
Miss Ellen Andrews ('Nell') (1950s. Later, 1954, Mrs. Bambridge – see Furniture)
Miss Daphne Mason ('Macey') (1958-1971)
Miss Brenda M. Goose (1960s. Later, 1965, Mrs. Rowland)
Miss Kathy McRann (1960s)
Miss Pat Fendley (1960s).
Mrs. Judy Gotsell (1960s)
Miss Claxton (1960s)
Mrs. Edith Ferguson ('Edie') (1960s)
Miss Jeanette Goldberg (1960s)
Miss Geraldine Kennedy (1960s)
Miss Anne Wright (1960s)
Miss Maureen Gostling (1960s)
Miss Mary Loasby (c1970) ('Saturday Girl')

HARDWARE: 1920-1971 (Cont.)

Mr. Framingham (1960s)
Mr. Michael Greenfield (c1965)
Mr. Clifton H. Hearle ('Cliff') (c1970-1971)

Front: Ellen Bambridge; Miss Claxton; Doris Eastwood. Back: Mrs. Chase; June Roberts; Brenda Goose; Daphne Mason.

Front: Kathy McRann. Back: Pat Fendley; Brenda Goose;
June Roberts; Paul Griffiths. (Les Spinks cut off at top).

HARDWARE: 1920-1971

Mr. Percy Cox (c1924-c1964) (Manager)
Mr. Charles A. Cook ('Charlie') (c1930s-1940s)
Miss Jean M. Pipe (1942-1946)
Mr. Barry Hall (c1960s)
Mr. Barry Purple (c1960s)
Miss Marion Pearman (Later, 1957, Mrs. Fordham)
Miss Anne Thurston
Mr. Ernie Cardew (1960s)
Mr. Walter F. Holland ('Bill') (1960s)
Mr. Trevor W. Clare (1960s)
Mr. Barry Smith (1960s-1971)
Miss. Anne Back (c1960s)
Mr. David Hipperson (1960s)

CHINA: 1920-1971

(Miss Florence May Finbow – see Pre 1920)
Miss Winifred E. Withers (1930s-1940s)
Miss Hazel Richardson (Later, 1954, Mrs. Loasby) (1939-1971)
Miss Beryl G. Causton (Later, 1953, Mrs. Kemp) (1950s)
Miss Margaret Munge (Ann) (1954-1956)
Miss Sybil Parker (c1955-1971)
Mr. Robin Crawshay Scott (1957-1971) (Manager)
Miss Bessie Simpson (1950s-1960s)
Miss Pauline Mott (Later, 1962, Mrs. Hall) (1950s-1960s)
Miss Yvonne M. Benefer (Later, 1968, Mrs. Whitehouse) (1960s)
Miss Linda J. Jakeman (Later, 1968, Mrs. Benefer) (c1965-c1969)
Miss Lynda Parker (aka Miss Joyce) (1964-1971)
Miss Noreen Foulsham (1966-1971)
Mrs. Joyce Benefer (1950s)
Miss Maureen A. M. Caley (Later, 1958, Mrs. Purdy)
Miss Beryl Canham (1960s)
Miss Janet Rudd (1960s)
Miss Mary Bird (1960s)

China department staff at King's Lynn Trades Exhibition, 1961: Robin Scott; Pauline Mott; Hazel Loasby.

DRAPERY: 1920-1971

(Miss Maggie Brookbank – See Pre 1920)
Miss Mary Kettlewell (née Grummett)
Miss Millie Hearle (c1930s) (Later, 1948, Mrs. Addison)
Miss Penny Riseborough
Miss Jean Franklin
Miss Jean Hall (Later Mrs. Smith)
Mrs. Pat Tidd
Mrs. Ethel M. Goodson.
Miss A. Sampson (c1938)
Miss M. Williamson (c1938)
Miss Mary Loasby (Daughter of Mrs. Hazel Loasby – see china department)
Miss Sandy Wheeler (1960s)

CHINA (Continued)

Miss Mary George (1960s)
Miss Ruth Simpson (c1967 – 'Saturday Girl').
Miss Janet Baker (c1967 – 'Saturday Girl').

Pauline Mott, Hazel Loasby and Doreen Mendham at Scott & Son's Trade Show stand, 1958.

DELIVERY: 1920-1971

(Mr. Joseph Dixon – See Pre 1920).
Mr. John Long (1930s-1940s).
Mr. Hendry (1920s-1930s).
Mr. Eric Peacock (1950s-1960s).
Mr. Reggie Mace (1950s).
Mr. Barry Booth (1950s-1960s).
Mr. Derek Brown (1960s).
Mr. Ray Fysh (1960s).
Mr. Barry Wilson (1960s).
Mr. Henry Futter (1960s).
Mr. David Lomax (1960s).
Mr. Colin Delph (late 1960s).
Mr. Fincham (1960s).

Doreen Mendham, second left, with her future husband Hedley Chapman, centre, and John Mitchell, right, on a day trip for staff and friends to Clacton.

Ethel Gill, Nell Bambridge, Doreen Mendham and Bill Holland, standing in front of one of Scott & Son's little Bradford fitters' vans, at the 1958 King's Lynn Trades Exhibition.

Jim Gathercole and Barbara Church.

SOUTH QUAY WORKS and WORKSHOP at PURFLEET STREET: 1920-1971

Mr. Albert Edward Smith (See Pre 1920)
UPHOLSTERERS:
Mr. Percy William Hall (c1919-1961)
Mr. Cyril A. Reeve ('Tom') (c1927-1971)
Mr. Harry Bushell (c1930s-1940s)
Mr. Albert Booty (c1930s-1960s)
Mr. Jimmy Jackson (c1930s-1940s)
Mr. Richard Holmes ('Dick') (1950s)
CABINET MAKERS:
Mr. Sydney John Rainbow (see Pre 1920)
Mr. James William Gathercole ('Jim') (c1930-1971) (French polisher)
Mr. John Anthony Mitchell ('Jack') (1950-1967)
Mr. John Gazley (c1950s-1971) (Later Carpet Fitter)
Mr. Paul Griffiths (1967-1971)
SEAMSTRESSES:
Miss Joyce Waterfield (c1950s)
Miss Barnard (c1950s)
Miss Anne Banham (c1950s)
Miss Diane Dexter (1962-1968)
Miss Ann K. Auker (Later, 1958, Mrs. Hornigold) (1950s-1960s)
Miss Barbara Church (c1960-1971)

Barbara Church, Cyril Reeve and Diane Dexter.

Vans at works c1925with: Joe Dixon; William Scott jnr; Mr. Hendry; Arthur Meggitt; and John Long.

CARPET FITTING: 1920-1971.

Mr. Graham Edward Carter. (c1930-1971)
Mr. Arthur Meggitt (See Pre 1920) (Part time 1960s)
Mr. Norman Borley (1960s)
Mr. Christopher Crawford ('Chris' or 'Biscuit') (1950s – 1960s)
Mr. John Gazley (c1960-1971) (See Cabinet Makers)
Mr. Richard Eke (Late1960s) (Son of 'Ernie' Eke)

CLEANERS: 1920-1971
Mrs. Gladys Sutterby (c1960-1971).

WAREHOUSE: 1920-1971.

Mr. William T. Green ('Billy') (c1930s-1971).
Mr. Jasper Smith (c1950s).
Mr. Roy Bloom (late 1960s)
Mr. R. Ellis (late 1950s)

Kathy McRann c1965

Albert Booty c1941

Sisters Gwendoline (top) and Muriel Green both worked in the office as manager. After marrying, Muriel came back as Mrs Browne part time during WWII.

DEPARTMENT UNCERTAIN: c1938

Mr. Edward Mott ('Ted')
Mr. D. Whitby
Mr. D. Pegg
Mr. Herbert Dowdy
Miss E. Johnson
Miss S. French
Miss R. Brock
Miss B. Simpson
Miss J. Lakey
Miss E. Webber
Miss A. Lawson
Miss V. Bray
Miss F. Jarvis
Miss Hilda M. Cowen
Miss J. Castleton
Miss I. Gordon

DEPARTMENT UNCERTAIN: c1950-1971

Mr. John Hughes
Miss Barrett
Miss Clarke
Miss Stella French (Later Mrs. Batterham) (c1960s)

Gwen Smith, John Bowers, Doreen Mendham, and Judy Claydon outside the warehouse in Purfleet Street. Behind them is one of Scott & Son's small fitter's vans. The top of the Custom House can be seen in the distance.

Albert Edward Smith. Started as an upholstery apprentice c1897 and rose to become Works Manager.

Hazel Loasby, Beryl Causton, Doreen Mendham and Maureen Caley.

178

ARTHUR MEGGITT – Scott & Son's longest serving member of staff (1899-c1963)

Arthur Breeton Meggitt was born at Aickman's Yard, King Street, King's Lynn, on 28th January, 1884, the eldest of 11 children.

Breeton was the maiden name of Arthur's grandmother. Emma Breeton married Abraham Stead Meggitt in Hull and they had four children. The youngest, Arthur's father Edward Breeton, was born in Spennymore, Durham in 1860. Within a few months of Edward's birth, his father Abraham died and his mother married Thomas Gamble, a policeman who had been born at Great Plumstead in Norfolk. Thomas brought the family down to King's Lynn where he took employment as an oil cake maker. Oil cake is what is left over from vegetable matter such as linseed, olives and soy beans after they have been pressed for oil production. The remaining 'cake' is commonly used for cattle feed.

Edward married Charlotte Barker at Postwick, near Norwich, in 1883 and he worked as a bricklayer and, later, a dock porter. Eventually, the family moved from Aickman's Yard and were living at Swiss Terrace, near to the railway crossing in Tennyson Avenue, in 1911. Later they lived at 28, Broad Street, King's Lynn.

On 1st February, 1899, Arthur entered into a five year apprenticeship as a cabinet maker with Scott & Son. His apprenticeship indenture (right) was signed by Arthur and his father Edward, and by both Thomas William and William Crawshay Scott on behalf of Scott & Son.

Arthur completed his apprenticeship and worked as a cabinet maker at Scott & Son's works on the South Quay until the outbreak of the Great War in 1914.

The war was to have a devastating impact upon Arthur's family; eight Meggitt brothers enlisted in the armed forces but only five returned.

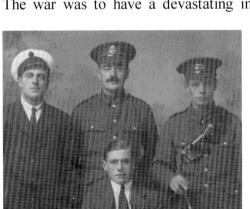

The photograph, left, shows four of the brothers who survived the war; Arthur, Abraham and William standing, with their brother Joe sitting in front.

Arthur joined the Royal Naval Air Service at the start of the war as a rigger in the kite balloon section. The balloons proved invaluable for naval scouting, allowing spotters to guide the gunners onto targets that could not be seen from the ship. Kept in specially constructed holds on deck, the balloons were inflated and allowed to ascend to the required height, controlled from on board by winches.

'The balloon's gone up' is an expression derived from the deployment of these observation balloons immediately prior to the commencement of a bombardment by the heavy guns. One of Arthur's jobs was to clean the balloon envelope and for this he had to remove his wedding ring to avoid snagging the material.

Arthur married Ethel Horsley in 1914 and their first child Ethel Maisie was born in 1915 but died in 1923 aged just seven. Their second child Mary died in infancy in 1916. Viola, their third child, was born in 1924.

The three brothers who died in the war were Richard Dring, killed at Gallipoli on 12th August 1915, aged 21, Frederick Charles, who died as a prisoner-of-war in Turkey on 8th January, 1918, aged 28, and Elijah Morris, who contracted influenza towards the end of the war and died of pneumonia at the age of 20 in hospital in Alexandria.

After demobilisation, Arthur started back at Scott & Son's works and was involved in the full range of cabinet-making tasks undertaken by the business. This included making new furniture both for sale in the shop and for clients, such as pubs and clubs and for offices.

During the Second World War, Arthur joined the Civil Defence Corps in Lynn, serving alongside another of Scott & Son's veterans, Albert Booty. In the photograph above Arthur, with a black helmet on his lap, is sitting one from the end on the left and Albert Booty is next to him with a white helmet.

After the war, the nature of the work changed. New furniture was limited to the utility brands and there was very little wood available for any to be made at the works in Lynn. However, there was a demand from clients for repairs and renovations and Scott & Son was one of the firms specialising in this service in Lynn.

Arthur was a skilled craftsman and he was also extremely versatile, being able to turn his hand to almost any practical job of work. Scott & Son were fortunate to have several such men and women on their staff and clients knew that they could rely on them to undertake work for them at their own homes. This would often extend to jobs that were not strictly within the scope of those offered by a furniture store. Scott & Son were often asked to send out a named member of staff to a client's home or work premises and Arthur's services were regularly requested. The wife of was one of Lynn's most senior and experienced solicitors, Mrs. Donald Jackson was a most formidable woman and would often call upon Scott & Son to send Arthur Meggitt round to her house to undertake a job of work. If it was the replacement of a pelmet or curtain rail, it was expected that the cobwebs and dust would be removed at the same time. On one occasion Arthur found that the job entailed filling the coal bucket for Mrs. Donald Jackson!

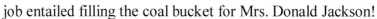

Several of Scott & Son's longest serving members of staff never really fully retired, continuing either full or part time at the shop or works. Arthur was one of these and, as the specialist work reduced, he took on a wide range of jobs, including carpet fitting. Arthur finally retired in about 1963. He and Ethel celebrated their 50th wedding anniversary in 1964 (above) but Ethel died soon afterwards and he moved to Costessey, on the outskirts of Norwich, to live with his daughter and son-in-law, Viola and Peter Betts. He died in 1973 aged 89.

FLORENCE DAWES (née Finbow) – Scott & Son's longest serving china department manager (c1902-c1960 and part time to c1967)

Florence May Finbow was born on 15th October, 1888 at King's Lynn, the daughter of Robert and Harriett. She had an elder sister and a brother, Frances Mary (born 1881), and William Masters (born c1885), and a younger sister, Ellen Maud (Nellie), who was born c1894.

Her great grandfather, William Finbow, was born in Sedgeford in about 1793 and his wife, Frances, was born in Burnham Thorpe in about 1785. William was an agricultural labourer and life was a struggle for the family. In 1851 they were living in Docking and he was listed as a pauper in the census. They had four children, Frances (c1816), William (c1823), who was Florence's grandfather, John (c1828), and Samuel (c1830). William jnr. was also an agricultural labourer. He moved to Old Hunstanton and married Frances Smith in 1849. Their address in 1851 was Sea Lane, Hunstanton, and William jnr. was working as an agricultural labourer. William jnr. and Frances had at least nine children, including Florence's father, Robert Smith Finbow, born c1858 in Hunstanton.

Florence's grandfather, William Finbow, died in 1888 at the age of 66. Her grandmother, Frances, continued to live at 61, St. Edmunds Terrace, Hunstanton for a few years and her son Luke came to live with her. She was granted Parish Relief and continued to stay with Luke after he married and started a family. She died in 1906, aged 83.

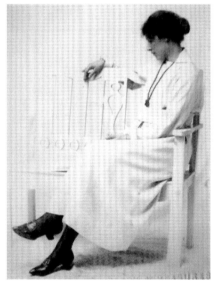

Robert Finbow married Harriett Hall in 1880 and their first child, Frances Mary, was born the following year. To start with, they lived with Harriett's parents, Charles and Mary Hall at 3, Garden Row, King's Lynn. Garden Row is off Windsor Road, next to the 'Live & Let Live' public house and the houses there were very small. Consequently, the accommodation for families with children must have been very cramped. By 1891 Robert and Harriett had moved the family into No. 10, Garden Row. Florence was two years old at this date and her brother William was five.

The principal residents of Garden Row were labourers and their families. There were roadmen, railway workers, bricklayers' labourers, a blacksmith, a seaman and several deal porters. These last were employed at the docks for unloading the cargoes of timber planks and stacking them in the storage yards. There was a small general stores in the street. The children of these labourers included a school teacher, hairdresser and some shop assistants. Robert was a sawyer who went to work at the engineering works of Frederick Savage where he became a saw sharpener.

Florence's mother Harriet died in 1902 at the age of 42, and her father married Elizabeth Keepe, a 37 year old nurse from London. Elizabeth died in 1946 and Robert continued to live at No. 2, Empire Avenue until shortly before his death in 1952 at the age of 94.

Charles and Mary Hall moved from No. 3 to No. 18, Garden Row. Charles died between 1891 and 1901 and Mary moved to Checkers (sometimes Checker) Yard off Norfolk Street where she was living in 1901. On census day that year Florence, aged 12, was visiting her. Mary Hall stayed at Checkers Yard until her death in 1912, aged 78. The Yard was near the Eagle Hotel which received a direct hit from a German bomb on 12th June, 1942, killing 42 people. It may be that Checkers Yard was also badly damaged in the blast.

In 1902 at the age of 14, Florence was given a job at Scott & Son by William Crawshay Scott. She worked hard in her first week as a china department assistant and lined up with the other staff to receive her first pay packet at the end of the week. She was rather taken aback when William Scott announced that he was not going to pay her what he had said he would when he gave her the job. Instead, he told her that, because she had worked so well, he was going to give her double that amount! There was no stopping Florence after that and she was destined to take over the management of the china department, a post that she was to hold for many years.

It would appear that Florence's elder sister Frances joined her in the china department at Scott & Son soon afterwards. Frances had been working as an assistant in a tobacconist's shop in 1901 but in the 1911 census both sisters were china shop assistants. Frances married Charles Blench in 1906 and may have left Scott & Son soon at that date or soon afterwards.

It was Florence's Proud boast that, while working at Scott & Son, she served three queens:- Queen Mary; Queen Elizabeth, mother of our present queen; and Queen Maud of Norway.

In 1943, at the age of 55, Florence married Theodore Ernest Dawes, a widower 24 years her senior. Theodore had been born in Syderstone in 1864. His father was a nurseryman, seedsman and florist and the business had been established by the family before 1800. Theodore specialised in the cultivation of rhubarb and was acknowledged as an expert throughout the country, becoming the champion grower in England and holding 14 medals for rhubarb growing. The wedding took place at East Winch church and Florence was given away by her father. Her brother-in-law, Stanley Linford, was best man. The reception was held at the home of Mr. and Mrs. Burfield, and William Crawshay Scott was called upon to make one of the speeches. Florence received presents from Scott & Son and the individual departments of the shop.

In the wedding photograph, right, courtesy of Rosemary Robson, William Crawshay Scott jnr. is standing second left. Sitting far right is the bride's father, Robert Finbow. Standing behind Florence is Ellen Linford and behind her is her husband, Stanley.

For three years Florence and Theodore lived at 378, Wootton Road, King's Lynn, which they named "Rhubarbia" but Theodore died on 12th April, 1946, at the age of 82.

Florence continued to live at 'Rhubarbia' and returned to work full time at Scott & Son as their china department manager. Even after her retirement, Florence would come into the shop for one afternoon per week and William Scott always took a wage packet round to her house at the end of each week.

Florence died towards the end of 1970 and several of her former colleagues from Scott & Son paid their last respects to her by attending her funeral.

MAGGIE BROOKBANK – Scott & Son's longest serving drapery department manager (c1919 – 1971)

Maggie Brookbank was born at 21, Providence Street, Lynn, on 20th October, 1905.
Her mother was Ellen Proctor, who had been born in Shouldham in 1865, the daughter of James and Susan. James Proctor was a carpenter and he and Susan had at least seven children. They moved to Lynn between 1871 and 1879 and set up home in 6, Victoria Street before moving to 10, Providence Street.
Ellen worked as a general servant until marrying Dennis Brookbank at Lynn in 1883. Dennis, who was 17 years older than Ellen, was a merchant seaman and the family moved about the country. They had about six children, the eldest of whom was born in Durham whilst the others were born in London and King's Lynn.
It appears that Dennis Brookbank died at sea sometime between 1891 and 1901. At this latter date, Ellen was still living at Providence Street in Lynn with four of her children and this was where Maggie was born and brought up.

By 1911, all of the older children, apart from Dennis jnr., had left home. Dennis was working as a traction engine stoker for a miller. Providence Street cannot have been the happiest of places in Lynn during the Great War because thirteen of the young men who left there to join the forces failed to return or died soon afterwards. Nevertheless, Ellen and Maggie continued to live there. Ellen died in 1929 at the age of 64 and Maggie had moved to No. 27, Providence Street by 1957. Not long after this, the houses in Providence Street were swept away in part of the slum clearance programme of the 1960's that included the redevelopment of the Hillington Square area of Lynn, between the Millfleet and Providence Street. Maggie moved into one of the new flats.

Maggie joined Scott & Son after leaving school and worked there until the shop closed in 1971. She soon rose to take on the management of the drapery department which supplied all manner of linens and furnishing materials. Working closely with the seamstresses and the fitters, Maggie and her assistants took orders for curtains and hangings which were made to measure and hung in the clients' premises. Many of these contracts were for offices, schools and other establishments, including church and village halls and at RAF Marham.

One of the more unusual contracts was for a huge quantity of net curtaining that was required for scene-setting for the film 'Operation Crossbow'. The old 'Central Hotel' in Purfleet Street had been bought by Scott & Son and was part of the hardware department. Some scenes in the film were acted out against the backdrop of the Custom House and the old Central Hotel became a café frequented by the German soldiers. The interior was draped in yards of net curtaining bought at the drapery counter of Scott & Son, and made up by the seamstresses in the workshop. William Crawshay Scott jnr. was convinced that the film company would not settle their account with the shop, but they did.

After Scott & Son closed, Maggie Brookbank retired from work but continued to live in Lynn. She died in early 1999 at the age of 93.

WALTER HART – Scott & Son's delivery driver in the horse-drawn era (c1895 – 1935)

Walter Carrison Hart was born in Lynn in 1861, the son of William and Elizabeth.
William married Elizabeth Carrison in 1852. He was employed as a merchant's clerk and had been living at Coronation Square with his parents John (also a merchant's clerk) and Sarah. William later worked as a shoemaker at 59, Norfolk Street, moving to Sedgeford Lane, by 1871.
Walter joined the Army in 1880, at the age of 19, serving for 12 years, principally in Egypt and the Sudan and being awarded two medals in 1882. Two years later he took part in the Nile Expedition, popularly known as the 'Gordon Relief Expedition'. Major General Charles George Gordon and his garrison of 7,000 men at Khartoum were besieged by the Mahdi's force of 50,000 and were desperately trying to hold out until the relief force arrived. Unfortunately, the expedition force of British and Canadian men were two days too late and found that every one of Gordon's men had been slaughtered. Walter was awarded the1884-85 Nile Clasp for his part in the expedition.
Having left the Army, Walter returned to Lynn and started working as a sugar boiler – making sweets and rock. His father had already quit the shoemaking business for a life on the road making rock with the travelling fairs. Robert Rudd Hart, thought to be Walter's uncle, had a confectionary business in Lynn at 114, Norfolk Street during the 1880's, so rock making was in the family.
Walter married Isabella Marie Hornigold c1887 in Lynn and settled in Heacham before moving to Surrey Street, Lynn, by 1891. Isabella was the daughter of William Hornigold, a fisherman.
By 1895, Walter had taken a job with Scott & Son as their furniture packer and horse-drawn pantechnicon driver. He was undoubtedly an extremely capable horseman and may have gained much of his experience from his service with the Army in Egypt and the Sudan, where he would have worked with horses and camels. The job required several different skills, involving the packing, loading and conveying of the furniture and household goods, many of which were quite fragile.

The management of the horses required planning and a knowledge of the routes that had to be travelled. The number of horses required would depend on the size and weight of the load and the topography of the route to be taken. On the road to Swaffham from Lynn there were five hills – these have long since been levelled out by the builders of the modern A47. Walter would have to calculate how many horses were needed to pull the load when the pantechnicon was full, allowing for the steepness of the hills that would be encountered before the first deliveries were made. Obviously, as the loads were dropped off, the pantechnicon would become lighter and it was a fine judgement as to whether an additional horse was needed at the beginning of the journey. Walter would pack the wagon each Monday and would then be away from Lynn for the rest of the week. Overnight stops had to be planned where the horses could be fed, watered and, if necessary, stabled for the night.
Walter and Isabella had at least 11 children and in latter years the family lived in Purfleet Street, in one of the houses bought by Scott & Son. When these houses were demolished to make way for Scott's new warehouse in 1935, they moved to 17, Saddlebow Road.
Walter maintained his interest in rock making and may have continued making it on a small scale throughout the time that he was working for Scott & Son. On his retirement in 1935, Walter became known as 'Lynn's Rock King', and was a familiar figure in the town. He was also well-known for his association with the British Legion and with the Ancient Order of Buffaloes and the picture shows him with his chain of office.
Walter Hart died on Saturday, 21st May, 1939, aged 78.

SCOTT & SON'S GREAT WAR HEROES

Several of Scott & Son's employees joined the armed forces at the outbreak of the 1914-1918 War, including Arthur Meggitt who served with the Royal Naval Air Service. The names of others who served are not known but the shop and, particularly, the works staff were seriously depleted during the war years. After the war, Arthur Meggitt came back to continue working at Scott & Son, as may some others, but some may have taken up other employment. Joe Dixon and Alfred Hall, who served with the Army and were badly injured, joined Scott & Son after the war.

Albert Victor Little, a cabinet maker, left Scott & Son in 1910 to emigrate to Canada, and joined the 5th Canadian Mounted Rifles. He was killed in action in France between the 15th and 17th September, 1916.

Two of Scott & Son's staff paid the ultimate price and lost their lives. Their stories illustrate how both older and younger men left their families to serve their country and the tragic impact that their deaths had on their loved ones and those who depended upon them. William Carter was one of Scott & Son's most experienced upholsterers. Aged 39, he was the father of five children, all under ten years old. In contrast to William, Frederick West was just eighteen when he left to join the Army. He had been taken on by Scott & Son as a young man, most probably straight out of school, and trained to be a furniture van driver.

William Edward Carter. Private 61365; 13th Royal Fusiliers. Died of wounds in France on the 15th April, 1917, aged 39.

William joined the Army in June, 1916 and was sent to the Western Front five months later. During the Arras offensive of 1917 he was wounded on 11th April and taken to the Canadian General Hospital where he died four days later.

William was born c1878 in Pimlico, London. His father Edward had been born in Shouldham, and his mother Susan came from Gayton. Edward and Susan settled in West Winch after a spell living in London, where William and his sister Amy were born. Four other siblings to William were born in West Winch. Edward Carter was working as a brewer's labourer in 1891 and William went to work for Scott & Son soon after that date, where he trained as an upholsterer at their South Quay works and continued working there until he joined the Army.

In 1905, William married Lucy Irene Newell from Stanhoe. They moved into 3, Pleasant Row, King's Lynn, off Windsor Road. They had five children; Lucy, Graham, Margaret, Doris, and Amy, who was just over one year old when her father died. Graham later worked at Scott & Son as a driver.

Frederick William West. Private 2565; 7th Battalion, East Kent Regiment. Died of wounds in Southampton on 11th September, 1918, aged 18.

Frederick enlisted on the 14th February, 1918, the day after his eighteenth birthday. He landed in France on 1st August but was shot in the neck by a sniper on 6th September. He was transferred to the University War Hospital in Southampton, where his mother was able to see him before he died. He was buried at Lynn cemetery on 14th September, his coffin being borne by six members of the Royal Defence Corps, of which his father had been a member.

Frederick's father was John, born in Darlington, who married Susan Newby, from County Durham, at Dickleburgh in 1897. John and his elder brother James worked on a farm at Seamere Green, near Watton in Norfolk, as a groom and a farm labourer respectively. The family later moved to Lynn where Frederick found employment as a driver with Scott & Son's new motor vans.

References:

'Lynn's Book of Heroes': Holcombe Ingleby c1921. Serialised in the Lynn News & County Press and copied into a bound volume held at Lynn Library.
(After the erection of the memorial to the dead in the Tower Gardens, King's Lynn, the committee who had raised the funds decided to spend the sum that remained on preparing a book containing the names and, wherever possible, a short account of the lives, of those who died in the war. The bound volume was presented to the Lynn Corporation and is kept in the Lynn Archives).

RECOLLECTIONS
OF
FORMER STAFF
& CUSTOMERS

SCOTT & SON – Recollections of former staff or their descendants.

Jenny Mitchell (daughter of Cyril Reeve)

My father, Mr. Cyril Reeve, known as Tom, worked for Scott & Son as an upholsterer for 45 years (1927-1972), in the works on the South Quay, with Harry Bushell and Albert Booty. Sometimes in the school holidays I would take my sandwiches at lunch time and go and watch him work.

Mr. Peak sometimes used to take me out in the delivery van in my school holidays, also Barry Booth. When Barry left he went to be a bus driver in London. I can remember Derek Brown as another van driver.

My husband's cousin, John Mitchell, also worked for Scott & Son, as a cabinet maker.

I have found two receipts for carpet and furniture that my dad bought for us when I got married over 40 years ago.

Muriel Browne (née Green)

Commenced working in the office at Scott & Son in 1932, leaving in 1938 but returning later to work part time during the Second World War. She worked alongside Edna Spinks. Her sister Gwendoline started there in 1928, leaving in 1936 when she married Norman Anderson and went to live in Luton. Marjorie Greeves worked in the office (c1938) before marrying James Guy. Other people working at the shop at about that date were: Miss Winifred Withers (china); Miss Irene Withers (office); Mr. Barry Purple (furniture); Miss D. Richardson (toys); Miss A. Sampson (drapery); Miss M. Williamson (drapery); Mr. Ted Mott, who lived in the end house on 'The Point'; Miss Joan Croucher (toys until she left in c1940 before marrying Mr. Maurice Scott); Mr. John Long (delivery).

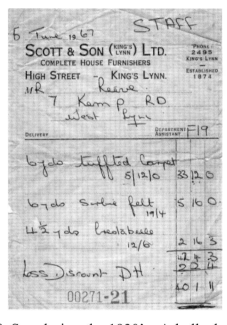

All the daughters of William C. Scott snr. were employed for a time in various departments of the shop, after finishing their education and until they left to get married.

There really was a 'Bull in a China Shop' incident at Scott & Son during the 1930's. A bullock that was one of many being led to market through the streets of Lynn had become very frisky and trotted off through Norfolk Street and High Street before entering Scott & Son through the china department and exiting at the back into Purfleet Street. The poor beast was cornered and shot. Apparently nothing was broken in the shop!

Jean Nunn (née Pipe)

Jean started work at Scott & Son in 1942, in the middle of the Second World War, when she was fourteen. She lived in Guanock Terrace, near to the 'Lord Napier' and opposite to Scott & Son's furniture warehouse with its big wooden doors. Her father was friendly with James Henry Martin who had a nursery at Goodwins Road, and whose daughter, Ivy, was married to William Scott. Jean believes that James Martin helped arrange for her to be offered the job. She was placed in the toy department but hated it. This was conveyed to William Scott via James Martin and she was immediately moved to the hardware department. She worked there with Charlie Cook and Percy

Cox and spent four happy years there. Charlie Cook lived at Terrington where he bred sheep dogs. Jean recalls that one lunchtime he took his sandwiches down to the South Quay but went to sleep in the sun. When he came back, late, to the shop, he was badly sunburned! After leaving Scott & Son he emigrated to South Africa. The illustration right shows the Guanock Terrace warehouse and the one below shows the Purfleet Street hardware window in the 1930's, with a display of wringers and suitcases.

SCOTT & SON'S WAREHOUSE, GUANNOCK TERRACE

Jean recalls that the gypsies would come round on occasions supplying Scotts with clothes pegs and potato baskets that they had made and which were sold at the shop.

There was a shortage of enamel ware at that time and people would queue down Purfleet Street hoping to buy some. Many were disappointed when the shop had sold out before they got to the front of the queue.

Each department had their own arrangements for tea making. The treat of the day was when Jean would take a jug over to Ladymans, at 39 to 41 High Street, for their morning coffee. Charlie Cook's daughter worked at Ladymans. Jean made tea for the men in the hardware department. A wartime drink was powdered chocolate and dried milk.

Percy Cox lived in Wootton Road and sometimes he would borrow Jean's racing bike to cycle home for his lunch. He liked the sporty look but did not get on very well with the bike!

The staff put out some stock for display in the arcade and this had to be taken back in before the shop closed in the evening. For metal repairs, items were taken round to the blacksmiths in Baker Lane. There was a shortage of mixing basins during the war and when the Globe Hotel sent for some replacements, they had to make do with chamber pots! They sold Ridgeons flower and

vegetable seeds. Raffia had to be plaited by Jean and hung in bundles for display. Oil lamps were still in common use, especially by people living in rural areas. Scott & Son supplied lamps, lamp glasses and wicks. These last had to be cut to length. Nails were sold by weight in paper bags. Other common items that were stocked included: step ladders; sugar soap; flower pots; linen lines; ironing boards; paint; string; and wire netting, which the men had to bring over from the warehouse in rolls. Wooden linen-horses came in single, double or treble fold. Jean would put them together with webbing hinges. 'Bungalow Baths' were still in common use and the staff would walk over from the warehouse with these on their heads.

The illustration below is from Scott & Son's catalogue for 1939 and shows their range of galvanised ware, including the 'Bungalow Baths' in three sizes.

Jean remembers watching the cabinet-makers making furniture in the workshop.

She recalls that the staff were lovely and that they were all very happy working there. Some others who were there then included, Bessie Simpson, Hazel Richardson, and Millie Hurl.

Mary Mathers (née Stoakley)

When I was about 18 months old, my mother was out shopping near the arcade entrance at the Purfleet Street corner. A large crowd had gathered outside Scott & Son because Queen Mary was inside the store. I was dressed in a royal blue velvet coat with white fur collar which my mother had made. When Her Majesty exited from Scott & Son via the side entrance she saw us and, touching my cheek, said to my mother "What a bonny child". Mr. Goodchild, the photographer, whose premises were on the opposite corner, was on hand to record the event. Some years later I joined Scott & Son's staff.

I came as office junior to Scott & Son in 1942. One of my jobs was to operate the telephone. This was a rather large box affair with buttons to all the departments. I had to make entries into the customer accounts ledgers and type quarterly accounts and business letters. Neither Mr. Will nor Mr. Maurice could give dictation, so I typed from hand-written notes. Mrs. Spinks was the office manager during my time. As office junior I had to make morning and afternoon drinks for the 'bosses'. In a back corner of the china department was a small partitioned area for drinks making. In the morning it was a wartime drink of powdered chocolate and dried milk, just mixed with boiling water. I can tell the story now: as chocolate and sweets were rationed at the time, I tasted a few spoonfuls of the mixture! The cups and saucers were 'Indian Tree' pattern.

Mr. Cox was the manager of the hardware department and also a Mr. Cook worked there. Miss Finbow was the manager of the china department. Later she married Mr. Dawes. (Florence May Finbow, the daughter of a farmer, born in Hunstanton in 1898, married Theodore E. Dawes in 1943).

The illustration below shows the arcade entrance to the china department c1930.

Moving from the hardware department, with frontage to Purfleet Street, you went through the china department on the corner into the main store with its front entrance to High Street. There were prams, children's furniture and toys – the sort that you see now on the Antiques Roadshow. Towards the back were the soft furnishings and carpets. The furniture was on the first floor.

Our office was situated in the centre of the store, with the cash desk and a glass partition. On the wall was a wooden plaque that read: "IF YOU HAVE NOTHING TO DO – DON'T DO IT HERE!" You had to go through the main office to get to the inner office where Mr. Will and Mr. Maurice were. During my time there I can recall the cashier 'Ginny' Bell, Bridget Green, an elderly lady named

Ermintrude and Mrs. Spinks. There was a staff room for tea breaks and where we could take our lunch.

The Purfleet Street warehouse has many happy memories for me. I was in charge of the customer accounts. Each member of staff had their own receipt book. This had a hard cover and contained duplicate bills: top copy for the customer; the carbon copy came to me. After entering the details into the ledger, the copies were numerically parcelled and filed into boxes for safe keeping. These were then transferred to the warehouse. This was my job and I would go there as often as I could. It was a delight to see all the beautifully decorated china stored there, providing replacements for all of our many local customers. During wartime the china department could only stock plain white china. I still have the very first gift I bought for my mother – a 'Sylvan' terrier. I believe it cost 17/6. The lift in the warehouse was hand operated – not the sort that you would find today.

We would receive regular visits from the accountant, Mr. Haddow of Messrs. Whiting & Whiting, Trumpington Road, Cambridge.

I used to cycle to work and would come into the passage at the back of the shop, entered from Purfleet Street. Inside on the left was the cabinet making workshop and polish shop and I can remember the glue pot being constantly heated – phew, what a smell!

'National Savings' started in the 1940's. My Monday morning job was to visit each department to collect from the staff. It was mostly 1/- each that they would put aside to buy the savings stamps. Each had their own savings book in which the stamps would be stuck. Having collected their money I would have to go to the post office to buy further stamps.

Mr. Maurice was called up into the army. Mr. Will ran the business on his own – doing his 'War work' on his home allotment where he grew vegetables and soft fruit. When I started, my wages were 10/- per week. Eventually, I decided that office work was not for me and I left in 1946, when my wages were £2 per week.

Mary Kettlewell (née Grummett)
I worked at Scott & Son from 1948 for a while, under Mr. Will, as he was known. He was a very good boss but had a very short temper and when angry a very red face! He was always fair to the staff.

Sometime during my time at Scotts I organised an outing to Great Yarmouth. I think it was the only one that we had but everybody came.

In the hardware department I remember Percy Cox, who was married to Mr. Will's sister (Florrie), and Charlie Cook. On the drapery counter there was Maggie Brookbank, Jean Franklin, Jean Hall, Mrs. Pat Tidd and me, Mary Kettlewell. In china there was Miss Bessie Simpson and Miss Hazel Richardson. Miss Peake and Miss Jean Bell were in the office and Horace Gazley was in furniture. In the workroom there was Albert Smith, Jimmy Jackson (French polisher) and John Gazley and at the Works was Albert Booty, Cyril Reeve, Arthur Meggitt and others.

I was married on 10th December, 1945. All of our furniture and bedding, pram, china, sheets and blankets were on dockets and we purchased them from Scotts.

John ('Jack') Mitchell
John trained in woodworking in the Air Force at Cranwell, making and repairing furniture and gliders.

On leaving the Air Force he joined Scott & Son as a cabinet maker and French polisher, starting on 21st May, 1950. The working hours were 8.30am – 5.30pm (5.00pm Wednesdays) and 8.30am – 12.00noon Saturdays, with 1hr 15mins lunch break (1hr. Wednesdays). There were 12 days paid holiday.

The workshop was at the back of the High Street shop, with access from the yard off Purfleet Street. There were three work benches but only two were used in his day (1950 – 1967).

In earlier years, the cabinet making and polishing was done at the South Quay works. On the ground floor of the works was the garaging for the vans. Above this, on the first floor, was the upholstery workshop, with a carding machine for the horse hair fill. On the second floor was the polish shop and on the top was a band saw with attachment for a circular saw. The machinery was all belt-driven, the power coming from a single-cylinder gas engine situated on the ground floor. The chair frames were bought in and then made up in the upholstery workshop. The works manager was Albert Smith. He undertook the cutting-out of the fabric for the upholstery and loose covers. In earlier times Scott & Son made pram hoods.

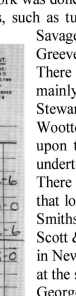

One of the upholsterers was Percy Hall. He seamed up the carpets. This work was done on the second floor of the warehouse in Purfleet Street. He had an aluminium leg, having lost his leg in the First World War. His party piece was to shock people by pushing one of the long upholstery needles though his leg!

There was a lot of repair work undertaken in the workshop, customers bringing in their broken furniture for repair. As a cabinet maker, John would also undertake the polishing. Jim Gathercole was a specialist French polisher. Scott & Son would undertake to make furniture to customer's requirements. Most of the work was done by hand. The only power tools were an electric drill and a saw. When special shapes, such as turned chair legs, were required, they would go down to Savages works. Blacksmithing work was put out to Mr. Jack Greeves in Baker Lane.

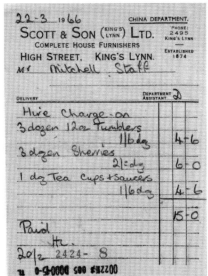

There was some public house, club and hotel contract work, mainly tables and chairs and stools. Some work was done for Steward & Patteson's inns. Seats were made for the New Inn at Wootton and for Wenns Hotel. Sometimes they were called upon to carry out repairs on clients' premises and they once undertook some repairs to the screen at the Pilot Cinema.

There was a warehouse in Guannock Terrace, next to a building that looked like an old chapel. It was near to the rear access of Smiths the bakers. John remembers it being full of old furniture. Scott & Son owned other property, including some small houses in New Conduit Street. Beryl Causton lived in one – she worked at the shop. They bought the Central Hotel in Purfleet Street and George Cook's engineering works at No. 8, which was demolished.

For a time the staff had a cricket eleven and they played one or two of the local cricket teams, as far away as Thornham.

John Gazley was in the cabinet-making workshop for a while and he used to make up the display stands. Other special displays were prepared as necessary, including a shaped wooden shell, painted blue, which was created as a backing for the huge display teapot that stood over the cash kiosk in the china department.

In the yard was a glue pot on a gas ring. The first job in the morning was to get this going and it was important not to let it boil dry. If it did it caused an awful smell!

There were three Bedford delivery vans and two small Bradford fitters' vans – replaced eventually with small Bedford vans (same chassis as the Dormobile). Scott & Son arranged for John to learn to drive and he would drive one of the small vans if he needed to go out on site. The Bradfords had very little power and struggled when fully loaded! The head driver, Joe Dixon, had received a head wound in the First World War and had a metal plate in his skull. The vans would be filled with a full load, including furniture stacked onto the tail-board. Sometimes the delivery drivers would have to take out the windows in a house to get the furniture in. On occasions they would lift the bedroom furniture onto the roof of the van and take it through an upstairs window.

John heard stories about the horse-drawn pantechnicon drivers. 'Old Hart' (Walter Hart) came from a Romany family and he would take the pantechnicon with a full load at the start of the week, returning at the weekend.

The deliveries were done by specific rounds: Monday was Littleport and Ely; Wednesday was Hunstanton area; Thursday was Terrington.

Brenda Skoyles (née Wilkin)

I was a ledger clerk from 1951 to August 1953. I left six weeks before my first child was born. In those days we had no calculators, but neither did we need any 'O' Levels to work in an office.

The shop had several departments. The china and hardware were almost separate shops, although you could walk through to the main shop. Drapery was in the main shop, although I believe they had their own till. Mr. Will and Mr. Maurice Scott had an office at the back, through our office.

We had an office under the stairs with a cashier nearest to the shop. She took all other monies through a gap in the glass panel. At the end of the day all cash was brought through to the cashier where it was checked. Profits were 33 1/3rd, the hardware being 20%. There was no cutting prices by 50% in the sales at that time.

I took the bank bag to the bank each day, carrying it quite openly along the High Street. It was a different world back then!

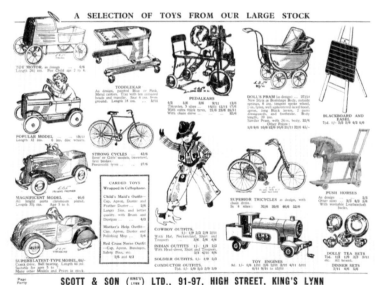

A SELECTION OF TOYS FROM OUR LARGE STOCK

SCOTT & SON (KING'S LYNN) LTD., 91-97, HIGH STREET, KING'S LYNN

At Christmas time a table was set up in the main shop and one of each type of mechanical toy was displayed there, so that customers could see what each one did when wound up. Any left over were sold cheaply in the New Year sale, which I believe was the only sale of the year.

There was a savings scheme for the staff. Each of the savings certificates was worth 15/-. Every time that we had saved for a certificate we were given one shilling towards the next one. After my baby was born, I bought myself a new outfit with the money that I had saved. I was also given a baby bath, which was sent to my new address in London. This had been ordered but had not arrived in the shop before I moved.

Although I did not like the office under the stairs, I do feel honoured to have worked for a firm who were honest at all times with their customers. I do not think that you would find that today.

My step father-in-law, Mr. Eddie Tomlins, worked for Scott & Son for many years as a driver's mate. He never held a driving licence, so was probably also employed in the warehouse. He retired in the late 1960's or early 1970's.

Margaret Green (née Munge)

My name was Margaret Munge (known as Ann) and I worked at Scott's china department from 1954-1956, when I left for a more lucrative job! I have been searching my memory for names of other china department members and came up with the following: Hazel (Richardson) the manageress who married Mr. Loasby; Mrs. Dawes, who used to come in about two days a week; Sybil Parker, who was an assistant, tea lady and feeder of the shop's cats, who lived at North Runcton; Pauline Mott, who joined the firm after me and became a good friend; Beryl Kemp, who may have joined after I left, whose husband Colin worked for my father-in-law; and Maureen Caley. I remember the two Mr. Scotts, William and Maurice. On the furnishing side I remember Horace Gazley. His son, John, would I think have been the store carpenter who put up the display boards and did painting jobs etc. From the furniture department I remember the manager Ernie Eke. The warehouseman was Billy Green. One van driver was Reg Mace, whose 'mate' Dick Holmes drowned in an accident in the Ouse.

Monday was the day for dusting all the fixtures – nerve racking! My wages were about 25/-.

Daphne Baylis (née Mason)

Daphne Mason was known as "Macey" in the shop – several of the staff had nicknames.

She started work at Scott & Son straight from school, aged 15, in 1958 and worked in the toys and prams department until the shop closed in 1972.

Daphne recalls the names of many members of staff and these are included in the list above.

June Ranger (née Roberts)

I left school Christmas 1960 and went to my first job in the New Year at Scott & Son. William Scott interviewed me and I worked under Maurice Scott and his son Alan in the furniture department. I was very happy over my 6 to 7 years there. Maurice was a very good boss. We were very afraid of William. You didn't dare stand about if he was on the warpath. It was a big loss when the store had to close.

(June provided photographs of the furniture department staff)

Paul Griffiths

I started work in the furniture and carpet department as a 17-year-old in 1962, having been at the local technical college for two years learning to be a carpenter. I opted out of that and had to get a job, so I joined Scott & Son at £5 per week. I left in 1966 and went on a Government training course to pick up the carpentry again. After that I had a few site jobs and was drawn back to Scotts in

Experienced Staff of Upholsterers, Polishers and Fitters for our Repairs, Renovations, Curtain, Carpet and Linoleum Fitting.   Estimates Free

1967 to take over from Jack Mitchell in the workshop, who had left to join Beresford & Hicks (furniture manufacturers) who had just relocated to Lynn from London. I followed Jack to Beresford & Hicks in 1971 when I needed more money to bring up two children.

I have some wonderful memories of my time there, working with such Scott legends as Horace Gazley, Ernie Eke, Margaret Brookbank, Graham Carter and Jim Gathercole. This was undoubtedly the happiest working time of my life, and I am still working in the furniture trade.

Lynda Parker (aka Miss Joyce)

I started at Scotts on leaving school aged 15 and my earliest memories are of being terrified and in awe of the older members of staff. I recall that I was instructed to call your father and your uncle Mr. Will and Mr. Maurice and also to address Robin and Alan in the same way. Pauline Hall and Hazel Loasby instructed me in my duties, as they had been working in the china department for some time. We all wore navy nylon overalls which attracted the dust. We only had one each and it had to be washed on Wednesday afternoon (we only had Wednesday afternoons and Sundays off at that time). One week, whilst ironing my overall I burned a hole in the front. My mother helped me to relocate the pocket over the hole and I wore this damaged overall for at least a couple of years without anyone knowing.

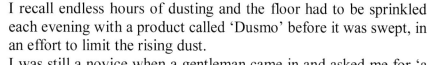

I recall endless hours of dusting and the floor had to be sprinkled each evening with a product called 'Dusmo' before it was swept, in an effort to limit the rising dust.

I was still a novice when a gentleman came in and asked me for 'a tin of elbow grease'. I almost directed him to the Hardware Department but realised just in time that it was a joke played on most new staff. The guy came from Humphrey's of St. Anne's Street (Fred S. Humphrey, Ship Chandlery) and I think he was put up to it by someone in the Hardware Department.

A lady by the name of Sybil Parker had apparently been working at Scotts for some time. She seemed like an 'old retainer'. She was a lovely lady but rather eccentric. By the time I started work she was employed only on a part time basis and used to wash up the staff teacups and help with packing and other odd jobs. She had had an interesting life, having come to North Runcton from London to work as a bus conductress during the Second World War. We were impressed that she had met Michael Caine the actor, who was also evacuated to North Runcton at that time.

The consequence of already having a 'Miss Parker' on the staff meant that I had to have an alternative surname. As my middle name is Joyce it was decided that I would be 'Miss Joyce'. This name stuck for the whole eleven years that I was at Scotts, even after Sybil retired.

I have very fond memories of Billy Green, the warehouseman. He was a tiny man with a big heart. Many times I would go over to the warehouse in Purfleet Street but could not see him there at first, but would find him in a large barrel or packing case. The crockery arrived in large barrels filled with straw – in later years in packing cases filled with wood wool – which were so deep that Billy could only empty them by getting inside. We had to go out of the main shop and across the road in all weathers in order to access the warehouse. We girls did not mind this on special Saturday afternoons when 'star' acts were due at the Corn Exchange. The entourage would always take the back road via Purfleet Street and I was lucky enough to see P.J. Proby – who was my idol at the time - arrive one Saturday. Goodness knows how many trips I made to the warehouse

that afternoon – I'm not sure how I got away with it!

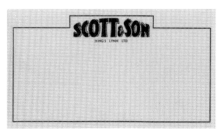

I loved working in the China Department and have had a love of beautiful things ever since. I recall helping Pauline Hall – the window dresser – and eventually was able to take on this role myself. The China Department had three windows, one of which was on the street side of the arcade. I remember helping set up a display in that window with the centrepiece of the most wonderful Royal Doulton figurine, which was approximately 18in. high and 24in. long. This was 'Princess Badoura' and she was sitting on an elephant and the painting of the fabrics which she wore was fabulous. It was the most expensive piece of Doulton that we had in stock to that date and Pauline and I had to carry it between us down the stairs and through the shop before placing it safely in the window. We were so nervous I'm surprised that we did not drop it!

Mrs. Dawes is another lady that I remember very fondly. She had been the manageress of the China Department and, although very elderly, came in one day each week (Thursdays, I think). She always wore a green suit and had her grey hair in a bun. She had a magnificent collection of Royal Doulton figurines and I used to wonder where she put them all. I was so sad when she died, and her funeral was the first that I had ever attended. Robin always vacated the 'office' when Mrs. Dawes was there – everyone had great respect for her. The office was a prefabricated tardis-like structure, which housed the cash register at the front, with the rear being closed off with wine-coloured curtains. All the bills were hand written and totalled up by the staff – duplicate bills being deposited on 'spikes' in the office. My mental arithmetic improved dramatically while I was there. I especially remember someone coming in to give us all individual decimalisation training in this little office. We were all so worried and could not think that it would possibly work!

The China Department's proud boast was that all items of tableware were sold separately. Many customers collected a set by buying a piece each week. The carrier bags were made from brown paper with a string handle. We wrapped most goods in newspaper – tissue paper being reserved for special items. Chamber pots were displayed along the topmost shelf behind the counter and we had to ascend a very rickety wooden ladder in order to get them down. Billy Green used to recall coming in from the warehouse carrying chamber pots when Queen Mary was in the shop! One section of the shop was called 'The Bar' – this was where beer, wine and spirits glasses were displayed for the customers who were licensed victuallers.

Diane Green (née Dexter)

I joined Scott & Son as a seamstress straight from school in 1962, working with Barbara Church until 1968. I had no qualifications or experience and learnt the trade as I went along. It was solely sewing work. Orders would come through from the drapery and furniture departments. These ranged from net curtains for houses to heavy velvet curtains for banks. The larger contracts included big blackout curtains for schools made from two lengths of double-width material sewn together. These had to be hand stitched down the sides. Other jobs included piping for mattresses and for leather chairs. When the Mart came to Lynn in February each year, there were often special orders for curtains for the showmen. We stitched pram hoods and aprons and the canvas for deckchairs. The binding for coconut matting had to be stitched by hand. When work was slack, we made up sand bags. All the curtains needed to transform the old Central Hotel in Purfleet Street into a café for the film 'Operation Crossbow' were made up by us in the workshop.

Anne Pease (née Ripley)

I worked in the furniture department (lino, carpets etc.) at Scott & Son for two years from August, 1969 until it closed in 1972, earning £5.02 per week! I thoroughly enjoyed every minute there, working for Mr. Alan and Mr. Maurice.

Some of the names that I remember are: Trevor Clare; Edie Ferguson (Toys); Mr. Spinks (only worked weekends); Bernard Tuttle (was at college and only worked holidays); Jeanette Goldberg (Toys); Penny Riseborough (Drapery); Mr. Carter (Carpet laying); and I really remember working with Daphne Mason. There was also Barry Wilson, a van driver, who always came to work in his slippers!

Sandra Clark

As a fifteen year old, in 1970, I joined Scott & Son, 'Complete House Furnishers' as a 'Saturday Girl' and stayed there for three years, working on Saturdays and in the holidays. It was my first job and I was paid the grand sum of 17/6d (75p!) for a day's work, which was a bit on the low side, because a lot of my peers were earning £1 a day! However, I thoroughly enjoyed it and still have a passion for china (I have far too much in my house). I think a large proportion of my earnings went back to Scotts!

One of the ladies I originally worked with was later employed by Robin Scott at Scotts China Shop in Norfolk Street.

At the old shop there were four Mr Scotts, the two (senior) brothers and their respective sons (cousins). To differentiate, they were called Mr. Will, Mr. Maurice, Mr. Robin and Mr. Alan.

The china department was on the corner fronting onto the High Street (which was not pedestrianised then). Behind the china department was the hardware department. To the right of the china department I think was the large carpet department and upstairs was furniture. My mother tells me they also sold toys up there. I don't remember going upstairs because at the age of seventeen I wasn't in the least bit interested in furniture!

The china department had its warehouse over the road in Purfleet Street, and took up the entire first floor. We also had storage facilities in 'the butcher's shop', which was to the left of the big warehouse (where the Showboat amusement arcade is now). My mother tells me that this used to be George's the butchers. Above the china department was the attic (which leaked copiously and had buckets positioned at various points around it to catch rainwater!). We also stored china up there too. Also upstairs we had a very small 'tea room' for tea breaks, which had about two chairs in it and an elderly lady called Sybil (Parker)was the 'tea lady'.

199

SCOTT & SON – Recollections of former customers or their descendants.

Jane Hurry (née Harper)

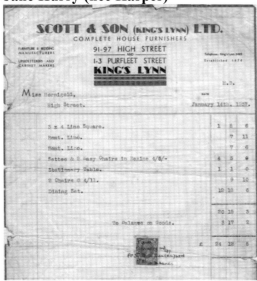

My four sisters and I were all born in Purfleet Street, at Nos. 10 and 11, which were two houses knocked into one (illus. right). The house, which was owned by Scott & Son, was opposite to the warehouse.

Our grandmother had the sweet shop, called Hornigold, next to Dales the pork butchers, at the High Street end of Purfleet Street, opposite to Scott's hardware and china departments.

I can remember Scott & Son very well; it is where we went to furnish our home. Although I do not have any receipts for any of my furnishings, I do have two receipts dated 1937 for furnishings which belonged to my late mother (one illus. above left).

Tom Fayers

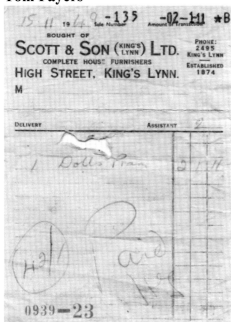

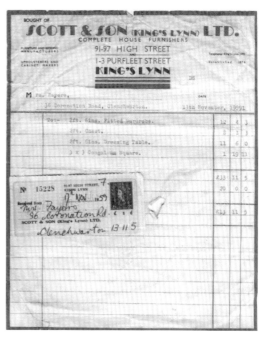

I came across the two invoices which I have copied for you. The first is dated 15th November, 1949 (illus. left) and is for £2/1/11 for a doll's pram. The pram was bought by my mother for my sister Agie. My mum used to get £4/10/- to keep our family of four children, so you can see that this was a huge expense. The second one is dated 13th November, 1959 (illus. right) and totals £33/11/5 for a fitted wardrobe, chest, dressing table and a Congoleum square.

Diana Smith (née Ebbs)
My uncle Frederick Dale had a shop, F. Dale & Sons, Pork Butchers in Purfleet Street, right opposite the side of Scott & Son.
I remember Scotts shop well in the High Street and siding onto Purfleet Street when I was a child in the 1960's. I went in there quite often and even remember buying my nana an 80th birthday present of a Pyrex plate costing 4/-, quite a fortune to me aged about ten. I still have it in my cupboard.
I remember Margaret (Brookbank) in the soft furnishings department, just about where Mothercare is now in High Street. I also remember the walkthrough arcade at the front of the shop, tiled in black and white floor tiles and the baskets of crockery laid out all along it on the ground. The outer windows on the offside of the arcade (fronting High Street) were filled with china and the staff had to cross the walkthrough arcade to get to them.
All sorts of crockery were available there, with ironmongery in the hardware shop. I remember going upstairs to the toys where there were rocking horses and big items and the bedroom furniture.

Daphne Harvey
I have a bill dated 14th July, 1936 for: Bedroom suite £4/18/6; Bed set of bedstead, mattress, bolster and two pillows £3/9/6; Dining set £5/5/0; Four chairs @ 3/11 = 15/8; Three yards Linoette @ 9 ½ d = 2/4 ½ ; Two and a half yards of lino @ 2/11 = 7/3 ½ .

Raymond Askew
In reply to your letter in the Lynn News, please find enclosed invoice (illus. over). This was for my late parents first home. They were married on 25th March, 1939. My father was a farm labourer at that time and I think £31/6/11 was a lot of money.

The items on the account, which is dated 9th March, 1939, are as follows:

Bedroom Suite	6/12/6	
Bedstead	2/7/6	
Spring Mattress	1/8/6	
Soft Mattress		1/7/6
Settee and 2 Easy Chairs in Rexine and uncut Moquette	10/18/6	
3 Dining Chairs @ 9/11	1/9/9	
3 Chairs covered in Green Rexine @ 2/6	7/6	
Drawleaf Table	1/9/6	
Ext. Kerb	7/11	
8 yds. Lino @ 2/11	1/3/4	
Down Quilt	2/18/6	
China Account	15/11	
TOTAL	**£31/6/11**	

Settee and two Easy Chairs, as design £10/18/6
Comprises Settee and two Easy Chairs covered in heavy quality Rexine, with Moquette seats and backs. All edges finished with thick piping. Variety of Coverings all colours.

DRAW-LEAF TABLE
Size 5 ft. x 3 ft. when open, 3 ft. x 3 ft. when closed. Polished legs and frame, and strong framed Whitewood top. 29/6

The illustrations, above right, show two of these items from the pages of the Scott & Son catalogue for that year.

Mary Billing

I have in my possession a receipted hand-written bill from when my late father purchased the goods for his home prior to his marriage to my mother in 1923.

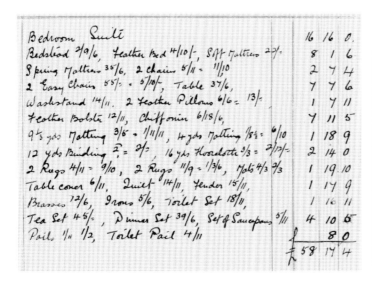

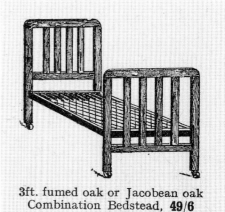

3ft. fumed oak or Jacobean oak
Combination Bedstead, **49/6**

Jean Barber

I have in my possession two invoices for furniture supplied by Scott & Son. The first is dated 23rd January, 1932, when my late parents set up home (below left). The other is dated 20th August, 1949 (on the following page).

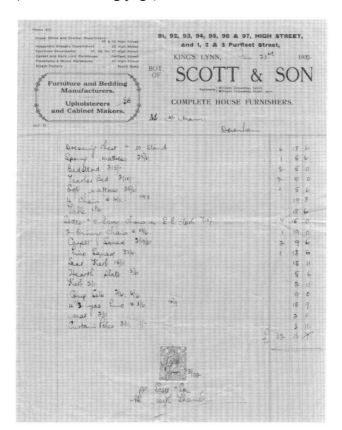

Oak Dressing Chest and Washstand as design, £6/18/6 the pair.
3 ft. low Dressing Chest has three drawers, large bevel-plate centre mirror and two reflectors ; 3 ft. Washstand has cupboard, drawer, rouge marble top and back, and fitted with towel rails.

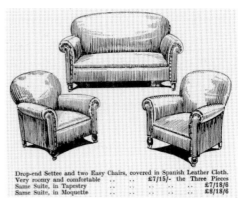

Drop-end Settee and two Easy Chairs, covered in Spanish Leather Cloth.
Very roomy and comfortable .. .. £7/15/- the Three Pieces
Same Suite, in Tapestry £7/18/6
Same Suite, in Moquette £8/18/6

The illustrations above right are from Scott & Son's catalogue for 1932 and show two of the items on the bill: the oak dressing chest and washstand (£6/18/6), and the drop-end settee with two easy chairs in Spanish leather cloth(£7/15/-).

Billheads, labels, business cards and wrapping paper.

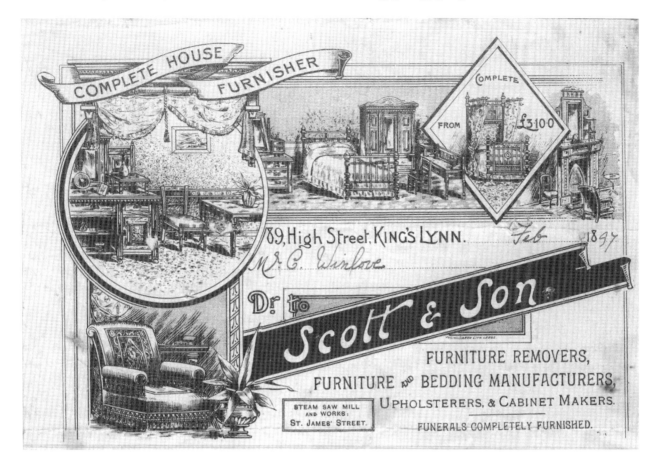

Above: billhead from 1897. This design, produced for Scott & Son by lithographer Julian Green of Leeds, may have been in use from the formation of the partnership in 1892. The shop at No. 89, High Street was rented and they owned the factory in St. James' Street.

Above: billhead from 1908. Scott & Son purchased Nos. 93 & 94, High Street in July, 1898. They bought the music business of J. H. Reddie at No. 42, High Street, in January, 1903. They moved out of the rented shop at No. 89 in about August, 1904. Following the fire at the St. James' Street factory, they had been manufacturing furniture and bedding at their new works on the South Quay since 1902.

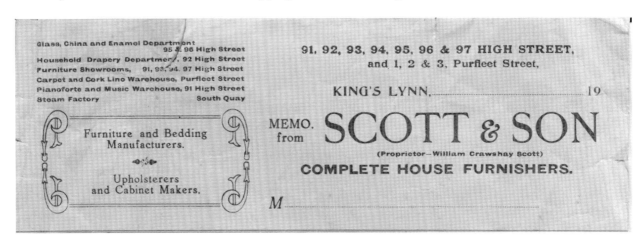

Above: a billhead from c1912. William Crawshay Scott was now the sole proprietor and his name had been added by hand. The business was now occupying Nos. 91 to 97, High Street.

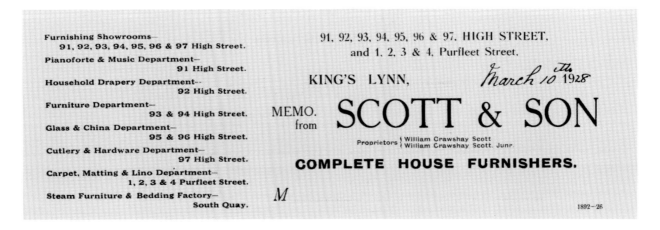

Above: billhead in use c1913-c1928. Nos. 1, 2 & 3 Purfleet Street were listed along with the High Street shops and William Crawshay Scott's name had been added as proprietor.

Above: the billhead introduced in March 1928 when William Crawshay Scott jnr. was made a partner, following his marriage to Ivy Violet Martin.

204

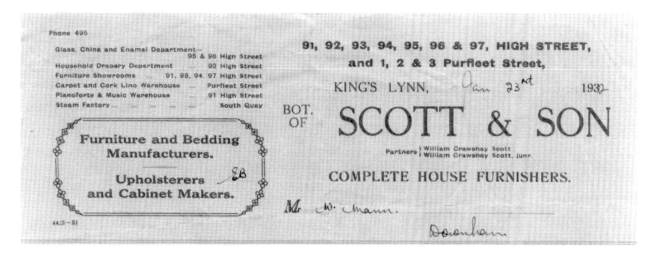

Above; billhead from 1932, listing the telephone number as 495.

Above: billhead from 1937, showing a radical change in design from earlier ones. The telephone number was 2495. The business is shown as having been established in 1874, but this was the date that Thomas William Scott first commenced on his own. Scott & Son was not formed until 1892. They were still advertising as furniture and bedding manufacturers and as upholsterers and cabinet makers.

Above: billhead from 1949. The style of lettering had been altered slightly from the previous example.

Above: billhead from 1967. The distinctive curved style of lettering for Scott & Son had been adopted for advertisements as early as 1944. It may be that it was not used for billheads until they had used up their stock of old style bill pads.

Above: China Department billhead from 1967. This was the only department to have its own till.

Above: business card from the 1960's.

206

Above: both sides of a label c1928.

Above: printed brown wrapping paper c1960's.

Index of names

213